THE GUN DIGEST® BOOK OF
RUGER
PISTOLS & REVOLVERS

PATRICK SWEENEY

©2007 Patrick Sweeney
Published by

Gun Digest Books
An imprint of F+W Publications
700 East State Street • Iola, WI 54990-0001
715-445-2214 • 888-457-2873
www.gunlistonline.com

Our toll-free number to place an order or obtain
a free catalog is (800) 258-0929.

Library of Congress Catalog Number: 2006935761

ISBN 13-digit: 978-0-89689-472-3
ISBN 10-digit: 0-89689-472-X

Designed by Jamie Griffin & Tom Nelsen
Edited by Dan Shideler

Printed in the United States of America

Dedication

Once again, as always, to Felicia.

Contents

Acknowledgments **5**

Introduction **6**

Chapter 1: A Visit to the Ruger Factory **8**

Chapter 2: Calibers **35**

Chapter 3: Pistols

    Part One: The Mk I **55**

    Part Two: The P89 . . . . **69**

    Part Three: The P90 . . . . **76**

    Part Four: The P94 . . . . **83**

    Part Five: The P95 . . . . **88**

    Part Six: The P345 . . . . **101**

    Part Seven: The SR9 . . . . **106**

Chapter 4: Revolvers

    Part One: The Bearcat **118**

    Part Two: The Blackhawk **123**

    Part Three: The Super Blackhawk **150**

    Part Four: The GP100 . . . . **160**

    Part Five: The SP101 . . . . **176**

    Part Six: The Redhawk **190**

    Part Seven: The Super Redhawk **200**

    Part Eight: The Old Army **218**

    Part Nine: The Vaquero **228**

    Part Ten: The Convertibles **241**

Chapter 5: Reloading for Rugers **247**

Chapter 6: Ruger Safeties **275**

Appendix: Serial Numbers **279**

Acknowledgments

As this book focuses on a single manufacturer, there aren't a lot of firearms manufacturers to thank. Beth McAllister and Ken Jorgensen of Ruger, in the New Hampshire office, were more than helpful. They sent me firearms, answered my questions, and even saw to my visit to the factory.

As for the ammo, Mike Shovel and Peter Pi of Corbon sent a truckload, as did Erik Leslie of Magtech. Jeff and Kristi Hoffman as usual sent two truckloads, and my local delivery people once again had sore backs for a few weeks. (You'd think they would be used to this by now.)

I'd also like to thank the numerous shooters, club members, and customers of my old shop who used, abused, wore out and had to rebuild their Ruger handguns. I learned a lot from their attempts to slay the armor-plated whitetails that seemed to populate "up north." Without the lessons learned there I would not be as amazed at the durability of the basic Blackhawk, Super Blackhawk, Redhawk and Super Redhawk revolvers, let alone the tuned and rebuilt ones from such master 'smiths as Hamilton Bowen.

The products of Sturm, Ruger & Co. may not have the tactical panache of some brands, but lots of shooters just want an unbreakable jeep, not a highly-tuned off-road Ferrari. For those guys and gals there are plenty of Rugers to go around.

Introduction

Why Ruger? Why not? Ruger hasn't built their reputation on competitions. They have occasionally done well along such lines, but that doesn't mean a whole lot to the police departments that buy and issue Ruger handguns. They don't have a long history, not by firearms manufacturers' standards, and thus the model changes that went into effect in 1921, that collectors obsess over, aren't there for Rugers. Not that there aren't Ruger Collectors. The RCA has many members and meets annually, and its members like to show off to their peers.

Ruger didn't go down the Commemorative path that some did, at least not until they started running into 50th anniversary years. But the Rugers that are 50th anniversary models are basically standard-production guns with a little extra marking or scrollwork. Not tarted-up guns with more money put into the commemorative bling than the gun itself cost to make.

But everywhere you turn, you see Rugers. You can't go to a range (with some exceptions) and not see a Ruger handgun. You can't go out handgun hunting without the other hunters at the club wanting to compare Ruger handguns. Go to a class for concealed carry licensees, and you'll be sure and see at least one Ruger there. Maybe it is simply the instructor's loaner gun, but there is one there someplace. If not that class, then the next one will have two Rugers in it.

They are everywhere. If you wanted a firearms symbol for something ubiquitous, the choice would be between an AK-47 or a Ruger handgun.

And they are durable. So durable that there are gunsmiths who do nothing but rebuild them to bigger calibers than Ruger ever made them in: .357s turned into .41 and .44s, .44s turned into .475s and .50s. So durable that no one talks about how to make them tougher. So durable that in twenty years of gunsmithing, the only Ruger handguns I saw broken literally had hammer marks or tire tracks on them.

That's not to say the Ruger handguns are universally loved. The price you pay for such durability is size and weight. Compare the Ruger Blackhawk to a Colt SAA, and the Blackhawk comes out looking pretty darned good. It is close enough in size that one holster with hold either. The New Vaquero is the Blackhawk-size frame with fixed sights, and is a great gun. But go up in size to the Super Blackhawk, and you're paying a ten-ounces extra price for a .44 Magnum revolver. The Redhawk, compared to an S&W M-29, is big. The Super Redhawk is monstrous.

Ruger pistols have always had a "rep" for being blocky. The P85 was about as close to being an ugly pistol as you could find without going overseas. But the newest models are almost sleek.

Bill Ruger himself got the company in trouble in some quarters for being a bit of a gentleman. That is, he wasn't up to speed on modern politics. When he grew up, politicians at least kept the veneer of civility up at all times. You could discuss things, work out a compromise, and if there was no compromise, then work out something that kept things going and people safe. Now, however, politics are a blood sport. He offered the opinion that perhaps a fifteen-round magazine was enough, and that maybe we all should just find some common ground there.

As an engineer and designer he was brilliant. But he wasn't so good at hearing the positions of politics. The anti-gunners would have gladly taken that position and run with it, resulting in ever-decreasing magazine capacity. ("The National Matches at Camp Perry only call for five-round strings. Who really needs any more magazine capacity than that?") He incurred the enmity of the anti-gunners for moving back from that position, and the lost allegiance of many shooters for having offered it.

But he kept designing and manufacturing, and his pistols came with fifteen-shot magazines as long as it was lawful to do so. When the Assault weapon Ban of 1994 "sunset" in 2004, Sturm, Ruger & Co. once again offered hi-cap magazines.

I've been shooting Ruger handguns since the summer of 1967. I think the only one I haven't shot in that time is the Hawkeye. Considering its rarity, that is not surprising. I suspect I'll still be shooting them forty years from now, provided I'm able to and it is still legal to. We may all lose the fight to time and old age, but we need not lose the fight to politicians who "know better" what is good for us. Buy a Ruger. Buy other guns, too, and make sure you join any (or all) of the groups that protect your right to own and shoot.

Chapter 1

A Visit to the Ruger Factory

I recently managed to use my powers of persuasion, wit and charm to get inside the walls of the Ruger plant in Newport. As with all such visits, it took some talking, as manufacturers are a bit reluctant to show things off. Not always for the reasons you might think. Most people, when I mention the work it takes to get inside, assume that there are secrets. You know, super-secret guns that are in-progress for the government, special designs that will beat the competition, or some über process that makes the company lots of money because the cost becomes almost nothing. (Then again, some people really think that the auto companies have bought up all the super-efficient carburetors that give cars 100 miles to the gallon, too.)

No, the main reasons the manufactures don't like to give tours are few and simple: danger, distraction and tricks of the trade.

A century ago this barrel would have been unproducible. Half a century ago it would have made engineers green with envy, and scratching their heads as to how it could be made at a reasonable price.

Bins of partially-completed handguns are all over the plant. The flow is planned but at times it can seem just a bit, well, chaotic.

It can be dangerous to walk around a manufacturing facility of any kind if you don't know what's going on. All kinds of equipment can be dangerous to be around, even with safety gates, lockouts and operators keeping an eye on you. There's also the fact that you haven't been briefed on the peculiarities of the plant in question. What if there is an emergency and you don't know which way to run? They can easily visualize you running straight into the multi-million dollar robotic equipment, getting killed, and closing the plant for the time it takes to a) get the authorities to do the investigation; b) clean up the mess and replace the tooling corroded by your splattering blood; and c) convince the insurance company that they'll never, ever, consider letting a non-employee onto the plant floor again.

As for distraction, who wants assemblers distracted, slowing down output, and perhaps making something not up to snuff? When I visited FN, they let me assemble one of the then brand-new FiveseveN pistols. I wasn't even out of sight when an assembler was tearing it apart, no-doubt to inspect and gauge every single part before re-assembling it. Was I offended? No, I had probably thrown him and the rest of the team behind schedule, and unless someone stepped in on the next performance review they were going to take it in the neck. That he checked over my work was simply a way to avoid future potential problems. I don't take it personally, and no, since then I don't ask to put something together. I make sure and ask before I even pick something up.

And the last, tricks of the trade, should be obvious. If someone has figured a way to save themselves from a production bottleneck, or speed up an otherwise time-consuming process, they sure don't want it spread to all their competitors. (Never mind that they've all probably already thought of the tricks themselves.)

So it isn't uncommon that I am presented at some point in the introductions and polite-conversation questions with the same problem on every plant tour or visit: "No pictures." Now in an ammunition plant, the "no pictures" ban is absolute, and for an entirely different reason. Ammo plants work with powder. Powder, unless the rules of physics have changed recently, is flammable. To save themselves from being blown to kingdom

come, ammo manufacturers use automatic fire extinguishers. Those units are slaved to flash detectors. Not smoke, but flash. Anything that fits the spectral definition, even a bit, of a flash-fire or powder detonation, sets off the fire extinguishers. Depending on the exact system used, the reaction is either a torrent of water that rivals the Johnstown Flood, or a rapidly expanding cloud of halon. You can tell which it is by looking at each work station: if there is a breathing mask and tank, it's a halon system. If not, it will be a wet day. Both water and halon stop production until they clean up the resulting mess. The manufacturer doesn't want an errant flash unit on a camera triggering the fire extinguishers, creating the mess, and halting production for a day or more. Oh, soon they will all

What you see in any modern manufacturing enterprise these days: row on row of CNC machining stations, all busily humming away.

Here we see twelve of the twenty-four machine-tool holders in this CNC machine. That means twenty-four different cutting, drilling (and if sophisticated enough) tapping tools to work on the parts in the parts cradle.

be water, as halon is on the list of eeeevil chemicals that deplete the ozone and as a result will turn us all into mutants.

Ruger does not make ammunition, but nevertheless when I walked in we had the same discussion/negotiation I've had lots of other places.

Ruger Official: "Oh – and no photos."

Me: "But I made that clear in the e-mails. These are for the book, and the reason for the trip."

Ruger Official: "Well, we'll have to call Ken then."

And so we came to this agreement: I would take all the photos I wanted, but I'd send the CD with them to Ken at Ruger. He'd look them over and discuss things with the production staff. Whatever they didn't want seen, I wouldn't run. As such, not an unusual arrangement, and one that seems to satisfy everyone involved. Those of you pouting about not getting to see the inner secrets of Ruger, and the things they wanted to hide, can satisfy yourselves with whatever conspiracy theories you can dig up on the internet. The end result on this trip? As per my usual process, I shot hundreds of images. They barely fit onto a CD, even as jpegs. Ken nixed two of them.

The modern materials that define Western civilization are steel, glass and concrete. Of those three, the only one really useful in firearms manufacture is steel. I imagine there's an engineering professor somewhere who will expand the "Concrete Glider" lab session to include a "concrete rifle" but for our purposes, glass only works in optical sighting systems, and concrete works in floors. To know about firearms, you have to know a bit about steel.

Investment casting produces parts that require much less machining. To make this frame from a forging, the forged lump would have to have had the cylinder opening milled clear and then broached to bet the tight corners needed for the cylinder to fit.

The hole for the barrel is already there on the casting. When the CNC machine cuts the frame face, and drills the barrel shaft to full diameter, it also taps the barrel shank hole for the proper threads for the barrel.

Steel

Steel, for an utterly basic definition (so basic it isn't much help in uncovering details), is simply iron with carbon in it. Now, the amount of carbon matters, but other things matter more. Like crystalline structure. Big or small crystals matter, and one or the other can be good or bad, depending on what your needs are. A good engineering school will have those seeking a mechanical engineering degree spending months working on the details of steel. If I may take a moment to make my position clear: modern civilization is not possible because of the efforts of philosophers, accountants, bureaucrats or god forbid, politicians. No, engineers (mechanical, chemical, electrical and civil) make modern life possible. I'll grudgingly add digital engineer to that, if we include programmers and exclude spammers. That buildings stand, vehicles run, water drains and the lights go on at the flick of a switch is something engineers make possible, not MBAs, managers, money gurus and political hacks.

Steel isn't easy. Not only do the many extra ingredients, called alloying agents (hence: alloy steel) change the properties of steel, the various combinations of them change it in unexpected directions. It matters when, and in what manner, they are introduced to the base iron. Before the American Civil War, "steel" wasn't really what we now know to be steel. It was a high-carbon iron. After the war, the Bessemer process allowed huge

After visiting the chambering machine, the cylinders are now ready to be fitted to a frame, timed and have the headspace and cylinder gap set.

volumes of high-grade steel to be made. You see, the iron ore has to have the impurities "blown out." That is, the iron has to be heated to a ferocity not possible prior to the Bessemer method. The Bessemer process involves a large vessel with molten iron in it, with air being blown through. The high-temperature oxidation removes the impurities by forming slag which is lighter than the steel. Once purified, then the molten iron can then have carbon and alloying agents added.

The beauty then? The Bessemer process produced pure iron, ready for alloying, in 15- to 30-ton "pours." Instead of one at a time steel parts, a foundry could produce ingots of ready-to-be-alloyed iron. Those ingots of iron could also be sent, still hot, to the alloying buildings, to be turned into steels.

Improving firearms has always been a goal, a goal of not just inventors and manufacturers, but armies and war departments. The first step on the modern path of high-grade steels (after the Bessemer process, which as we said allowed huge quantities of high-grade steel to be made) came in 1913 when English metallurgist Harry Brearly, discovered that adding chromium to low carbon steel gives it stain resistance. It didn't take long for "stain-less" to become stainless. Adding a minimum of 12 percent chromium to the steel makes it resist rust, or stain "less" than other types of steel. The chromium in the steel combines with oxygen in the atmosphere to form a thin, invisible layer of chrome-containing oxide, called the passive film.

This is the same process that makes aluminum and titanium rust-free. However, in the case of those two, the process can be (for aluminum) enhanced or (for titanium) a real headache. The sizes of chromium atoms and their oxides are similar, so they pack neatly together on the surface of the metal, forming a stable layer only a few atoms thick. If the metal is cut or scratched and the passive film is disrupted, more oxide will quickly form and recover the exposed surface, protecting it from oxidative corrosion. That's why a freshly-polished stainless gun looks different than it had before, and will soon again. Give up the polishing and admit defeat. Metallurgy is against you. Iron rusts quickly, and because atomic iron is much smaller than its oxide, the resulting oxide forms a loose rather than tightly-packed layer. The resulting "film" has no strength and flakes away. The passive film on a metal requires oxygen to self-repair, so stainless steels have poor corrosion resistance in low-oxygen and poor circulation environments.

In seawater, chlorides from the salt will attack and destroy the passive film more quickly than it can be repaired in a deep-water or low oxygen environment.

The lesson there is that a firearm in a seawater environment, under water, may rust more quickly than it would in the air, with salt spray.

Types of Stainless Steel

When an alloy of steel contains more than approximately 10-1/2 percent chromium it can be classified as a stainless steel. As you would learn in any aforementioned good engineering school, the three main types of stainless steels are austenitic, ferritic, and martensitic. These three types of steels are identified by their microstructure or predominant crystal phase. (It would be obvious to the engineering

Cylinders for the wheelguns are all turned from bar stock. Here a rack of single-action cylinders are off the profiling machine, and ready for the chambering machine.

Ruger Super Redhawk Alaskan frames. These have been cut from the mould "tree" and are ready to go into the holders and then the CNC machine.

student in the second week, as those are the names of the same types of non-stainless steel.) Austenitic steels have austenite as their primary phase (face centered cubic crystal). These are alloys containing chromium and nickel (sometimes manganese and nitrogen), structured around the Type 302 composition of iron, 18 percent chromium, and 8 percent nickel. Austenitic steels are not hardenable by heat treatment. The most familiar stainless steel is probably Type 304, sometimes called T304 or simply 304. Type 304 surgical stainless steel is an austenitic steel containing 18-20% chromium and 8-10 percent nickel. Also found here are tableware, the familiar "18/8" markings on your knives, forks and spoons. Ferritic steels have ferrite (body centered cubic crystal) as their main phase. These steels contain iron and chromium, based on the Type 430 composition of 17 percent chromium. Ferritic steel is less ductile than austenitic steel and is not hardenable by heat treatment. Martensitic is where all the action

is, as far as firearms are concerned. The characteristic orthorhombic martensite microstructure was first observed by German microscopist Adolf Martens around 1890. Martensitic steels are low carbon steels built around the Type 410 composition of iron, with a minimum of 12 percent chromium,

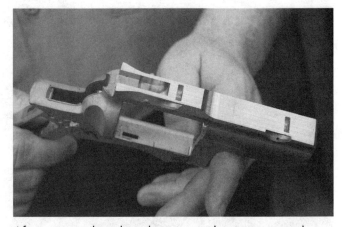

After one machine has done its work, you can see that the topstrap, scope rings and sight area have been machined. Also, the bottom has been machined. Now that the top and bottom are done, the next machine will clamp the frame on those surfaces and machine in the middle. (You've got to hold the parts somewhere.)

and 0.12 percent to 2.0 percent of carbon. They may be tempered and hardened. Due to the high carbon content of the steel it responds well to heat treatment to give various mechanical strengths, such as hardness. These steels are all magnetic.

Martensite gives steel great hardness, but it also reduces its toughness and makes it brittle, so few steels are fully hardened. A brittle part is not useful.

Type 416

Similar to Type 410 (the basic alloy in this line, and thus the one all others of its type are compared to) but has a bit of added sulphur giving improved machinability. Available in industrial quantities in bar form, you can also order it in many other shapes. Just ask your local steel mill for multi-ton order pricing. 416 is a common firearm stainless steel. It

is relatively easy to machine, it can be heat-treated. Many handgun barrels on the aftermarket are made of 416 stainless. Since it can be hardened, it can be made tough enough for firearms. Since it has a relatively high alloying content, it is much more resistant to corrosion than carbon steel.

There are also other grades of stainless steels, such as precipitation-hardened, duplex, and cast stainless steels. Stainless steel can be produced in a variety of finishes and textures and can be tinted over a broad spectrum of colors.

But we aren't done yet. Passivation is the removal of free iron from the surface of the stainless steel. This is performed by immersing the steel in an oxidant, such as nitric acid or citric acid solution. Also known as a "pickling bath." Since the top layer of iron is removed, passivation diminishes surface discoloration. There is some dispute over whether the

The fixture allows the fitter to file at the exact angle needed. The padding on her wrist keeps the bench top from irritating her wrist.

Contrary to what some think, Ruger parts are hand-fitted. They're just designed to require less of it than other designs.

A rack of SP101s in .357 Magnum, barrels fitted, as they travel through the plant.

corrosion resistance of stainless steel can be enhanced by the process of passivation. While passivation does not affect the thickness or effectiveness of the passive layer, it is useful in producing a clean surface for a further treatment, such as plating or painting. On the other hand, if the oxidant is incompletely removed from the steel, as sometimes happens in pieces with tight joints or corners, then crevice corrosion may result. Most research indicates that diminishing surface particle corrosion does not reduce susceptibility to pitting corrosion.

Aluminum and titanium can be a real hassle in this regard, while stainless is not helped much. Passivating aluminum is done only as a precursor to anodizing. Passivating titanium is a waste of time. Those who finish or re-finish firearms simply dunk aluminum, then clean the pickling solution off, and

insert the parts into the anodizing tanks. No big deal. Titanium can't be so processed without putting the whole setup in a non-oxygen atmosphere. Titanium apparently oxidizes so quickly that the time it takes to get the parts from the pickling tank to the plating tank is enough time for them to at least partly oxidize, and thus produce a blotchy finish.

What does all this have to do with a factory visit to the Ruger plant? Notice the repeated mentions of "good machinability" or "easy to machine" or "relatively easy to machine" when discussing steels. If you're going to forge steel into roughly-shaped parts, and then machine away everything that isn't a frame/cylinder/barrel, you'd better be paying attention to machinability. However, if you're casting parts, and using surface grinders, belt sanders and other shaping methods, you can use tougher alloys that are not so machine-able. The carbon steel most notable in this regard is 4140 steel. In carbon steels, it is a 0.4 percent carbon content steel, with a percentage point of chromium, and added molybdenum and manganese. Unlike say, a 1040 steel, which had the same carbon content, but no chromium, no moly, and less manganese, a 4140 is much more resistant to corrosion and abrasion. Both can be heat-treated but after heat-treat the 4140 will be much more durable. For a long time barrels were made of 4140 for its strength, while receivers and other parts were made of other less-alloyed steels such as 1040.

In using the investment casting method, Ruger was able to make the whole firearm out of 4140 or better steel. Since they didn't have to machine large portions of the forgings away (as in the forging/machining manufacturing route) they could make

the parts from much-tougher alloys. One example from a different manufacturer is the Browning Hi Power. The frame forging comes out of the forges as a red-hot piece of steel weighing several pounds. More than 90 percent of it is machined away. In order for the machining process to happen in a reasonable time, and with acceptable tool life, the steel has to be, in the words of custom gunsmith and first-rate shooter Bruce Gray, "made of the finest velveeta cheese." The Hi Power had a reputation as a relatively light-duty handgun. Where the 1911 could be fired 100,000 times or more with occasional slight gunsmith ministrations, the Hi Power was viewed as a 15,000-round gun max.

When FN switched the frame to a casting, to allow them to make a .40 S&W Hi Power that wouldn't come apart in a few thousand rounds, they

Once each frame has its trigger guard fitted and they are surface-finished together, they stay together.

Once cranes and trigger housings are fitted to the frame, the package can go off as a set to the belt-sander for the Ruger surface finish to be created.

used the same frames in their 9mm. The Hi Power Mk III they sent me went through 23,000 rounds without a fault, except for two malfunctions: one an ammunition fault, the other a magazine fault. Ruger, making pistols from castings from Day One, can expect much more than a mere 23,000 rounds through theirs, given correct ammo and proper maintenance.

Newport, New Hampshire

Located in the southwestern part of new Hampshire, Ruger's Newport plant is a huge place. You need a lot of room when you're making thousands of guns a week.

In the plant tour I started with castings in bins. The casting plant is a specialized building for a specialized process, and they start before dawn. By the time I arrived, they were done for the day. The castings get pulled from the bins and bolted into machining trays. Modern manufacturing does not involve rows of dedicated mills and lathes. Instead, companies use what are known as CNC machining centers: computer-controlled mills that perform more than one operation on a part. The systems are so well-designed now and computer control is

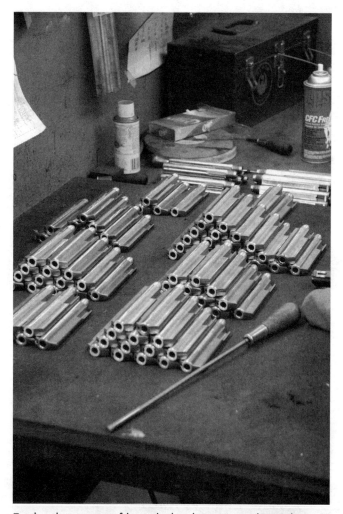

Each pile is a set of barrels that have "timed" on the test fixture to the same index. Doing this makes the assemblers' job a whole lot easier.

so cheap and effective that the machine reads the bar codes attached to each cutting tool. It knows the "offset" for each tool, which is measured at the toolroom and entered into the database. "Offset?" you ask. Let's take a simple end mill, say a one-inch cutter. It is supposed to be 1.00" (or 1.000", depending on how much you pay for it) in diameter. The tool room measures it and find that it is actually 1.05" in diameter. (In some places, such a tool would be sent back to the supplier with a sharp note about "off-spec cutters.") I am not commenting from direct observation of Ruger practices. It would be rude of me to ask such details, and it would be sloppy of the tool room people to answer. The tool room people slap a bar code sticker on the tool and its holder, and note in the database that it is actually 1.05" in diameter. When the CNC machining station picks that cutter out of the tray to cut with it, it knows to "offset" (that is, take into account) each cut by the .05" excess diameter of the tool.

But it gets better. From experience with their alloys, the toolroom people know how fast a tool wears. And after cutting "X" linear inches of steel, that tool will most-likely be 1.04" in diameter, and probably dull. The machine will note the lengths cut with that tool to the database, and when it reaches "X" linear inches of steel cut, the operator will replace the tool in the tray with a new one.

The number of cuts that can be made on a part held in a fixture are limited by the number of tools that the machine can hold or swap in a reasonable

time, and the cleverness of the people who program the cutter paths. Regardless of how big a machine you have, or how clever your programmers are, it is typical to have to put a part through two machines. After all, you have to clamp the part somehow, somewhere, and you can't very well machine the part where it is clamped. While the flats, slots, and pin holes are being machined/drilled, the CNC station can also be threading the frame for the barrel.

The castings that come in are frames, slide, barrel in some cases and other large parts. However, cylinders of revolvers are not castings. As cylindrical parts they are much more easily fabricated on automated lathes. As with the CNC machining centers, the CNC lathes have tool trays, and the machine picks them up (or they are pre-loaded on multiple arms) for the cutting tasks that particular

This assembler would probably be happy to show off, and make something to really impress a gun writer. But those pesky accountants want him busy making lots and lots of really good revolvers for the rest of you. So, no special guns for gun writers, alas.

part needs. In the case of the cylinders, bar stock of many feet are loaded into automatic feeders. Each bar is rolled out of the feeder and into the trough that feeds it through the lathe head. Inside the closed compartment, the machine hoses it with lubricant (in multiple garden-hose volumes) and turns the cylinders to their near-finished dimensions. They come out as gleaming cylinders, but lacking chambers. From there they go to another machine that puts the finishing touches on the bearing surfaces, and reams the chambers. Single action revolvers then get the ratchet cut, the locking slots cut, and are sent on to assembly.

Double-action revolvers need a few more steps. Once the cylinders of the DA guns are reamed, they have a ratchet/extractor star fitted, drilled and pins pressed home before final fitting of the ratchet. They

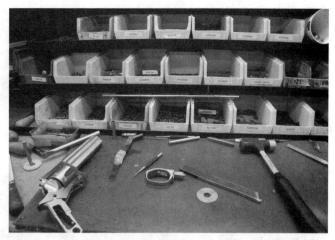

Here you see the assembler's bench, with all the parts bins arrayed, and tools at hand. Aspiring gunsmiths should pore over this photo and identify each tool and its purpose.

then go on to assembly.

Meanwhile, their frames and cranes have been passing through other machines for the milling, drilling and lathe-turning operations they need. The barrels have also been going through either an automated lathe or a CNC station. The single action revolvers, since they use cylindrical (mostly) barrels, can have their barrels cranked out by automated lathes. There, the outside is profiled, the shank turned and threaded, and the muzzle trimmed. The double-action revolvers, since they use profiled barrel and not cylindrical ones, have to have theirs carved on a CNC station. But, by means of a clever adaptation, the CNC station can also cut the shank to diameter and thread it. All very cool to watch – though you're watching through window of the machine and past firehose-level volumes of cutting lubricant.

Barrel Fitting

Even with all the precision of CNC-turned barrels and mill-cut barrel seats, barrels and the frames they go into cannot be cut to the last tenth of a thousandth to fit. They have to be hand-assembled,

The machine rest, for accuracy and remote proof-test firing.

A bin of barrel blanks, ready for their trip into the profiling CNC machine.

and that is where an interesting bit of hand-fitting comes into play. As we walked by one of the barrel-fitting benches, I noticed the workman spinning barrels into a fixture and then unscrewing them and placing them into piles. He was turning them

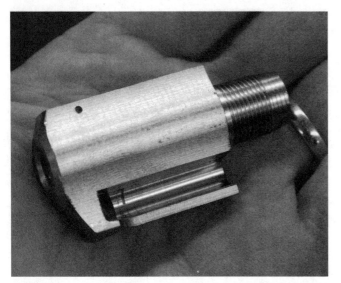

The double action revolvers need a profiled barrel, so they take a lot more machining.

into a threaded fixture and noting just how far they "clocked." That is, did each barrel spin around until the front sight was at ten o'clock, Noon or two o'clock? Each would be placed in a different stack.

Then as he worked on each frame, he had a selection of barrels to work from. Grab a frame, put it in the assembly fixture and spin on a barrel. What, it doesn't turn up far enough? Faced with a barrel that won't spin up far enough, the gunsmith with just that barrel and that frame is faced with a dilemma. He can either really apply torque to the barrel clamp, and thus force the barrel to turn enough. Or, he can remove the barrel and then file the frame or barrel to take metal off, allowing the barrel to spin around further until it comes back up to where it should be for proper torque. Most gunsmiths go directly to the "remove metal" part, as you can break a frame trying to torque a barrel in too tightly. The Ruger

The single action revolvers only need a simple cylindrical barrel, so the automated lathes crank them out like there's no tomorrow.

Here you see the individual tool-holders of your typical CNC machine. The holders are precisely ground to exacting standards that you'd scoff at if I told you. OK, how about this: one-tenth of a thousandth of an inch is considered a sloppy-fitting tool holder in some circles.

assembler? He just unscrews that particular barrel, puts it back in its stack, and tries again with a barrel from a "later" (as in "clocks up later") stack. Or, if the first barrel clocks too far, he picks one from a stack that clocks earlier. At the end of the day he only has a few frames and a few barrels that require filing,

instead of the every-other-one task of treating them all as matched pairs from the get-go.

The clever assembler or engineer who thought of that system should have received a bonus. It happened so long ago that no one remembers who thought it up and when. At least not without a lot of

Once accustomed to the alloys used, a Ruger assembler (any assembler) can file, stone and fit parts with a speed other gunsmiths can only envy.

research, which we couldn't do, standing in the aisle between assembly stations.

Then the barrel/frame combo gets a cylinder fitted. At this step it is easy, as the only two variables are the distance from the back of the cylinder to the front of the frame, and to the back of the barrel. Once the cylinder gap has been set, the racked revolvers head off for internals.

Now, the process is a bit more complicated when it comes to double-action revolvers. There, the crane has to be fitted to the frame before anything else. Then the cylinder gets fitted to the crane and the frame. Then, the barrel gets installed. Since the cylinder is already fitted to the frame and crane, the only step left for the DA revolvers is setting the cylinder gap.

Cylinder Gap

We make a great deal of fuss over cylinder gap. The amount needed is very easy to describe: enough so the powder residue on the cylinder face doesn't bind against the rear of the barrel. However, there's more to it than just that. Too much gap and you can have a loss of pressure. You can also have lots of gunk sprayed to the sides (called "spitting") on each shot, which can be bad for other shooters. It can be anything from annoying to hazardous. As you shoot,

you gradually wear the rear of the barrel and peen the bearing surfaces of the cylinder. You increase gap. And endshake. If you try to take a revolver with too much endshake, and fit it with a tight gap, you'll get cylinder rub. If you have a worn barrel rear (also known as the forcing cone) and you remove all the endshake, you could end up with excess gap. Removing endshake basically means forcing the cylinder back to take the slop out of it.

Neither condition is good, and either requires the ministrations of a gunsmith. If you shoot your revolver enough to get to that point, you should consider the wear as part of the cost of that much fun, and have it taken care of.

Internals

Once a revolver (the New Hampshire plant does wheelguns, the Prescott plant does pistols, with occasional overlaps) gets a part fitted to it, they stay together through the plant. DA revolvers with fitted cranes stay together until they get cylinders, barrels and internals, on to packing and shipping. Walking through the plant I had to constantly walk around racks of "in-process" guns. Here was a rack of frames, there frames with barrels. Being wheeled down the aisle were DA guns with cranes, and there were racks of complete guns waiting their trip to the test-fire plant.

Internal fitting happens at two stations. Or, I should say, there are two different streams of internal fitting you could map in the plant. The first is single action revolvers. Since there is no trigger guard to be fitted (at least not like the DA guns) the internal fitting is simply assembling the hand, hammer, trigger and associated parts into the frame. The assembler also ministers to the "minor" aspects of timing and trigger pull.

The double action guns are a bit more involved. First the trigger guard has to be precisely fitted to the frame. Yes, the curve of their joint is precision-machined on CNC machines but they still require a bit of hand-fitting. Each frame is mated with a trigger guard. If the line matches perfectly (a common occurrence as the CNC machines are well-serviced) then the sets are re-racked. If they do not, the assembler takes a few strokes with a file to make sure they do match.

The Ruger Finish

Once the rack has the trigger guards fitted, it would be wheeled off to a jaw-droppingly impressive machine. Oh, I suppose by the standards of someone who thinks in terms of computer-controlled machines, or huge size, would not be impressed. But for me, looking it as a big machine that does a simple job effectively, cleanly, and without a whole lot of technology, it is impressive. The receiver finish machine is a relatively simple, old-technology (by the standards of the CNC crowd) machine that imparts the distinctive Ruger finish to each stainless revolver.

Here is the belt sander finishing machine. There's something like twenty feet of belt in there, all coming down to caress the sides of the frame and trigger guard of the Ruger revolver in the fixture.

Racks of finished Bisley-gripped Super Blackhawks, ready for test-firing and boxing up.

Basically the machine is a movable fixture in which each revolver is held. (Pairs of them, in fact.) The finishing machines? A powder belt sander. Except the belt on this thing is something like 20 feet long, and at its contact point rotates around a pivot wheel that is about four inches in diameter.

The wheeled end of the machine rises and lowers, with the belt whipping through, while the pivoting fixture lifts, moves and just about pirouettes. The belt sander thus imparts that distinctive brushed-stainless finish that we've all come to know as only a Ruger finish.

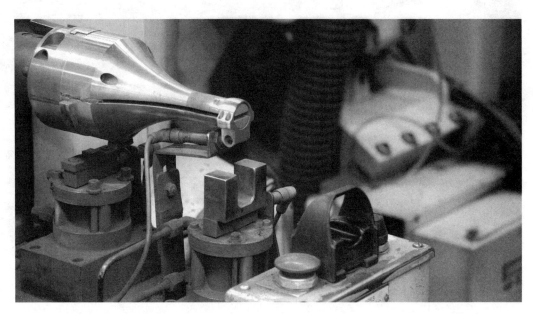

The ring machine and its holding arm. That's a finished ring on the arm.

There's a little SP-101 in there, getting prettied up.

Once all the racks at the finish machine are done, they are sent back to the assemblers and then they all come off one-by-one for internals.

There, the assembler first fits the internals into the trigger guard. As the entire package comes out as one assembly, he/she can simply install everything and check function. Then, it goes into and out of the frame several times as the assembler adjusts timing and trigger pull.

I watched one assembler who was quite fast and effective. In many filing jobs your gunsmith will approach the task with careful, graduated filing strokes, repeatedly measuring and testing. But then, the task your gunsmith is doing is practically a one-of-a-kind job. It may be years before he has to do that exact same operation again, or it has been years

since he's done it before. If he screws it up it could be quite expensive.

The assembler is dong the same thing, over and over again. Once he or she gets a feel for the hardness of the steel Ruger uses, filing is a much better quantified process. Having worn out more than a few files myself, I can tell you that once you know how a task goes, you can even account for the wear on the file. The assembler I watched was like a chain-saw filer. Something needed fitting, it would get one, two or three full-power filing strokes then be checked for fit. Then one more, and he was done. Quite impressive. Each revolver would be fitted, timed, and then go back on the rack. The parts were in bins in the front of the bench, and the assemblers would pull one out from each bin as needed.

An easy job. Pull the finished ones off and put them in the "Finished" bin. Then put the next rough-machined ring set on and hit the trigger to send it off.

The next rough-machined one on the arm, and the operator getting ready to hit the trigger.

Scope Mounts

The big thing early in my career working at the gun shops was the change in Ruger scope rings. Like all other rifles (bear with me here) the Ruger M-77 originally used drilled and tapped screw holes in the receiver, and a bolted-on based for rings. I don't recall if the "round top" Rugers used the Remington receiver contour or the Winchester, but Ruger did use a common shape for their rifle, which made it easy to fit bases, as you could simply use one of the common ones already on the shelf.

But that wasn't good enough for Bill Ruger. You see, four little screws are not a very secure way to hold a scope in place. That we've been getting away with it for decades doesn't make the system any stronger. So what Ruger did was make the rings such that they had their own clamp built-in, and dovetails and a Woodruff key made as part of the ring. Then, they changed the receiver, so it had a pair of flats, with slots for the key and notches for the clamping lugs. Now a Ruger rifle had Ruger rings that were more durable than the scope itself.

In working at the shop I saw more than a few damaged scopes and a handful where the screws had simply snapped, launching the scope from the rifle. We had a photo of John the shop manager (wish I had a copy) sitting at the shooting bench. He was holding his large-caliber rifle in one hand, and his scope and rings in another. Streaming down his forehead was a river of blood, from where the scope had bounced off his skull after leaving the rifle when John had fired it. That was the kind of occurrence Ruger wanted to prevent.

The ring system did just that. There was only one problem: they couldn't make the rings fast enough. When the system was unveiled, and for some time afterwards, you got a set of rings with the rifle.

Rough machine ring sets ready to go to the machine.

Period. Lose the rings, and getting another set was a major hassle. Spares? Fuggedaboudit. It was all they could do to keep up. The rings would have been perfect for the handguns, and the rapidly increasing handgun hunting segment, but they could barely keep up with the rifles.

So Ruger installed the first piece of automated equipment, which they still have and which is still in use. As automated machines go it is primitive, slow and probably hard to keep running smoothly. (At least compared to the self-maintaining, self-servicing, auto-notice "hey, I need my oil changed" CNC machines of today.) It also requires a dedicated operator. The process is simple: the rough-machined rings are matched-up to bases. They have four Philips-head machine screws locked in to mate the pair and keep them together. The operator sits in his comfy chair and as the machine bring an arm around he plucks the finished ring off and sets it aside. He then places a rough-made ring on the arm. As the multi-armed machine rotates around, each arm brings it to a machining/polishing station, where the finish dimensions are cut and the surfaces polished and matched. After completing a rotation each ring is done, and the operator plucks if off, sets it aside, and installs the next rough ring set.

The machine sped up the ring manufacturing process so much that Ruger could offer extra rings for sale, make handgun models that could take them, and make the life of gunsmiths soooo much easier. Ruger rings became so common, and obviously were so durable, that I had the occasional customer asking me if I could machine his or her rifle or handgun to take the Ruger rings, even though they had not been so-made to start with. I tried it once, on a scrapped Ruger handgun. (Always, ALWAYS do your R&D on a scrap gun if at all possible.) The steel Ruger used was hard enough that I clearly needed a bigger machine than was available to me. So I dropped the idea.

It shows what a (at the time) large investment in machinery can do for a company. To have tried to increase production with individual machines and machine operators would have been cost-prohibitive. But one automated machine, simple by today's standards, made the rings a common commodity. The

next time you're in a gun shop and see Ruger rings on the pegboard, you'll now know why they are so common.

Finishes

One of the big advantages to using stainless for so many firearms is the complete lack of finishing chemicals. The stainless surface needs only be given whatever polishing or brushing that results in the desired finish. The belt-sanding trick Ruger has produces the distinctive brushed finish. The carbon steel guns require a hot-dip blueing, but one updated by the decades of experience and advances in chemistry. The interesting finishes are the ones that are newer. The "titanium" finish on the stainless guns like the Super Redhawk we tested is a new one, and is done in a manner so secret I couldn't get in the area of the plant that did it. I can only surmise that they've found a way to control oxidation of stainless (sort of the opposite of the passivation method discussed earlier) and thus use a bead-blast and oxidation combo to produce the dark gray finish.

The color case-hardened finish on the Vaquero is another advance in chemistry. Alloy steel can't

Without timing and sorting barrels, the assembler might have to resort to turning the shoulder back, as a custom gunsmith is doing here on a bull barrel for a custom caliber installation.

The custom fit also involves setting the cylinder gap on the turned-back barrel. After all, if you advance the barrel a turn, it comes further out of the frame towards the cylinder.

In extreme cases you have to chase the threads to make the last ones fit the frame after setting back the barrel shoulder. All this work is avoided by sorting barrels. Smart guys and gals, those Ruger folks.

be case-hardened, at least not by any method that produces colors. So to give the investment-cast alloy steel Vaquero receiver a swirling color like the color case-hardening is another secret method. As far as I know, no custom gunsmith has figured out how to duplicate either finish. So if you have a Ruger with one of those finishes, and you do something to scrub, wear, remove or otherwise plate-over those finishes, the only way to get them back is to send it to Ruger.

Which leads me to a tangential subject.

Ruger Repairs

If you send in an Old Model Blackhawk for the new upgrade, you'll get all the old parts back. But if you have done anything to change the factory-original Ruger, those changes might be removed/put back to original, and that could be pricey. Or, Ruger might not do it. If you send in a Blackhawk that has been hard-chromed since it left Ruger, they might not work on it. If you send in an old .357 Magnum Blackhawk that has been re-built to .44 Special they may not work on it. Or the price of repairs might include a new cylinder and barrel, back to .357 Magnum.

Ruger has been sued more than any other firearms maker. Not because they are less competent, but because they have more money. Look, I'm not insulting lawyers when I point out that they sue people who have money. And only people who have money. Ruger is touchy about altered Ruger products, and cannot have anything leaving the factory that has been changed from the design they intended.

If you had their legal bills, you'd be touchy too.

So if you have a Ruger you want to send in for repairs it might be a good idea to send a letter describing the situation to them, and asking for a quote or at least feedback on your needs.

To return to our story:

Test Fire

Each and every Ruger handgun gets test-fired. The description given me was "Each one gets a chamber-full of proof loads." Thus, a rifle gets a proof load and then some standard ammo on whatever schedule called for. Ditto pistols. But revolvers get a full five or six (depending on how many they hold) proof loads. A proof load is an

Not only are the individual proof loads headstamped as such (and the brass melted down and recycled after one firing) the heads are dyed red to makes sure no one confuses them with regular ammo.

A rack of fully-assembled GP100s, each loaded with six proof loads, ready to get their initial shooting.

industry-standard cartridge (loaded by the ammo companies) that has its specifications very carefully defined and rigidly controlled. Basically, it is a load of (around, it varies from caliber to caliber) 130 percent of the normal maximum working load of that caliber. As an example, the maximum working load of a .44 Magnum cartridge is listed as 34,000 psi. Most factory ammo will be under that, by enough of a margin that even the hottest load in a particular production batch won't exceed the 34K figure. (Or not by much, nor very often.) Most reloaders will keep their loads in the 28K range, if not for recoil then simply because 34K all the time wears a gun faster. A proof load? We're talking on the order of 44,200 psi. One thing I noticed right away in the old days when I was working in radio broadcasting was that few if any DJs listened to the same music off the air that they played on the air. If you think test-firing guns sounds like a cool job, trust me, it wears quickly. The people in every single test-fire bay I've ever seen look at it as a fun job, but a job nevertheless. And often they do not do much shooting in their spare time.

A percentage of a production lot of guns are clamped in the machine rest and checked for accuracy. If there is anything wrong, the offending handgun is torn down, inspected and the cause uncovered. Then the whole batch is inspected to find out if any of the others have the same problem, and if so, they are fixed.

Last, they are boxed, with a fired case (required by so many ignorant state legislatures), the owner's manual, lock and other accessories.

Gun Writers' Guns

While I was at the plant, I asked if they could show me the room with the "gun writers' guns." You know, the hand-selected, hand-built guns that get sent out as cherry-picked samples to wow us with their performance. That got a laugh. Folks, there is no such room. Not at Ruger, and not at any other firearms plant I've ever been in. When we ask for guns, they simply send a shipping notice to the stockroom. There, someone grabs the model the shipping notice asks for, wraps and labels it, and off it goes. I know I'm going to hurt someone's feelings here, but the "gun writer sample gun" is the same kind of urban myth as the 100 mpg carburetor, or the engine that runs on water. Ain't no such thing.

Chapter 2

Calibers of Ruger Handguns

If you're going to make handguns for the American market, you'd better make them in the most popular calibers available. However, Ruger has made some combinations that are far from common, and even unique.

The .38 Special comes in a variety of flavors, and also works just fine in .357 Magnum chambers. Left, a .38 Special 158-grain lead round nose. Center a 200-grain .357 Magnum load, and on the right the super-hot 125-grain JHP in a .357 Magnum.

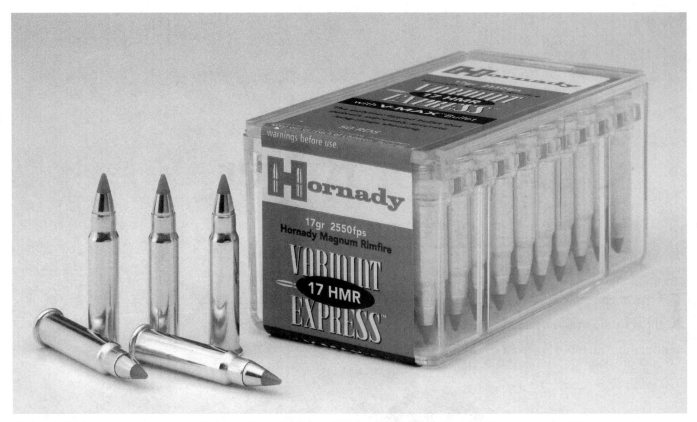

The powerful new propellants available today make the .17 HMR one of the most accurate, hardest-hitting rimfire cartridge available.

.17 HMR

The little .17 came about from the requests of varminters for something better than the high-speed .22LR loadings. Created by necking down a .22 Magnum to take (obviously) .177" jacketed bullets, it offers higher velocity, flatter trajectory and better accuracy than the high-speed .22LR loadings. The ballistics are on the order of 17-grain bullets at 2500 fps, and 20-grain bullets at 2300 fps. These are far past the typical high-speed .22LR, with its 32-grain bullet at 1300-1400 fps. The much better ballistic coefficient of the little .17 means it has both a flatter trajectory and greater retained velocity at range.

The Ruger Single Six is currently the only handgun in the Ruger lineup where you can get the .17 HMR (Hornady Magnum Rimfire) cartridge.

.22LR

By far the most common, and highly-produced cartridge in America, if you make a firearm and you don't make a version if it in .22LR you're probably not going to be in business long. First developed by Smith & Wesson before the Civil War, the rimfire .22 has gone on to be the one cartridge you can count on everyone having fired. Unless your exposure to firearms is exclusively from having been in the military, you will have shot a .22LR at some time in your shooting experience.

Apparently a lot of it, as the last production figures I read on the .22LR had annual production (and thus consumption, as few shooters squirrel away cubic feet of .22LR ammo) had production over 2.1 billion rounds a year, and that figure had remained steady for a number of years. I suspect that the reason it hasn't gone up is a combination of two factors: First, the existing .22LR machinery is probably working at full capacity in every plant that makes rimfires. Second, the latest surge of surplus ammo has occupied some of that "plinking" ammo expenditures. While the two are not comparable in any other way, the .22LR and 7.62X39 cartridges share one thing in common: they are (or were, until the 7.62 got scarce) common and cheap. So plinkers who might have been satisfied with just a .22LR expedition, topped off by a box or two of hunting-rifle ammo, now spend money on a case of 7.62 for their SKS or AK. That discretionary ammo money comes out of the .22LR end of things.

Still, two billion .22LR cartridges! If every person in the USA got a portion of that, it would be a fraction less than nine rounds for each of us. Since there are many who do not shoot (apparently New York, LA and other cities are full of people who don't shoot) then we can alter that. The last figure I saw was that there were something on the order of 59 million adults who own firearms. That puts the .22LR ammo distribution at an average of 36 rounds per shooter.

Since those of us who shoot shoot a lot (the last time I went to the range and shot some .22LR I put about 400 rounds downrange) some of you are obviously slacking. Still, that's a lot of ammo to be made, and shot, each year.

The very first Ruger firearm, the Mark I, was (and still is) a .22LR. You can also find the Ruger Mk II and Mk III in .22LR, as well as the .22/45. In the revolver line there are the SP-101, Bearcat and Single Sixes to be found in .22LR.

.256 Winchester Magnum

A single-shot cartridge made for a special Blackhawk called the Hawkeye – single-shot in that the Hawkeye did not have a cylinder, merely a rotating loading block. Load it, fire the shot, open it and extract the case, load it and fire again. Why go to all this trouble? Because the .256 was a .357 Magnum case necked down to accept stubby little .257" bullets. In a standard cylinder each round as it was fired would press back as the shoulder of the case expanded. In a few shots you couldn't rotate the cylinder. So Ruger made the Hawkeye as a single-shot. Except it was even stranger than you'd think. The swinging block wasn't the chamber. The chamber was cut in the end of the barrel, and the swinging block was simply the breechblock, with an extra long firing pin inside it, to fire the round. For all that you got a 75-grain stubby bullet with not much of a ballistic coefficient, at 2300 fps. Not much of a varminter, nor a barn-burning hunting round.

Ahead of its time, the Hawkeye was a commercial dud, one of the very few Ruger has offered. Collectors now go crazy about them, as only 3,104 of them were made.

.32 H&R Magnum

The old firm of Harrington & Richardson is now remembered only for two things: a popular line of inexpensive revolvers made in the latter part of the 19th and early part of the 20th century, and the cartridge they tried to use as a "bootstrap" to lift them out of their problems in the 1980s. It is derived from the old .32 S&W Short and .32 S&W cartridges, lengthened and run at much higher pressures. The extra length was to preclude someone putting the new high-pressure cartridge into one of the old guns, which were not designed for anything like the pressures of the new Magnum. As a small game and low-recoil defense cartridge, it has a lot

The .32 offers a lot of options. For great accuracy, .32 Long wadcutters are superb. The common and usually cheap .32 Short or .32 Long are great plinkers. The .32 H&R Magnum (on the right) is a sharp little defense round that you should not take lightly.

to recommend it. It has not, however, found wide acceptance in the marketplace. One place where you can find it is on the Cowboy Action Shooting circuit. There, however, it isn't shot as a Magnum but as a super low-recoil competition load. Where a factory defense load for the .32 Magnum would be in the 85-grain JHP bullet at 1100 fps, a Cowboy load (which must be both a lead bullet, and under 1,000 fps) would be a 105- to 115-grain bullet, and probably going a sedate 750 fps.

Any revolver chambered in the .32 Magnum can also use the .32 S&W and .32 S&W Short cartridges, meaning there is a lot of cheap practice ammo lying around on closet shelves in the US.

The Ruger firearms to be found in .32 Magnum are the SP101 and the Single Six.

.32-20

The high-speed predecessor to the .32 Magnum, the .32-20 originally was a black powder cartridge from the 1880s. It ranked third behind the .45 Colt and .44-40 in total production in the Colt SAA revolvers. Apparently a lot of cowboys back then felt adequately equipped with a .32 revolver. The original loading was a bit light by later standards, and the ammunition companies loaded a special hi-speed version, which was not to be used in handguns. If the .32-20 was plenty stout enough, why the .32 Magnum? Two reasons: one, there were a lot of old guns that could chamber the .32-20 that should not be fired with a modern version. So upping the pressure, even using a special case marked with the now-standard "+P" markings for over-pressure loads, would not have worked. There would have been too many old guns busted, and owners potentially harmed. Two, the .32-20 was too long to fit in the cylinder of the H&R revolvers of the early 1980s. So H&R teamed up with Federal and made a new cartridge.

Another concern was the reloadability of the old .32-20. Reloading was going strong by the 1980s, and the older cartridge, with its bottleneck case shape, could be a real pain in the neck to reload. By using a straight-wall case, Federal and H&R could be sure that the new case would be a snap top reload. And so it is.

The .32-20 can be found in the Single Six S32X Special model, with cylinders for both the .32-20 and the .32 Magnum. Also, if you really wanted one you could get a Blackhawk in .30 Carbine fitted with a new cylinder in .32-20 (the bore diameters are compatible) and run up some really wicked-hot loads.

.30 Carbine

When the Blackhawk in .30 Carbine was introduced in 1974, the shooting world was still awash in surplus .30 Carbine ammo. It was possible to do a lot of shooting for not a lot of money. That the Blackhawk with a long barrel and in .30 Carbine proved to be a very useful (and fun) varminting cartridge didn't hurt. It has been in production ever since then, with a short hiatus in the mid-1990s.

The .32-20, here flanked by a 9mm and a .38 Special. You can see from its length that it would have been a tight fit in any revolver initially made for the .38 Special and only the .38 Special. Thus the invention of the .32 Magnum by H&R, as their revolvers did not have cylinders long enough for the .32-20. In the right revolver (can anyone say "Ruger Blackhawk convertible?") the .32-20 can do anything the .32 Magnum does, and more.

While the surplus .30 carbine ammo (at least the cheap stuff) has long since dried up (we shot it all!) the Blackhawk in .30 Carbine is still a hot ticket for handgunning varmints. Since the cartridge is capable of impressive ballistics for a handgun, you can count on a flat trajectory and high velocity out to as far as you can reasonably hit. There is one caveat, however, and that is you'll have to wear plugs or muffs even while hunting. The Blackhawk in .30 Carbine is loud. Loud even by rifle standards. Yes, we all "know" that hunters don't hear the shot, they're too focused on their game to notice little things like muzzle blast. But it still happens. This

The .30 Carbine is a loud, loud round in a Blackhawk. But it is a flat-shooting cartridge that does everything the .32 Magnum and .32-20 wish they could.

isn't an exercise in philosophy and debate like the tree falling in the forest. And, in varminting, you're going to be doing more shooting. At least if you're good at it. Where a deer hunter might fire less than a box of ammo in a hunting season, quite a few less if he doesn't practice and is a good stalker, a varminter might fire several hundred rounds. Those shots take their toll, especially the .30 Carbine. The Blackhawk, even with a long barrel, is much shorter than the 18" barrel the .30 Carbine was designed for. Thus the muzzle blast is at a higher pressure than other handguns cartridges would be from the same length barrel.

Loud, flat and fun.

9mm

Developed for the Luger Pistole M-1908 for the German Army, the 9mm is one of the most common centerfire cartridges to be found. The original Luger used a .30 cartridge, but that wasn't big enough. The Germans asked the designer, Georg Luger, to open the bottleneck of the case to as large a size as it would take, and that became the 9X19, 9mm Parabellum,

9mm Luger, and all the other names it has gotten over the ensuing century.

The cartridge is quite efficient. You would be hard-pressed to get a bullet of that size and weight up to a similar velocity in any other case, and not be using a lot more powder to get it. Compact, it can be fit into a wide variety of pistol, submachine gun and carbine platforms. As compact as it is, those platforms will hold a lot of bullets, one of the premier attractions of the 9mm.

It was not, however, held in high regard here in the States. Not for decades. Not until the high-crime 1970s and the advent of hi-capacity pistols. When your choices are between the 1911 with 8 rounds total of .45 ACP, and a plethora of 9mm pistols that hold much the same, why choose smaller? There were a few early hi-cap pistols, like the Browning Hi-Power. But most were like the quirky MAB-15, or unobtainable, like the CZ-75. When S&W came out with the M-59 in 1974, and ammo makers started making hollow points that actually expanded, then the 9mm got a lot more popular. So much so that by the mid 1980s Ruger had to have a pistol, and unveiled the P85. but it took a bit of time to get going. (So much so that when first we heard of the new Ruger pistol, its model designation was the "P84.")

The 9mm is so common it threatens to overtake the .22LR as the most common cartridge to be found at ranges.

Ruger has the 9mm equation down pat now. You can get a Ruger revolver in 9mm. The Blackhawk convertibles have been made in .357/9mm, and the Security Six and SP101 have been made in 9mm. Then there is the impressive listing of pistols: P85, P89, P93, P94 and P95. A lot of 9mm bullet launchers to choose from.

As if that wasn't enough, the Ruger PC (Pistol caliber) 9 and PC-40 carbines use Ruger handgun magazines. And a final 9mm entrant is the Ruger SMG, an improved Uzi built here in the USA for use by law enforcment.

.357 Magnum

Developed and unveiled in 1935, as an evolution of the .38-44 High Speed loadings of the .38 Special, the .357 was then more than most shooters could handle. Or so the hype went. (You think hype is new? I think the Romans invented it. If they didn't

they refined it to dizzying new heights.) Shooters of the time were told it launched a 158-grain bullet at 1400+ fps. Maybe in the pressure barrels, but not in any revolver, then or now.

By the mid 1950s it was seen as a hot load, but one an experienced shooter could handle. And after all, any revolver chambered in .357 could also handle .38 Specials so it was natural that the first Ruger centerfire handgun would be offered in .357 Magnum.

Simply the .38 Special case extended 1/10" and run at much higher pressures (nearly double, with the .38 at 18,000 and the .357 at 34,000 psi), the .357 Magnum in the long run proved to be too much for earlier revolvers designed as .38 Specials. The S&W K frame, originally a .32 and .38 (first rolled out in 1899) proved to be a tad fragile for a steady diet of .357 Magnum ammo. So much so that S&W had to develop the L frame, an amalgam of the K frame .38 and the N frame .44 sizes, to withstand

Bullet weight for the .357 Magnum were traditionally 158 grains, as these all are.

The .38 and .357 are so simple to load for, that dies for them are commonly in the top tier of best-selling loading dies. To make ammo for the .38 is easy. Just read up first, so you do it safely.

the pounding of the then-popular law enforcement loading of a 125-grain JHP at Magnum velocities.

The Blackhawk had no such problems. I've never heard of someone shooting a Blackhawk in .357 Magnum loose, at least not with normal, sane loads. There's always someone convinced that the safety margin built into cartridges and firearms is actually a conspiracy to cheat them of the shooting fun that extra recoil, noise and velocity are guaranteed them by the Declaration of Independence. So you can always find someone, somewhere, who has broken any gun, no matter how tough. Some of them are actually proud of it.

The .357 Magnum can be found in Ruger revolvers both single action and double action. The original Security Six, the later GP100, SP101 and even the big Redhawk. But not the Super Redhawk. The Blackhawk (obviously) and the Vaquero both Old and New, but not the Super Blackhawk.

.38 Special

Any Ruger that uses the .357 Magnum also uses the .38 Special, but some models take the .38 only. The SP101 can be had in .38 Special-only versions. I can only imagine that they are there for some shooters or some agencies that requires .38-only revolvers, and which cannot (or are not allowed by regs) to also accept the .357 Magnum.

.357 Maximum

This one lasted for just a few years. In the late 1970s and early 1980s metallic silhouette was a hot new shooting game. Basically you're shooting steel knock-down plates out to 200 meters. To shoot well you needed an accurate handgun that shot flat enough to 200 meters to make sighting relatively easy. It had to deliver enough power at 200 meters to knock a steel ram silhouette off the pedestals. And since a standard course was 40 rounds and a full course was 80 shots (you couldn't make up misses) you didn't want something that would make you punch-drunk from recoil before you were done.

Some shooters were stretching the boundaries of the .357 Magnum by either using heavier than standard bullets, or special hard-cast bullets that were loaded long to get more case capacity.

Developed by Remington and offered in a special Blackhawk with a longer cylinder, it lasted three years in the Ruger catalog: 1982 - 1984. The cartridge did everything it was supposed to: it launched a .357" bullet at impressive velocities, to the rams and beyond. It knocked them down just fine. However it also created gas-cutting in the frame. When the bullet jumps the gap between the cylinder and the forcing cone of the barrel, the superheated gases jet out of the gap behind the bullet. This jet of gases slams into the topstrap of the frame. On most guns it creates a hard-crusty powder residue. On some it cuts the steel surface a bit, and then stops. It stops because the extra distance created by the cutting is just enough to reduce the cutting action. Also, the surface becomes rough and the scale shields the underlying steel from further cutting. On the .357 Maximum it cut deeper, and faster, than on other calibers. Ruger asked Remington to change the loading, Remington asked Ruger to change the design or alloy, and the shooters asked for more guns. No one got what he wanted, with fewer than ten thousand guns made.

.38-40

The .38-40 is another cowboy cartridge dating back to the post-Civil War era, when the whole

The .38-40 is a cartridge with a great history, and can be found amongst cowboy action shooters. It doesn't do anything the 10mm doesn't (and the 10 can do more) but it does it with a lot more style and nostalgia than the 10mm does.

idea of self-contained cartridges was new. Despite its name (which was originally the .38 WCF) it is neither a .38, nor did it take 40 grains of black powder. It came from necking the .44-40 down to .40 caliber, and so the case designation came from the "40" of the .44-40 – which is close to but not the same as the case size as the .45 Colt. The case size is so close that specialty ammunition manufacturers could make the old "Five-in-One" blanks for movie productions back when the staple of movie productions was Westerns. Those blanks would work in .45 Colt, .44-40 and .38-40 handguns and rifles. Thus five in one.

The .38-40 exists today solely due to the efforts and nostalgia of cowboy action shooters. I think also to their parsimony. Collectors of Colt SAA revolvers will jump all over .45 Colt and .44-40 specimens. But the .38-40? Big yawn. After all, ammo was hard to find, they were common and not really rare, and often not accurate. So, if you were a would-be cowboy action shooter, and needing some real Colts, wouldn't you shoot a pair (they need paired guns) of .38-40s? Since you could get them for a lot less than the .45 Colt and .44-40s the collectors were fighting over?

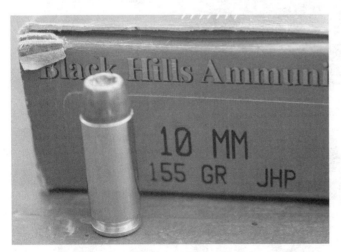

You can get some really screaming rounds in the 10mm. Black Hills (among others) offers a 155-grainer that easily goes over 1250 fps from a pistol or revolver.

The one good thing of the .38-40 is the bullet size. The cases are fragile, hard to reload, and prone to random acts of reloading and functional suicide. (They crack, crumple and lose tension without warning, and at high rates.) The accuracy can sometimes be hard to improve. But the bullets are .400" for jacketed and .401" for lead. This is the same size as the .40 S&W and the 10mm. Which is not a great surprise, as the developers of the 10mm cartridge used .38-40 bullets (but not cases) to experiment with and create the new cartridges.

The .38-40 is found in convertible Blackhawks, paired with the 10mm.

10mm

A pistol cartridge developed in the 1980s for the Dornhaus & Dixon Bren Ten. As originally loaded it was hot. Hot. HOT. The Norma loading was a 200-grain bullet at 1200 fps. At that it was an autoloading pistol that was just a step behind factory .44 Magnum loadings. Even in the (next step) American loading a 180-grain bullet at 1200 fps it was a stout number. So much so that the FBI, who had declared after April 1986 that the 10mm was going to be the new FBI cartridge, found they couldn't swing it. Not to be disparaging, but the FBI is a law enforcement agency composed of accountants, lawyers, statisticians and focused on white-collar crime. They are not a bunch of fire-breathing SWAT cops. The idea that they could get every (or even a significant minority) of their agents to qualify with a kick-ass cartridge like the 10mm was absurd. Compounding the problem was the 10mm case. Designed to fit into a 1911-sized pistol, it was as long as a .45 ACP. That meant it would only fit into a full-sized pistol. Short-statured agents had a heck of a time just wrapping their hands around the resulting big guns.

In their efforts to get agents qualified the FBI kept asking for ever-softer loadings in the 10mm. When they got down to the point of asking for a 180-grain bullet at 950 fps, the engineers at S&W and Winchester put their heads together. The big 10mm case, run at such a low level, had a lot of airspace in it. If they would just shorten the case, and move the bullet back, to eliminate that dead air, why they could fit the resulting cartridge into a 9mm-sized pistol. And the .40 S&W was born.

Ruger has never made a 10mm pistol. Only revolvers, and those were only the convertibles in .38-40 and 10mm – actually only New-Model convertibles, as by the time the 10mm was unveiled (and the .38-40 had had its resurgence) the factory had switched over to the New Model.

.40 S&W

As you just read, the .40 came about because the 10mm was "too much." I call it the Goldilocks cartridge, as the arguments for decades before the 10mm had been between the .45 ACP (the "too much" cartridge of an earlier generation) and the 9mm (the "too little" contender).

Advocates of the 9mm pointed out that anyone could shoot it, that it was plenty good enough, and that a whole lot of people had expired from having been shot with a 9mm. The .45 (to their point of view) was too much, it kicked too hard, the guns were too big, they didn't hold enough ammo, and worst of all, the advocates of the .45 were also all 1911 advocates, and a "cocked and locked" pistol was just unsafe. Advocates of the .45 pointed out how the 9mm was a poor "stopper" (reliably expanding bullets were still new in the early to mid 1980s) and

The .40 S&W is rapidly becoming, if it isn't already, the most common police pistol cartridge in the US. If you can't find a box of .40 in your local gunshop, it is only because all the hoarders have bought it in expectation of the next ammo price increase.

you needed all those extra bullets and then some to make up for the poor effectiveness of the 9.

The 10mm was to be "more but not too much" but you have to wonder who was reading the ballistic tables in the FBI head office when they settled on the 10.

The .40 was the compromise, and has turned out to be a decent-enough cartridge. When it comes to revolvers, the .40 to the 10mm is not in the same league as the .38 to the .357. You cannot use .40 S&W ammo in a revolver unless it has been modified to use full-moon clips. Unlike the .38/.357 which headspaces (stops dropping into the chamber) on the rim, the 10mm and the .40 headspace on the case mouth. As the 10mm is significantly longer than the .40, the .40 will drop past the reach of the firing pin.

So you can have a Ruger in .40 only in pistols, unless you have an extra cylinder cut for your .38-40/10mm Blackhawk, one that is .40 S&W only. The only reason I could see doing that is if I had a limitless supply of free .40 ammo available, and a burning desire to shoot it though a single action revolver. As neither of those is likely to happen (I got the "shoot a single action all day" part out of my system decades ago) I can't see having Hamilton Bowen make me a .40 cylinder for a Blackhawk.

.41 Magnum

The .41 was to be the "in-between" cartridge of the hunting and law enforcement set. The .357 Magnum was good, but many wanted more. The .44 Magnum was too much for use on the streets, at least as seen by some. That didn't keep the Detroit PD and other agencies from authorizing its use. A good idea, the .41 would have had a better chance if it hadn't been last. The .357 came out in 1935, the .44 Magnum in 1956, but the .41 didn't arrive until 1964.

With a case the same length as the .357 and .44 Magnums, running at the same pressures it fits into the same guns, and uses .410" jacketed and .411" lead bullets.

When it came out the obvious revolver for it was the Blackhawk. And so you could get a lightweight big bore in 1964, if you "settled" on the .41. By then

The bullet weights and choices in the .41 Magnum may not be as expensive as that of the .44, but you can find plenty to keep you happy. The common weights are 210-215 grains, in a lead SWC or JHP. The low end is 170 grains, the top end is the 250-265 grains.

Ruger had shifted the .44 to the Old Model Super Blackhawk, and you had a bigger gun for the bigger bullets. When the Redhawk came out in 1980 there were still enough shooters using the .41 to warrant offering it in the .41, but no models introduced since then have had the middle magnum as an option.

If you want the lightest possible single action in a big bore, your choices are a Blackhawk in .41 or .44. It's a toss-up as to which the collectors will deprive you of first. The .44 is certainly a more-popular option, but the collectors won't leave the .41s alone for long.

.44-40

Another grand old cowboy cartridge this one ranks second only to the .45 Colt in sales in the Colt SAA. The .44-40 is an oddball, in that it is (basically, but not exactly) a necked-down .45 Colt, to take bullets of .427" diameter. As such it is an odd size. The Ruger convertibles that took the .44-40 thus has to be a compromise. The .44-40 bullets (and thus the grooves) should have been .427" while the .44 Magnum called for .429-.430" bullets. The compromise was .430" for modern bullets and standard pressures in .44 Magnum loadings and letting the .44-40 soft lead bullets "slug up" to the slightly larger groove diameter.

.44 Russian and .44 Special

The Russian and the Special are to the .44 Magnum as the .38 Special is to the .357 Magnum: shorter cases but with the same case, rim and bullet diameters. Cowboy action shooters like to use the shorter cases. With the soft loads they use (they are not allowed to load anything but lead bullets,

Left to right, the .44 Russian, the .44-40, the .44 Special, and the .44 Magnum. With the right convertible you can shoot all these from one Blackhawk.

and those must be less than 1,000 fps) the large case has lots of extra air space. Extra air space is bad for consistent ignition. So the short cases let them load light and still have consistent pressures for reliable accuracy and function. The Russian and Special rounds simply fit into the .44 Magnum chambers, and the bullet makes the jump without any problems. However, as with the .38 Special, if you do a lot of shooting with the shorter cases, you should scrub the powder and lead residue out of the chamber (the gap between the shorter cases and the end of the chamber) to keep the Magnums from sticking when you fire those.

.44 Magnum

The original big-bore hunting cartridge for the modern hunter, the .44 Magnum is a result of the

experimenting of Elmer Keith. What he did was take the .44 Special, design a bullet that protruded more out of the case in a useful way, and then loaded it with the then-new progressive powders that gave more velocity at lower pressures. He also upped the operating pressure from the 17,000 PSI of the original .44 Special, up to something in the upper 20,000 range. This was hard on the guns, but the results were worth wearing out guns. He could boost a 240-grain lead semi wadcutter to close to 1,200 fps. Properly loaded, it was accurate enough and powerful enough to make handgun hunting more than just a stunt. The .44 Magnum came about in the 1950s, where the case was lengthened to preclude the use of the new ammo in the old .44 Special guns, and the pressure was upped to reflect the improved steels, heat-treatment and powders available.

The low end of the .44 Magnum bullet weights is 180 grains (not in this lineup). Handgun hunters want something better, so they start at the traditional 240-grain lead semiwadcutter (left) and progress up to the heavyweights, in the 315 to 325 grain weight range.

The Ruger Blackhawk almost beat the S&W Model 29 to market (although it wasn't called the M-29 until later) and was more durable. However, the shooters of the time found the recoil of the relatively light Blackhawk a bit much, and Ruger introduced the Super Blackhawk in 1959.

Since then, each big-bore revolver Ruger has brought to market has included the .44 Magnum as a caliber you could select. The Blackhawk, Super Blackhawk, Redhawk, Super Redhawk and Vaqueros are all Ruger handguns you can have in .44 Magnum.

Loaded to the extreme end with heavy hard-cast bullets below the pressure ceiling, it performs wonders of perforation on game animals.

.45 Colt

The original big-bore metallic cartridge handgun round, the .45 Colt (not "Long Colt") began in 1873 with the Colt SAA and its Army contract. For a long time it was the most powerful handgun, and when the .357 Magnum came out in

1935 some argued it still was. The basic ballistics are supposed to be a 255-grain slightly conical lead bullet at something on the order of 900 fps. However, you'll most likely find it with a flatter-nose bullet and down in the upper 700s as far as feet per second go. Either is a hammer of a round. However, soft lead bullets don't penetrate as well as hard-cast bullets do, so the hunters use those instead.

Starting with the Blackhawk in 1971, the .45 Colt has been in the catalog ever since. The Old Model Blackhawk was replaced with the New Model Blackhawk, but the .45 Colt remained in the catalog. As at the time there wasn't much other choice, so I can see why it sold well. (And still does.) Back in 1971 you had few choices: you could shell out the big bucks (for 1971) for a Colt SAA. It may work when it arrived, and it may need work. It will be a wait in either case. Getting one from S&W was not an option, as they didn't make the N frame in .45 Colt in 1971. Oh, you could special-order one, but unless you had an inside connection your order wasn't going to happen.

The other choice was to buy an import. However, the imports of that time had all the faults of Colt and then some. It was after all a century-old design by that time. And the overseas makers were not as up to speed as they are now. Today you can get a .45 Colt cowboy gun for a lot less than a Colt (say, three Italian clones to one Colt gun), count on it working properly, and even have options in finish and caliber.

The Blackhawk was the start of yet more handgun hunting. The results of handloaders' endeavors on the Colt are detailed in the Blackhawk chapter, but the summary is simple: loaded properly, in a gun that can take it (almost any Ruger qualifies) the .45 Colt makes a bigger hole deeper through any critter than the .44 Magnum does.

Can't do that with an SAA. The .45 Colt can be found in the Old and New Model Blackhawks, the Redhawk and the Super Redhawk if you load your .45 Colt ammo into the cylinder marked ".454 Casull."

.45 Schofield

The Schofield is the reason some call the Colt the "Long Colt." It was introduced after the .45 Colt as a military cartridge for the big S&W No. 3 topbreak revolver, and to distinguish it from its big brother some shooters began referring to the .45 Colt as the "long Colt." It serves the same purpose for the cowboy action shooters that the .38 Short Colt and .38 Special do in a .357 Magnum, and the .44 Russian and .44 Special in a .44 Magnum revolver:

The oldest centerfire handgun cartridge, and still in regular use, the .45 Colt has a lot to offer. Especially in the ultra-tough Ruger revolvers.

The .45 Schofield is a short .45 Colt. You can shoot a Scofield in any revolver chambered for the .45 Colt, or .454 Casull, and it will work just fine.

short case, less dead air space with light loads, and more consistent ignition.

.45 ACP

Manufactured in incredible volume, the .45 ACP has been a staple of shooters since 1911. It was the autoloading pistol answer to the .45 Colt. A century ago cavalry was still important. In a military engagement, stopping a cavalry charge was paramount, for if you didn't they were through you, behind you, and then things got really bad very quickly. The newfangled autoloading pistols were neat in that you could fire a lot of rounds quickly. But a horse or rider might not even notice a .30 Mauser bullet unless it hit bone. No, to stop a mount you needed a big pistol. The .45 Colt, by 1910, had

been doing that for almost forty years. Those in charge of things were not going to give it up lightly. So the new pistol was going to be a .45, and it was going to have a performance as close to the .45 Colt as possible.

Thus the .45 ACP (Automatic Colt Pistol) began life as a 230-grain FMJ at 825 fps. Plenty hot enough, and not something you need to improve on. Not that that keeps ammo manufacturers from trying.

When the expanding bullets for 9mms began appearing in the late 1970s, I predicted that we'd see them for the .45 ACP. Why? Because if the .45 is better than the 9mm when they are loaded with "hardball" (full metal jacketed bullets) then the .45 would still be better if loaded with the hi-tech hollowpoints of the time. And those who favored the .45 were not going to be stuck with hardball if the 9 guys were all getting fancy jacketed hollow points.

And so it was. The result is that we have an almost embarrassment of riches when it comes to the .45 ACP. First we have the Blackhawk in a convertible, where you can use either .45 Colt or .45 ACP ammo. Then there are a plethora of pistols. The P90, the P97 and the P345 all are .45 ACP models, and cover the size from full to compact.

.454 Casull

Full-throttle recoil, anyone? The Casull comes from Dick Casull, who wasn't satisfied with the performance of any handgun cartridge. Beginning in the late 1960s, he blew up Colt after Colt improving the ballistics of his round. I remember reading an article in the early 1970s in *Guns & Ammo* about how he was loading "triplex" loadings to get the performance he wanted. Triplex: a layer of one powder over another, over another. The bullet compresses the powder column, preventing mixing of the three different powders. The first layer combusts, igniting the second, which in turn ignites the third. The idea, back before we had the current generation of progressive-burn powders was to get more of a

With the right bullet the .45 ACP expands, which makes it great for defensive use. As a hunting cartridge that same expansion might be a hindrance.

slower burning powder to combust in the relatively small handgun case.

As I said, he blew up guns. So before anyone gets the bright idea of emulating him, the new powders negated his need to use that clumsy, dangerous method.

We now have powders that work as a single charge, and the result is a hand-crunching level of recoil that you have to experience to believe. The crunch comes from the velocity of the bullet. To get more penetration from a .45 bullet you need to push it faster or make it heavier. As the top-end hunting loads of the .45 Colt (for Rugers only) already maxes out weight, the .454 Casull can only do more by going faster. Ouch.

For reloading the .45 is quite versatile, accepting bullets from 152 to 255 grains in weight.

In the Ruger lineup, the .454 Casull can be found only in the Super Redhawk. Indeed, shooting it in any other platform would be abusive, as you need the weight of the Super Redhawk to deal with recoil.

.480 Ruger

To get more from the Super Redhawk Ruger had to get bigger. The only option was to jump up in size to the .475 range of cartridges, but the likeliest prospect, the .475 Linebaugh, had mechanical problems. The main one was the rim size. If left to the Linebaugh rim, the cylinder could only hold five rounds, but the potential cylinder diameter would permit six. So Ruger teamed up with Hornady for a Ruger-named cartridge and slimmed the rim down in diameter do it would fit in the cylinder.

The ballistics are impressive, but only if you need to be whacking big critters with a handgun. For applications not requiring such power, it is awesome and a little bit scary.

If you plan to shoot a .480 Ruger, do yourself a favor and work up to it. Start with a .44 Magnum and mild loads, then gradually increase them. Switch to a .454 Casull, and then finally jump to the .480 Ruger.

The Rare and the Lacking

As they are relatively new to this handgun-making business, Ruger does not have a long track record of calibers adopted, abandoned and thus collected. But there are some. One caliber that collectors keep an eye out for is .38 S&W. Not .38 Special, but the older cartridge. The .38 S&W is a shorter and slightly fatter cartridge, with the nominal bullet diameter at .360" instead of the .357" of the .38 Special/.357 Magnum. It was the British sidearm caliber after WWI and until the adoption of

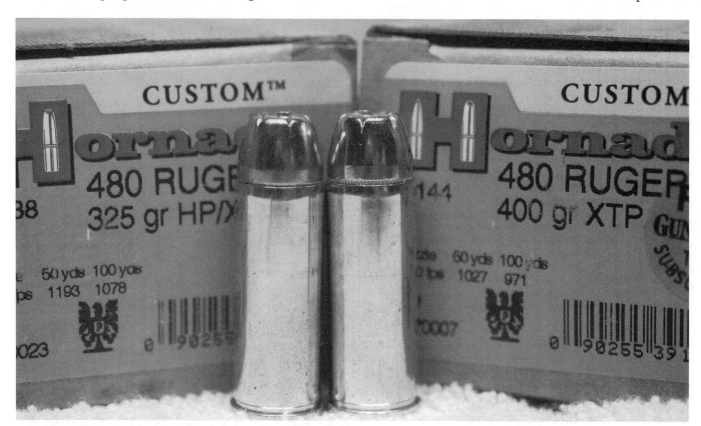

The .480 Ruger can be had in two bone-crushing factory loads; the 325- and the 400-grain XTPs from Hornady. If you need more (my wrists ache at the thought) you can use hard-cast bullets that are even heavier.

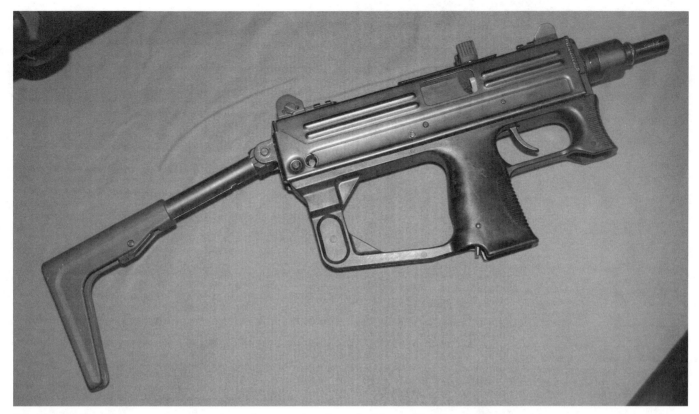

The funnest Ruger may not be a handgun, but it is chambered in 9mm. The Ruger SMG is a blast.

the 9mm with the Browning Hi Power. Apparently Ruger made a batch or several batches of revolvers in .38 S&W for export. The police of a country (or countries) that were former British colonies needed sidearms, and to keep the ammunition common they requested Security Sixes in .38 S&W. As it would only take a different broach on the barrel-making line and a different chambering reamer on the cylinder-making CNC, such a caliber change would be simple to make.

Another caliber change that I have heard of is .30 Luger. Some countries allow firearms ownership, but not in "military" calibers. So the .30 Luger would pass muster in some locations while its descendant the 9mm Luger would not. This is even simpler, as it would require only a different barrel and a recoil spring to match. The roll marks on the slide might have to be changed to show the caliber, and then again, maybe not. (If the slide rollmark is only a model designation, then the caliber wouldn't be there.)

If such guns were made for overseas sales, how would they be here? Ruger, as any prudent manufacturer does, would make more than they needed. If you need (for example) 100 of something for a contract, you set out to make 105 of them.

The 10mm is a long .40 to most people. Historically they came the other way: the .40 is a short 10.

The Ruger PC Carbines use Ruger pistol magazines, and shoot 9mm or .40 (not interchangeably) and are loads of fun.

Then, if parts get scrapped in the manufacturing process, or rejected due to cosmetics, you have spares. Add in the required for collectors early serial numbers, the company reference library/vault, and you have spares left over. Usually those spares would be shipped to a wholesaler and they would have to get them sold. Given the ready collectors market, "extras" of a short run or a special contract would be snapped up by collectors.

Calibers that I've neither seen nor heard of in a Ruger revolver include the .38 Super and the .357 SIG. The Super needs a .45 ACP-length magazine, so it could only be in a few pistols and none of the 9mm ones. The Super today is a competition cartridge, used by shooters in USPSA/IPSC competition, and none of

the Ruger pistols are suitable for use as an Open gun. (The most common by far uses of Super in USPSA/IPSC are in Open guns.) The .357 SIG is essentially a necked-down .40 S&W, and it is used primarily as a self-defense cartridge. And mostly in law enforcement at that. While I have heard of some Ruger pistols being chambered in .357 SIG for one or another law enforcement agency contract bid, I have not heard of a .357 SIG Ruger pistol running lose for collectors to snap up.

As for the rest, the rarities, the custom-made calibers, I suppose there are Rugers out there chambered for them, but only because someone has a Ruger and a chambering reamer. Or a Ruger and a barrel blank (in the case of a pistol) they could carve into a barrel. So if someone offers you a Ruger chambered in 9mm Federal, or .400 Corbon, be careful. It may be the collector's gem of a lifetime. And then again it may be a deal that is too good to be true. And as we all know, if something seems to be too good to be true, it usually is.

While it lasts, surplus 9mm ammo is a great way to feed your Ruger pistol or wheelgun. Once it dries up you'll have to prowl the big-box discount stores for 9mm on sale, or load your own to get cheap 9mm plinking/practice ammo.

— PART ONE —
The Mark I
AND ITS PROGENY

The Mark I was the first Ruger firearm product. Now, it may come as a shock to some of you, but there was a time when target shooting was considered a real sport. Not the outdoors counterpart to a video game, but something people did – even to the point of having firearms teams in schools. ("Ohmygod, did he just use the words "firearm" and "school" in the same sentence? Isn't there a law against that?") My dad shot on his high school rifle team, before going off to war. And his high school (if it still stands) was in the middle of a large city (Detroit). Apparently even New York City had smallbore rifle teams in the high schools even as late as 1969.

After WWII, there were a lot of target shooters. And they had a problem. The two big names in target shooting, at least in the .22LR part of it, were Colt and High Standard. Colt was still recovering from the war. They had basically worn out their machinery producing the weapons we used to win. Then, in the late 1940s, Hartford flooded. The river overran its banks, and the city (the plant was in the

The longer sight radius and extra weight of the Hunter model let you shoot more accurately. Put a scope on it, find the ammo it likes best, and you'd be *the* furry-critter killer of the woods.

The 22/45 grip angle is the same as, and the contours are close to, the 1911.

The 22/45 has the magazine catch right where we all expect it to be. The 22/45 makes a very good practice gun for someone using a 1911.

city) was under water for days. A short bath doesn't necessarily hurt a lathe or a mill, but either takes a whole lot of TLC before you can turn it on again. Colt had a lot of lathes and mills.

The Colt Woodsman had been designed by John Moses Browning. As a work of art it is beautiful. As a manufactured product, it was expensive. When there wasn't anything else to pick from, it was *the* pistol to have. But the design was firmly rooted in the early 20th century design period from which it came, and requiring machined forgings and hand fitting.

High Standard had a good pistol, but it wasn't a large company. The High Standard was, from an engineer's viewpoint, the same as a Colt Woodsman. The parts didn't interchange (not even the magazines) but from a design aspect they differed a lot less than two brands of internal combustion engines do. And both of those makers had a bigger problem: how they made handguns. Both used forgings or flat stock, and machined the receiver from a lump of steel. Then, they machined guide slots for the bolt onto the frame, and machined a bolt from bar stock or forgings. To work well, the rails and slots had to be in the right place, straight, lined up to the bore, and just the right size. To be accurate required tighter tolerances than those required for merely working reliably. And as if all that wasn't enough, the barrel seat had to be bored in just the right place on the frame, threaded, and a barrel screwed in. Then the barrel was profiled (or not) had a chamber reamed and an extractor cut made.

All very expensive. And requiring lots of skilled labor. Bill Ruger went at it differently. First of all, he didn't make the frame from a solid lump of steel. He had the two halves of the clamshell of a frame stamped out of steel. Then, while they were securely held in a fixture, the two halves were welded along the seam. The result was a frame that annoyed the purists, but was loved by the masses. A .22 LR has so little power that the extra strength of the solid frame was wasted. A sheet metal (thick sheet metal, however) was more than strong enough for the job of being a .22 pistol frame.

Oh, while I'm digressing, perhaps I might point out a historical curiosity that makes many modern engineers, manufacturers and shooters scratch their heads: steel quotas. Imposed during WWII to ensure that the plants making war material got first dibs on what they needed, there were still quotas on steel through the middle 1950s. In the five years between WWII and Korea there hadn't been time to lift them. When the Korean War started, they were enforced to ensure again the war effort got what it needed. Colt and High Standard, using large pieces of high quality steel (from which they machined a big percentage), were under a lot more pressure for steel than little old Ruger. Ruger only needed sheet steel, heavy gauge. They didn't produce a lot of scrap. Of course, as a brand-new maker, getting on the list of "supplied to" manufacturers was more than a little difficult. But

The adjustable sight of the Hunter lets you dial in your sights and be sure you need not use Kentucky windage.

Fiber optics tubes for installation in the front sight. And if the Ruger colors don't do it for you, there are a lot more to choose from.

Store the spares in the supplied tube.

they managed.

But, it got better, from an engineering standpoint. The barrel was turned on lathes to the desired profile. No flats, no ribs, no extra "stuff." Colt and High Standard barrels required a lot more work to be ready for fitting to a receiver. By the time of the late 1940s, lathes and threads could be "clocked." That is, you can cut the threads on a screwed-in part so it stops and tightens exactly pointing the way you want. The extractor cut could be made before assembly. The front sight slot, too. The receiver the barrel was screwed into was fashioned from seamless steel tubing. No elaborate machining, and as few a number of fixtures as you can imagine. Just take the tube stock off the truck, test it (just to be sure it is the alloy you ordered, and what was marked on the shipping crate) and then start feeding it into the automatic lathes. If you buy in large enough quantities you can even have the mill make the tubing very close to your desired final dimensions, so you don't even have very much work to do reaming the inside or turning the outside. The bolt was made from round stock. No elaborate machining to create a bolt and the slots for its rails in the receiver.

Now, in all this I've glossed over a lot. Take the

bolt, the last part mentioned, for example. Were you to make a new bolt for a Mark I, you'd have to mill the feed tang (that doohickey on the bottom of the bolt that strips a round off the magazine as the bolt goes forward, also called the pickup rail) and the hammer access, turn the recess for the cartridge rim, cut the extractor slot, drill the extractor spring hole, drill the takedown hole, drill the firing pin retaining hole and mill the firing pin slot. That's a lot of machining, but a whole lot less than you'd have to do for the bolt on a Colt Woodsman.

The Ruger sold for less, and it sold like hotcakes. The company placed an ad in *American Rifleman* and started selling them right away. Back then, there weren't that many magazines devoted to firearms. There were hunting magazines and men's magazines. (Unlike the magazines that would later be termed "men's magazines," the earlier ones simply were devoted to hunting and adventure stories.) If you placed an ad in *American Rifleman* in 1949, you could be sure that people who shot and competed would see it. They did, and they bought. They bought in numbers so great that it was only a year later that the Target version of the Mark I came out. Once there was a pistol that could compete with the big names, the game was over. The new wave of

Here you see the lock being locked.

experimenters would devote their efforts to making better sights, triggers, grips and even barrels for the Ruger. And why not? You could spend a bit of money on buying a Ruger, and then have a gunsmith completely overhaul it, and you'd still have a total bill for gun and labor that was less than the base cost of a Colt or High Standard. Competitors want to win. Less money spent on a handgun meant more money spent on practice ammo or going to competitions. A lesser investment in a base handgun meant it hurt less to experiment and learn as you went. The people who just wanted to plink and have fun outside, who were very price-resistant, found the Ruger plenty good enough for them.

Oh, there were drawbacks. The Mark I did not have a bolt hold-open. Once you expended the nine

The 22/45 Mark III Hunter comes with a scope base, and is already drilled and tapped for the base. Bolt it on, add rings and a scope, and you're styling.

No, not a tack-driver, but it is after all a plinking gun. If you want more accuracy, start with a trigger job and then test for the ammo it likes.

The new Mark III that looks a lot like the very first Mark I model. And nestled in the plastic box is a spare magazine. Would that more .22 makers had a spare in there. You don't want to run dry in the middle of a plinking session.

rounds in the magazine the bolt did not stay open. Nor was there even a way to lock it open. The nine rounds? The original magazine for the Mark I was derived from the High Standard magazine. (Hey, it was that or use the Woodsman as the starting point or design a new magazine from scratch, which was a lot more work than the fledgling firm of Sturm, Ruger & Co. was willing or able to undertake.) The High Standard had a reputation for greater durability and reliability than that of the Colt, so that was what Bill started with. Once selected as the starting point as a Ruger-designed and fabricated magazine, it happened to only hold nine. As competition with .22LR pistols back then (and now) only requires five shots per string of five, holding nine was not a problem. Some years later that was changed to a nice, even ten shots that

would fit into the magazines. And on the Mark II, they added a bolt hold-open.

If you disassembled the Mark I and then were a bit sloppy in handling the receiver, the hammer could swing forward of its usual stopping point. Getting it back, and reassembled, wasn't a hassle once you knew how. However, putting disassembled Rugers back together was a staple of many gunsmiths, myself included. I could count on several in the off season, and a bunch more after hunting season. Guys would take their Ruger Mark I (or II) up north to the hunting cabin. Sometimes during the trip they'd plink, and if it rained they'd clean their guns. (The smart ones, anyway.) You do the math: three quarters of a million hunters go north each year in my state alone. How many have Rugers? How many shoot them? How many take them apart to clean them? How many can't get it back together again? Those were the ones I'd see, come January or February. There were quite a few.

One fault the Ruger Mark I did not have was fragility or unreliability. I never saw one brought in "not working" that wasn't broken, have parts missing, or abused. Simply being dirty didn't stop the Mark I. I even heard from one of the competitors at the World Shoot in South Africa in 2002 about Ruger handguns. Gun clubs managed to get their hands on a bunch of Ruger Mark I pistols before the anti-apartheid embargo came down on them. (For those who slept through History in school, when the government of South Africa was still engaging in apartheid, the western world closed off all outside trade. An embargo.) Those Rugers were there to stay, but there weren't any new ones coming in. Most went to gun clubs, where members could check one out, shoot on the

club range, and turn it back in.

As you can imagine under those circumstances there was no such thing as "cleaning" or "preventive maintenance." So those pistols got shot and shot and shot. The magazines required the occasional weld fix here and there to take care of the cracks. But the pistols kept going. Some had logged round counts up near a million rounds. (Not too hard, really; one shooter each weekday fires two boxes, 100 rounds a day, with two shooters each on Saturday and Sunday. Just over three years of that, and you'd have shot a million rounds.) Despite such performance, an endorsement from the South African club shooters would not have gone over well in some circles, so the word never got out. But lots and lots of shooters here know the Ruger Mark I as an utterly reliable .22LR pistol.

The Mark III is all that and more. First, let's take a walk around the basic Mark III pistol. One

The bolt, ejection port, receiver, most everything is just as is was when the Mark I was introduced.

change the Mark III introduced was the relocated magazine catch. While the old style, with the mag catch at the bottom of the frame, worked just fine, shooters objected. It wasn't the way other pistols worked, not the way "real" handguns worked. A real handgun has its magazine catch on the frame, right behind the trigger guard, where pushing a button causes the magazine to drop out. So, on the Mark III, following the lead of the .22-45, the mag catch got moved to the "correct" location. A slight digression: the magazine catch on a handgun could be anywhere. If designers a century ago had placed the magazine release on the rear of the slide, that would be the "normal" location for it. One might argue that a better place for it would be on the frame on the right side, not the left, where the trigger finger would actuate it. That way, your finger would have to be off the trigger to perform any other function.

Above the magazine catch is the bolt hold-open lever, simply a stamped steel lever that pivots under the left grip panel and is pushed up by the magazine when the ammunition is gone to block the forward movement of the bolt after it has recoiled from the last shot.

Behind it, behind the grip, is the safety. On the original, the safety was simply a button that rode up or down, and when up it locked the Mark I and prevented it from firing. On the Mark III, it serves a dual purpose: it acts as a lock, too. The Mark III (and the 22/45 Mark III) both have locks that works like this:

Make sure the pistol is unloaded. Push the safety up, and using the supplied key, lock the mechanism. The key? A simple hex key/wrench that you use to unscrew the "lock" which is a threaded button. When you lock by unscrewing the button, it rises up into the clearance hole for the safety,

Unlike the Mark I, the Mark III has the magazine catch in the "normal" location we all expect: behind the trigger guard.

The safety is not only solid and reliable, but on the Mark III it is also the safety lock. Not, however, a speed safety.

below the slot of the safety. You cannot push the safety down once the lock is engaged. To unlock, screw the button in, and you now can move the safety. The question of is the lock on or off is pretty easy to determine: If you can move the safety the lock is off, and the mechanism will fire when you wish it to. When the safety is off, the button is inside the frame, and cannot back out and tie things up.

If you really are of the opinion that a mechanical lock of some kind for storage is a good idea on handguns, then this one is about as simple, effective and non-disastrous as possible. "Non-disastrous," you ask? The aforementioned politicians rarely consider that some people keep guns around for defense. A safety lock that could inadvertently lock and preclude the use of a defensive firearm is not a very good one. The Mark III is a secure and dependable one, even if it isn't a quick one.

The Mark III comes now in blued and stainless finishes, with bull or fluted barrels, and even with scope mounts already attached. (Or ready to be attached.) Through the years the various Marks could be had with barrels from under four inches to over ten, blued and stainless, skinny barrels and fat ones, and with fixed or adjustable sights. Indeed, a collector could keep busy doing nothing but collecting variants of the Marks and their progeny.

In the course of the book I had a chance to try two brand-new Ruger .22LR pistols: the Mark III and the Mark III 22/45. Needless to say, I did not undertake anything so filled with hubris as to conduct a "reliability" test of them. It would take tens of thousands (perhaps over 100,000) rounds to determine anything like a "mean time between failure" rate. Even given the low cost of .22LR ammunition, it would be an expensive undertaking, and consume a great deal of time, to be able to tell

The Mark III also boasts a bolt hold-open lever.

you with certainly one thing: They are Very Reliable. At the current ammo costs, 100,000 rounds of common .22LR ammunition would run about $1,900, sales tax not included. I'm sure I could get a volume discount, buying a hundred thousand rounds at one time (If I had the storage room) but get real. A hundred thousand rounds, two grand in ammo, three quarters of a ton in weight, just to say "Yep, those Ruger Mark Three's are really reliable guns." Not something I need to do.

But plinking and testing for the readers, now that's fun. The Mark III sent me was a blued model, skinny barrel with fixed sights. Pretty much what you'd expect to find as a beginner's gun from Ruger, since that day now sixty years ago when the first one left Southport. Function? One hundred

percent. Accuracy? Again, pretty much what you'd expect. .22LR firearms are notorious for being picky about ammo. Serious target shooters test their guns with all the ammo they can, and when they find something that it is particularly accurate with, they buy lots of it. And they buy that one lot of it. As in production lot. Then they practice with the cheapest most-accurate ammo, and used the absolutely most-accurate ammo in competitions. So, my using plain old "buckets o' bullets" bargain ammo (in this particular situation, Remington) and getting four-inch groups at twenty five yards should not be surprising. No, the real ammo selection work would be done on a bull barrel model, after trigger work. Were I looking for a more-accurate load, I would not be doing it with a four-inch skinny barrel fixed sight Ruger with a factory trigger.

Not that there was anything wrong with the trigger. It just wasn't the "half an ounce over the rulebook" trigger I'd use in a match.

22/45

The Mark I was for a long time a really cool gun. And a really good one. But it had a problem. Well, it had a "problem." You see, the guys (and gals) who shoot Bullseye do so with three guns. The full 2700 course is fired with a .22LR, an "any Centerfire" and a .45 ACP handgun. Typically, the "Any Centerfire" is another .45 ACP. That way, they can use the same gun for two-thirds of the course, and have the same trigger, grips, etc. Additionally, the Service category is fired with a .45 ACP 1911. (The Service Teams now use the Beretta 9mm M9/

M-92, but that is a different story.) So a shooter going to the national Matches would use the same pistol in three of the four categories. Or two pistols with minor differences, and none of those differences being the grip.

The grip shape and angle of the Mark I differs from that of the 1911. So shooters would have to switch grip shapes and angles, trigger feel and pull, between categories.

So in 1992 Ruger unveiled the 22/45. It was partly evolutionary and partly revolutionary. The evolution was that it incorporated a polymer frame. By 1992 that was no-longer news. But that the new frame was the same angle, contour and size as a 1911 frame was. No one had made anything new for Bullseye shooters for a couple of decades at that point.

When the Mark III was announced for 2004, the 22/45 (which uses the internals of the standard

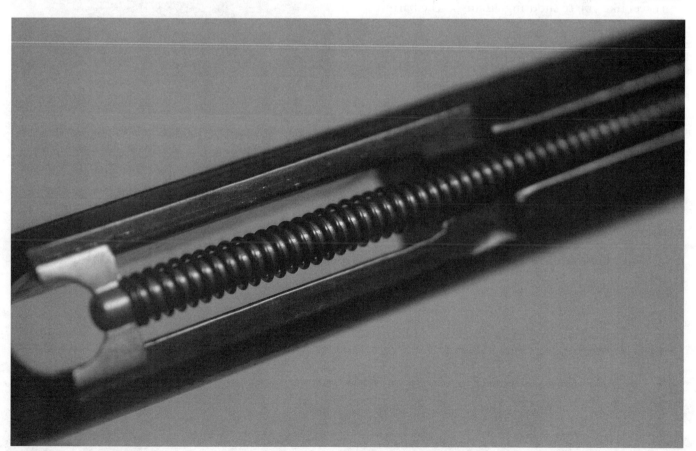

The recoil spring on all Marks rides on its own guide rod and is self-contained. No need to worry about launching the spring across the room when you take it apart to clean your Mark I, II or III.

Here you see the bolt hold-open lever. And just behind it the safety and below that the lock access hole.

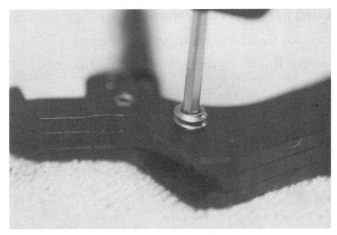

The safety lock of the Ruger Mark III (as seen when out of the pistol, for clarity).

Marks) also became the 22/45 Mark III. You can now have the 22/45 in blue or stainless, and in Bull Barrel or Hunter version. I elected a stainless Hunter, just because I wanted to see what a fluted long barrel handled and shot like. In a word: nice. The fluting takes the weight down enough that you don't feel like you're shooting an anvil. The barrel length aids aiming not because longer barrels are more accurate, but the longer sight radius helps you line things up. I was able to shoot much tighter groups with the Hunter than the shorter-barreled Mark III I had along at the same time.

The Hunter also came with a scope base and screws, and the receiver is drilled and tapped for them. If you want to install a scope, you just bolt in the base, attach rings and a scope, and off you go. As with the Mark III (it is, after all, a Mark III with a polymer frame) the 22/45 Hunter has a locking mechanism. The front sight is a Hi Viz fiber-optic sight, and you get a selection of fibers in colors for your selection. I left them alone, as I

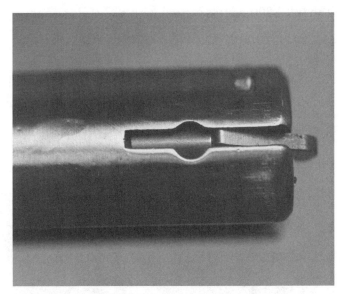

No one has ever had cause to complain about the extractor on the Ruger. Except those who take it out to clean the bolt. Leave it in, hose it with degreaser to get the gunk out, and lube it up when you reassemble.

prefer plain black, but I'm sure there are shooters out there with favorite colors. Since the tube sizes of fiber optic sights are pretty standard, you can find just about any color you want to fit.

Ruger .22LR pistols. They've made a bazillion of them – why don't you already own three?

— PART TWO —
The P89

The P85 from Ruger was awaited with much anticipation. Initially it was to be the "P84." However, design and production problems took longer to solve than anticipated, and we waited. And waited. Back in the 1980s, Ruger had a reputation for using gun writers as part of the marketing department. The common wisdom was that they'd show a gun writer a prototype, and let them play with it and take photos. He'd then write an article, letting the world know about the upcoming Ruger firearm. Then, judging from the feedback from the readers (and orders from dealers and wholesalers) they'd plan their production schedule. It was a pretty cynical view of the company from the buying public, but it was a commonly-held belief. Now that I've been on both sides of the curtain (so to speak) I can see where that viewpoint might take hold. It isn't true, but it sure can look that way from the reader's point of view.

In addition to the lock, owner's manual and two magazines, the P89 comes with a magazine loader.

The P89 isn't a tack-driver, but it is plenty accurate enough for everything else.

The first time I saw the P85 was at the local Sheriff's Department indoor range. I was shooting in the winter PPC league back then. I had started out shooting a box-stock S&W M-19. I soon progressed to using a Colt 1911 in .45 ACP, and with it I carried a 596 average. (600 was "clean.") As the one shooting the "big boomer" and the only one shooting an auto, I was relegated to the right side of the firing line. After I found the lower-recoil limits of functional reliability with the .45, I built a Colt in .38 Super to find an even-softer shooting gun. With that gun I upped my average to 598. (And like an idiot I experimented, and experimented until that nice little blaster was broken scrap. I should have left it alone, but I was young and curious.)

As the resident "pistol expert" in the league (the Sheriff's Deputies all carried issued M-15 S&Ws,

in .38 Special) I was given the task of shooting the P85 for accuracy the night it showed up in 1987. All I can say is, I was underwhelmed. And yes, that was an early winter evening in 1987. The P-84 had taken some time to work out, and even the new designation was out-of-date by the time you could lay hands on one.

The P85 followed the Ruger design imperative of over-engineering. In a revolver you can do that and get away with it, as people are willing to go larger to get the power a .44 Magnum or larger can deliver. But in a 9mm pistol, over-engineering simply makes for a big pistol. The thing was a brick. And not very accurate. We later found out that a manufacturing process that allowed for lower-cost barrels was the problem. Simply, the barrel-making line was turning pre-rifled barrel blanks into cylinders with a shank

The P89 barrel is a Browning link-down style, and the guide rod does nothing but guide the recoil spring.

on the chamber end. The casting department was making rectangular chamber castings. The casting would be bored-out and have a hole drilled in the top. The shank of the barrel would be pressed into the rectangular casting, and then the two plug-welded though the hole. Then it would be finish-machined and have the chamber reamed to adjust the headspace. A fast and inexpensive way to make barrels, but one that produced barrels of only average accuracy. That process was quickly scrapped, and the old barrels were replaced under warranty.

The grip was large, the slide was large, the lines were blocky. But the P85 sold, and sold well. At the time, the suggested retail price on an S&W 469, a 14-shot 9mm, was $482.50. The Ruger listed at $295. Now, retail wasn't what anyone paid, then or now, but still, the Ruger was selling (when you could

find it) for not much more than half of what a Smith & Wesson was selling for. There were a whole lot of people who didn't care about sleek lines, but who wanted a gun for defense that didn't cost a lot.

The P85 was developed in part because Ruger needed a pistol in the lineup, but also because the

The Ruger 9mm magazines are hell for tough, hold fifteen rounds, and are made of stainless steel.

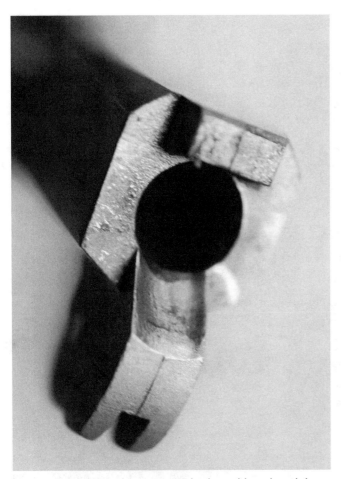

You can see the mold seam on the barrel hood and the lug below the feed ramp. The ramp is polished – no seam there.

government was looking for a 9mm pistol to replace the 1911s that were wearing out. So Ruger did their best to make the deadline with a product that would be selected. The Beretta was selected. The P85 then went through a series up upgrades and improvements. The big one is the Mark II and Mark IIR models, which have upgraded safety mechanisms. The Mark II has an active firing pin block, and the ones stamped Mark IIR have had the new parts installed afterwards. As with the Blackhawk, Ruger vigorously sought out and offered free upgrades to owners of the original P85 to bring them up to the new design standard.

The P85 lasted from 1987 to 1992, when it was overtaken and replaced by an onslaught of new Ruger models. Its direct replacement was the P89, the subject of our inquiry here.

The P89 was unveiled in 1993. Ruger pistol lines are named after the year development is begun, not the year the guns are unveiled. (I suspect the

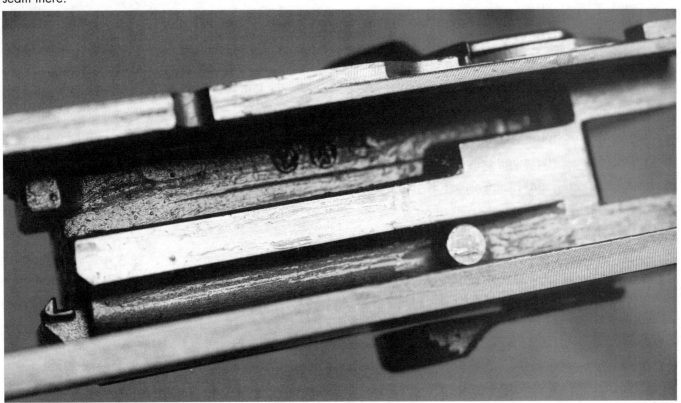

The slide has a solid back, and you can see the firing pin safety plunger keeping the firing pin in check.

The extractor is big, external, and did I mention big? No worries about empty cases getting yanked out of the chamber here.

The front sight is pinned into place, in the shoulder created by the investment-cast slide. If you ever break it, it will be easy to replace that sight blade.

process fell a bit behind with the very first one, and the "tradition" then became "development" and not "unveiling." But I've been accused of being cynical on other subjects, too.) It differed from the P85 in that it was designed from the start to have the active firing pin block parts in it. Indeed, it was designed around the new parts. It also featured re-sculpted slide and frame, a new safety lever design, and the new-manufacture barrel, the welded P85 having long been changed to a different one. The new barrels were made from investment castings. The cast rough-shape barrel is profiled, bored and broached for rifling.

One thing that was retained on the P89 (and all Ruger centerfire pistols) is the takedown method. You have to unload it and remove the magazine. Line up the disassembly notch on the side of the slide and push the slide stop out. Then push down the ejector plate. You can now pull the slide off. This method avoids the need to dry-fire he pistol to take it down, and also keeps the rear of the slide solid, without any slots through it to clear the ejector as it comes off the frame.

The P89 uses an investment cast aluminum frame, and a carbon steel or stainless steel slide. You can have your P89 in blue or stainless, and any

caliber you want so long as it is a 9mm, and with any sights so long as they are fixed. The P89 is most definitely the price-point pistol of the Ruger line. That does not, however, make it a "cheap" gun, nor an unreliable piece of junk. It is unbelievably rugged, reliable and reasonably accurate. I'm not sure anyone makes a replacement match barrel for a P89, but why would they? The P89 is not meant to be taken to a PPC match or shot in a USPSA/IPSC or IDPA match (although it wouldn't do too badly in the last one). It is meant to be the lowest-cost solid defensive arm that you can buy. Ruger wants that part of the market with this gun, and they have it.

The barrel is not one of the new-design types that uses the recoil spring guide rod as the cam for the barrel unlock. It is a pure link-down Browning design, and combined with the somewhat high bore axis, the P89 is a bit whippy in recoil. Not that the recoil is at all hard or tough to deal with. I mean, we're talking a 32-ounce 9mm with a hand-filling grip.

The grip contains the double-stack magazine that holds fifteen rounds of nine-millimeter ammunition. The magazines, like the pistol, have a stellar reputation for reliability and durability. The bottom plate design, with the baseplate retention rails folded in, does not allow for a magazine extension. So you won't be able to expand your Ruger mags past fifteen rounds. If Ruger makes magazines with a greater capacity than that, they keep them a deep-dark law enforcement-only secret. For I have never seen one or heard of one. You can get higher-capacity magazines from Mec-Gar, who makes 17- and 20-shot magazines. The Ruger P85, P89, P93, P94 and P95 magazines are all the same. So if you have one of those models, a magazine that works for one will work for all.

The late Bill Ruger got himself in some hot water with the rest of the firearms community some years back when he offered the opinion that fifteen rounds was enough. As the biggest competitor at the time was Glock, with a 17-round magazine, this was seen as a back-door attempt at cutting off his competitor, and "collaborating" with the anti-gun crowd to forestall further legislation. Nothing came of it; the assault weapon ban of 1994 is old history, but some shooters won't let go. I know some who will not only not own a Ruger, but also won't have one in their houses, because of that misstep.

The current MSRPs of the P89 are $525 for the stainless and $475 for the blued. As with all things sold in the good old USA, you can find them for a lot less than that if you shop around. The original P85 started the "300" prefix, and the P89 picked up where the P89 left off, near the end of the "304" series. (It wouldn't surprise me to find that somewhere, a Ruger collector has, or is searching for, the "bookend" Rugers: P85 serial # 304-88012 and P89 serial # 304-88013.) Since then, the "you can't buy a good 9mm for less" Ruger sales plan has obviously worked: the serial number prefix is currently in the "315" block. That includes the original single action/double action models, the decocker and the DAO models of the P89.

The P89 Ruger sent me was a stainless, SA/DA, in (obviously) 9mm and with fixed sights. It has

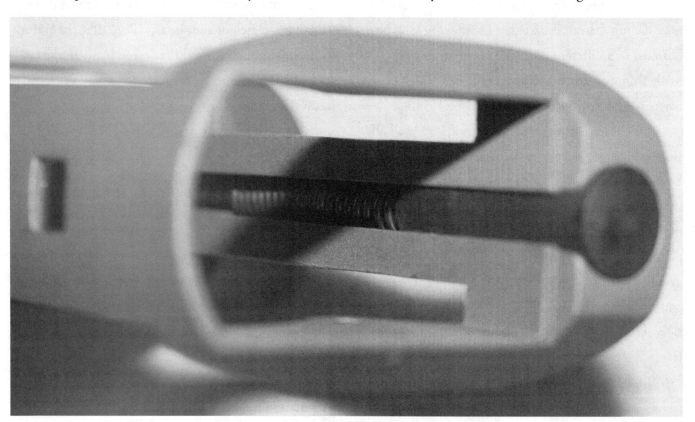

The cast aluminum frame of the P89 holds the mainspring in place, not the grips.

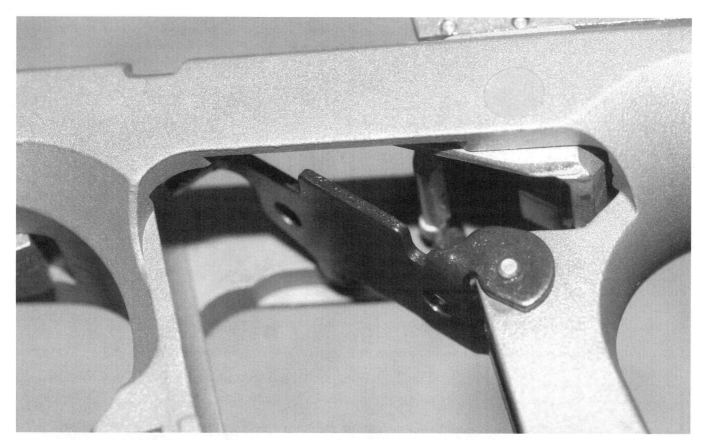

The ejector is also the takedown lever; once you get the slide back and the slide stop pin out, simply push it down (as shown here) to remove the slide.

the Ruger plastic grip, and came in its box with two magazines and a magazine loader. Not that you really need a loader for Ruger magazines (some other brands can be quite tough to load) but it is a nice addition. In shooting it shot a lot better than I recall that P85 of twenty years ago, but it still wasn't a PPC gun. Still, six shots in three inches on a freezing-cold day with a light dusting of snow coming down is plenty good for me.

I did not even think of conducting a "reliability" test with the P89. That it could chew through case after case of ammunition has been proven many times in the last couple of decades. That Ruger parts are so stoutly designed and fabricated that I could shoot this gun for the rest of my life and not have

anything break is also a given. Running it over with a car would not make it stop, and I think you'd have to go well past the pall-peen hammer as an impact device to do more than break the grips. Speaking of grips, the grips of the P89 show its age: they do not retain the firing mechanism. And they cannot be exchanged for differing backstrap sizes.

The P89 is what it is: a solid, dependable 9mm pistol that has long since paid back Ruger for its tooling costs. You can find them for not much money, all over the place (and yes, there are ten-shot magazines for those of you who live in Kaliforniastan or the People's Republic of New Jersey). The P89 will simply never let you down.

RUGER

— PART THREE —
The P90

At first glance you'd think the P90 was another P89. Close, but no cigar. As with the .22LR cartridge, if you're to be taken seriously as a firearms manufacturer, and you make centerfire pistols, you have to make one in .45. To make 9mms, but not something in .45 ACP, is almost heresy in some circles. So, Ruger designed the P90, which in the accustomed fashion, wasn't available until 1991. The design looks easy enough, right? Take the slide and open the breechface and fit a .45 barrel in place of the 9mm one. Then re-proportion the frame for a single-stack magazine, and you're done, right? (Things like that are what make gunsmiths crazy. Any conversation that start out with the would-be customer saying "All you have to do is…" always end badly.)

The .45 ACP has a lot more energy. The P90's slide had to be made slightly larger (a tenth of an inch or so) higher and thicker to give it more mass. The greater energy also requires a different geometry in the link and cam area. Typically, 9mms

It looks like a P89, but it isn't; it's in .45 ACP, and it's a P90. Two mags, manual, all the goodies.

Use good-quality ammo (which Black Hills definitely is) and you can get consistent groups from your P90. Or any pistol, for that matter.

The P90DC has a spring-loaded decocking lever where the safety is.

built on .45 pistols require much-lighter recoil springs than their .45 counterparts. Manufacturers adjust the cam angles, distances and proportions to account for the differences in energy, rather than simply install lighter or heavier springs. The smaller magazine let Ruger designers make improvements to the P90 from the P89 (which even the most-ardent Ruger fan will admit is the precursor to the P90). The trigger bar is brought inside the frame, and several parts can thus be eliminated.

As a result, the P90 has a smoother and lighter DA trigger pull than the P89. The ambidextrous magazine release of the P89 was changed to one that could be switched from one side to the other. While ambi mag catches are all the rage, then and now most shooters do not use them as ambi catches. They use them from one side, and that's the side they stick with. So being able to switch sides has the same effect

as an ambi mag catch, but with fewer parts. And, the single-stack magazine of the P90 is not as "happy" with the Ruger ambi catch. All the more reason to use the switch-side P90.

The P90's magazine, for reasons known only to Ruger, is not the same as the 1911's. When they heard rumors of a Ruger .45 pistol, legions of fans were aflutter with the thought that they could use 1911 magazines. Again: close, but no cigar. I imagine (Ruger is close-mouthed about this, as they have been with other subjects) that Ruger was not at all happy about the idea of their pistol being subject to the reliability (or lack thereof) of some brands and eras of 1911 magazines. I'm sure they could foresee nothing but P90 after P90 being returned because "it isn't reliable" – and with many of those shooters not bothering to mention that they were using grubby "two for ten dollars" on-sale gun show 1911 magazines. And they did, after all, have a certain amount of experience in designing magazines for their own pistols, right?

The P90 was the first Ruger pistol to have the high-mount decocking lever/safety that also was spring-loaded and returned to horizontal. Why is this a big deal? The traditional DA/SA safety lever stayed on in the Safe position. You had to push it up to unlock the pistol and fire. In manipulating the slide in a malfunction clearance or in struggling with someone, you could push the safety down and thus not have the pistol available when you needed it. By putting the lever up the shooter had move leverage to pull it down to decock. By spring-loading it, the shooter is sure the pistol is ready to fire when needed.

As with all things, there are those who object.

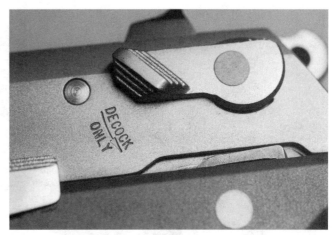

Press it down and the hammer falls but the gun doesn't fire. Let go, and the lever springs up and you're ready to go.

Some view the "safety down" position as a good one, and there have been cases where it was good. Police officers are subject to gun-grabs by miscreants, offenders and paroled felons. There have been a

The magazines look like, and are similar to, the ubiquitous 1911 magazines. But they are different, and you can't interchange them.

The extractor is big, the barrel clearly marked and the serial number in the right place. Must be a Ruger.

number of documented cases where the officer was saved because the bad guy couldn't get the safety up. However, there is as much risk that the safety will be down when *you* need it. If you carry such a pistol you should practice your draw so you reflexively push the safety to the Fire position when you draw. If not, get a pistol like the P90, with the spring-loaded safety.

The standard P-whatever front sight: a cast base and two roll pins holding the front sight blade in place.

As with the P89, the P90 has an investment-cast aluminum frame and can be had in the traditional DA/SA, and the decocker, but no DAO. Also like the P90, your choices are blued or stainless slide. As for the rest, you get a 4-1/2" barrel, fixed sights, polymer grips, and all the efforts of Ruger to make a reliable and rugged .45 pistol. MSRP on the P90 is a bit higher than that of the P899, but then you're getting a bit more steel and a much bigger caliber. The start of the serial number was with the "660" prefix in 1991, and sales have been brisk enough that in the ensuing fifteen-plus years they have gone into the 663 series. (What they'll do in another ten-twelve years for a prefix, I can only guess. Skip it?) In 2003 the P90 serial numbers were rolled in with the P97 serial numbers, so you will see overlaps there in the later-production guns.

The P90DC sitting on my desk is a stainless, decocking-only safety. In handling and function it is like all other Ruger centerfire pistols. The takedown is the same as well. The magazine is similar in shape to the 1911 magazine so many of you are familiar with but the front profile is blunter. The magazine is just about as long, front to back, but the radius is wider at the front. I have run into problems with some .45 ACP JHP bullets, with aggressively wide openings. The front flat is wider than some magazines can take. Conversely, I have run into problems with one 230-grain FMJ, in that the bullet is at the maximum overall length for the .45 ACP, and wrestling them into the Ruger can be a hassle. But only rarely is this an issue. In either case, my first suggestion is, and I'm not kidding: don't use that ammo. There are plenty of ammo choices you can make. There is nothing so special, or cheap, that you have to put up with it not-quite-almost-fitting the magazine. Switch ammo.

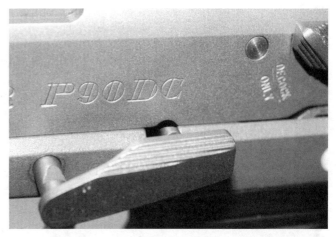

Line up the clearance notch in the slide and you can pull the slide stop out to start disassembly.

I know I've said this before, but it would be hubris to suggest I can shoot enough to test a Ruger pistol or reliability. Or durability. So I simply amused myself with learning how well it shot (very well indeed) how accurate it was (nice) and what the recoil was like. (Not bad.)

The function of the P90DC was, as expected, 100 percent. It tossed the empties a good 10-12

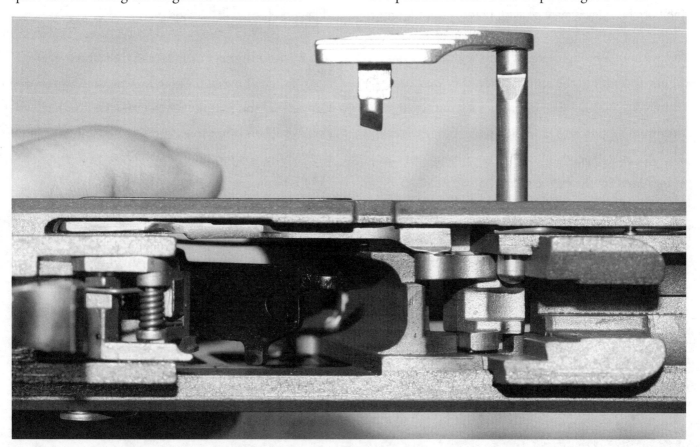

The slide stop lever stays in the frame when you go to take the slide off.

The barrel is a investment casting, bored, reamed, broached and then profiled to fit the slide.

feet without abusing them. While they would not all have fallen into the same bucket, they were not scattered to and fro. The magazines fell out when they were supposed to, and didn't when they weren't. The accuracy depended (as in so many cases) on the ammo I fed it. The classic accuracy load of a 200-grain laser-cast lead semi wadcutter and Vihtavuori V-310 would shoot nice clusters. I could often get a two-inch group from that load at twenty-five yards. With out of the box 230-grain hardball, just under three inches was a good best group. Mostly it shot three to four inches at twenty five yards. Considering

that it isn't a Bullseye or PPC gun, that the trigger has a bunch of over-travel (an unavoidable aspect of DA pistols) and that the temperature was in the low twenties when I shot those groups, I was plenty happy with what I got.

At 34 ounces the P90 has enough heft to keep you from getting beaten up by recoil, but not so much you feel like you're carrying a boat anchor of you select one as a carry gun. If you want an inexpensive .45 ACP pistol, you should consider it as a carry gun. It's a Ruger, so of course holster makers make holsters for it.

RUGER

— PART FOUR —
The P94

T he P94 is a continuation of the P85: an aluminum-framed pistol in 9mm and in .40 S&W. It was meant as an "in between" pistol in size, falling between the full-size and bulky P-85 derivatives and the compact 9mm-only P-93 pistol. First appearing in 1994 (and breaking the string of models that arrived the year or so after their "name" year), the P94 offered shooters something that before 1994 was not common: an inexpensive .40 S&W pistol. It may seem odd in today's world, where everyone makes a .40, and .40 ammo is everywhere, but when it first appeared the .40 was far from common. Yes, S&W was making .40 pistols, and Glock was certainly cranking them out, but it wasn't all sweetness and light.

The intention, from both the cartridge and firearms designers, was to shoehorn the .40 S&W into a 9mm platform with as little modification as possible. After all, it was an "in-between" cartridge, right? It was a robust 9mm, and you could certainly make a 9mm work with a .40 case, right? After all, hadn't the experimenters been doing

P94, two mags, loader, manual, sturdy box: you get a lot for your hard-earned dollars when you buy any Ruger pistol. You get a lot in a .40 when you buy a P94.

The standard safety. Push it down and it drops the hammer without firing, stays down, and prevents the pistol from firing even if you pull the trigger.

just that for (by that time) fifteen years? Well, yes and no. It certainly is "easy" to make a 9mm pistol take a .40-caliber cartridge, if a skilled gunsmith is doing the fitting, design and modifications. I don't count myself amongst the top tier of custom gunsmiths, but I certainly mulled over the possibilities. I elected not to not because I hadn't the skill to do it, but because I couldn't justify the time and cost of doing so. It was cheaper, in the end, to simply buy one so-modified by the factories.

The first few years, the gun makers struggled to make a 40 pistol that would stay together, that would be reliable and that would not mangle the brass. Ruger had done that with the P94. The earlier P-91 had also done that, but it was a bit larger in dimension and for bigger, too.

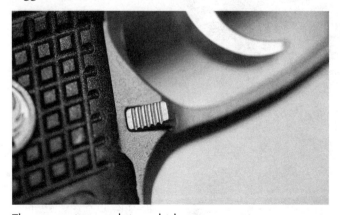

The magazine catch is ambidextrous.

The takedown is the same for all: once you've lined up the notches, push the slide stop out.

The one big thing the P94 was noted for was that it was a ten-shot-only pistol. The Assault Weapon Ban of 1994 mandated that all magazines, except those made for law enforcement, could hold a maximum of ten rounds. Ruger had the intention of making and selling them as fifteen- (9mm) and eleven-shot (.40) pistols. At the time, eleven shots was the norm for a metal-framed pistol in .40 S&W. But soon after they were offered, the AWB was signed and went into effect. The magazines were changed to ten shots each. Standard Ruger fifteen- and eleven-shot magazines work just fine in the P94s.

When the AWB expired in 2004, the P94 was dropped from the lists. Ruger had designed and offered much newer and more attractive 9mm pistols since then, so there really wasn't any reason to keep it round. Also, there is the psychology of gun shops and gun buyers to consider. For ten years, the Ruger P94 would have been seen in the display cases of gunshops as "The Ruger ten-shot AWB model" and when the AWB sunset, who would want one of those? Not entirely rational, perhaps, but a real consideration. The P944 still remains, but there is a small market for a relatively compact, ten-shot .40, so it sells well enough to keep on the lists. The P94 was dropped, which is a bit of a shame. However, it doesn't do much that other Ruger

This is about all you need do to clean your P94.

models don't do, so clearing out the catalog now and then is a good thing.

As with the other P-series pistols, the P94 has an aluminum frame with a stainless slide and your choice of traditional DA/SA, decocker and DAO trigger mechanisms. As with the earlier P pistols, you could have your choice of barrel length and sights as long as you wanted a (roughly) four-inch barrel and fixed sights.

As with the other P series (P85, P89 and P90) the P94 uses a Browning linked tilt-barrel system, and a separate recoil spring guide rod. The safety is right where you'd expect it to be, but the slide caught my eye in one particular detail: the cocking serrations were cast in the mould. Usually the slide, whether forged, bar stock or cast, has the cocking serrations milled into the surface. The ones on the P94 sent me were quite clearly cast, not machined. Ruger has obviously not been

asleep when it comes to advances in casting technology.

Also quite clearly, the P94 sent me does not correspond to the parts diagram of the P94 they show in the parts order sheet. On the parts sheet, the P94 clearly has a Browning barrel. If you look closely at the photos you'll see that the P94 I have here at Firearms Abuse Central uses a cam barrel and guide

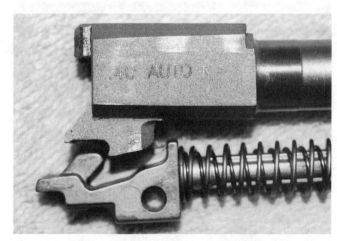

The new-style barrel and recoil spring guide rod. The guide rod is the cam that unlocks the barrel.

rod camming lock system like that of the P944. As a further puzzling item, the Ruger information from their web page lists the P94 as a 9mm pistol. And yet the one in my hands is clearly a .40. The solution to the mystery is simple and readily solved: the web page is not quite up-to-date and the owner's manual shows the Browning-link barrel and non-cam guide rod because it is a one-size-fits-all manual. It covers the P85, P90, P94 and P944.

The conclusion I take from this is that I might have sent back a collector's dream: a factory-made P944 that had a P94 marked slide. Or, they still had a few P94s in the warehouse, and when I asked for pistols somehow one of them got added to the mix. I'm sure the hardcore collectors will get to the bottom of things in short order.

Cast-in grasping grooves and an extractor that is tougher than old boot leather.

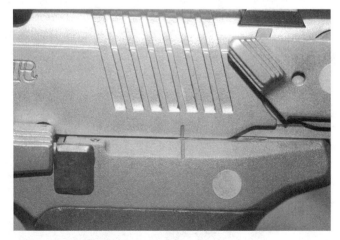

To disassemble, you simply unload, remove the magazine and line up the notches in the slide and frame.

In production from 1994 to 2004, the P94 was a decent seller. It looks like they made just about 70,000 of them – which is why I was so surprised to see one arrive on my doorstep with the rest of a shipment of Ruger handguns.

Other than that, it appears an utterly normal P94 in outline, in the magazines it uses and in performance. The P94 differs in one detail from some of the previous P-series pistols in that the forward part of the extractor is held in place behind a small web left in the exterior wall of the slide surface. I imagine that is there to provide the extractor a bit more purchase on the rim of a .40 case. Even with a heavier slide and heavier recoil spring, the slide velocity of any .40 pistol based on a 9mm pistol is going to be higher than it was before the change.

The magazines shipped with this P94 show the clear difference between the .40 and 9mm tubes. The 9mm tubes (as seen in the P89 I had at the same range session) are clearly stamped with a stiffening and constricting rib while the steel of the tube was still flat. The rib makes the interior the correct size for a stack of 9mm rounds. The .40 tube almost appears to have been creased after folding, which may well have been the case if they were redesigned as ten-shot magazines after having been set up originally as eleven-shot

With the guide rod doing the barrel cam tasks, the frame can be made a lot simpler and also take stress off the slide stop pin.

magazines. But why still have ten-shot mags in this day and age? Two reasons would be Kaliforniastan and the People's Republic of New Jersey. Some places, you still can't have mags larger than ten rounds.

In felt recoil, the P94 felt like what you'd expect a 33-ounce pistol to feel: with the standard 180-grain FMJ at moderate velocities we all love to plink with, not much at all. Fed something stiffer, like one of the Corbon 135-grain screamers, it was downright snappy. However, the wide grip of the hi-cap frame spreads the recoil. Even after a couple of hundred rounds of the Corbon, your hand doesn't feel like it has gone through a petting session with a dull-toothed Labrador retriever.

Should you buy a P94? After all, they aren't made any more, they aren't in the catalog and they aren't the latest and greatest. Me, I see those as pluses for the savvy buyer. So it isn't in the catalog – so what? Ruger made seventy thousand of them. They aren't rare. It is a derivative of the P-85 series and its progeny, so it isn't like spare parts will ever be a problem – that is, if you ever break something. Yes, it only holds ten shots of .40, but it takes the regular .40 magazines, so you can have eleven shots if you want. If you have to have the latest and greatest, you have to expect to pay for it. If you want a night-stand gun, something reliable and inexpensive, the P94 is a good option. You can probably find one now and then used, at a good price. It won't let you down.

P944

The P944 is Ruger's current catalog item for the category of ten-shot .40 S&W pistol. It came out

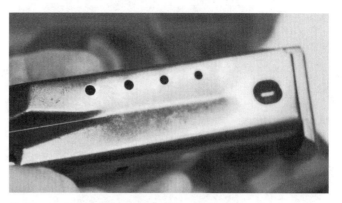

The P94 magazine, which differs from the...

...magazine for the P89.

the year after the P94 and differs in the barrel cam (instead of the Browning link) and has always been a ten-shot 40 S&W pistol and nothing else. A little bit of searching turned up a Ruger P944 under the display glass of almost every gun shop I queried. For a gun that has been in production for just over twelve years, and doesn't have knock-your-eyes-out numbers on the serial number lists, it seems you can find one anyplace you go. I now wonder how many of the "P89" Ruger pistols I've seen but not really looked at at gunshows, in gun shops, and at ranges are really a P944 that I wasn't paying attention to?

The P94 apparently didn't stop being made. It just turned into the ubiquitous P944.

— PART FIVE —
The P95

The P95 is yet another evolution of the P85/P89 series. The original, the P95, came out in 1995 as a DAO pistol. For quite some time, before the striker-fired design pistols took complete control of the pistol market, the makers of traditional designs struggled to produce pistols that worked like a striker-fired (OK, a Glock) pistol but used their existing mechanisms. Once the DOA was up and running, the decocker version came out in 1996. Only in 2001 was there a traditional SA/DA version of the P95. 2001 also saw the serial number prefixes folded together. Prior to 2001, the various pistols had had their own prefixes. The DAO started in the 340 series, the D (decocker) had the 311, and the P89 used 304. But in 2001, all the pistols were put into the 314 serial number prefix. And no doubt each was issued a serial number block for production purposes.

The P95DC comes in a hard plastic storage/transport container.

And to top it all off, the P95 magazines also work in the PC9 carbine. I just heard they are to be discontinued, so if you've always wanted one, get it while you can.

The P95DC is your basic, standard-sized, hi-cap 9mm pistol, with Ruger's legendary reliability.

The big deal about the Ruger P95 is that it does away with the slide rails. Well, not "does away" with them entirely, but what the design team at Ruger was able to do was eliminate the steel inset rails that the Glock and other pistols are known for. Instead of steel inserts that stick out, and the slide rides on, the P95 has polymer rails that the slide rides on. Obviously, to make the rails strong enough you would have to make them a lot larger. The already bulky proportions of the Ruger help here as the polymer rails can be made larger without actually increasing the proportions of the pistol. If anything, Ruger made it slimmer and better-proportioned. Indeed, compared to the original P85 (which looked like a brick with a muzzle) and later P series pistols, the P95 is downright handsome.

The slide is the typical Ruger investment casting, machined (actually, surface-ground and belt-sanded) to shape and finish, and mated with the polymer frame. The front sight is held in with a pair of roll pins while the rear is a fixed blade in a dovetail. Your choices are few, but clear: you can have your P95 any way you want, provided you pick blued or stainless, and you want a 3.9" barrel and fixed sights. You can have a manual safety or a decock system, and you will get an ultra-reliable 9mm.

The mag catch is the P85-derived ambidextrous design. The serial number is in a metal plate inset in the frame down by the magazine well and permanently bonded to the polymer frame. If there is any internal stiffener moulded into the frame, it does not surface at any point I can see. Obviously if there is one it has to have been held in place somehow, but I can't see it. Nor would there need be one, if Ruger used an appropriate polymer for the frame. Also, you can have your P95 with either a standard dustcover, or a dustcover that has an integral light rail on it.

As with all Ruger pistols, the feed angle from the magazine to the chamber is admirably straightline, and the disassembly is the same as all: you lock the slide back and push down the ejector flange, then remove the slide off the front of the frame.

The P95 Goes to War

OK, so the government bought the Beretta M-92 back in the mid 1980s to replace not only the 1911s that were "wearing out" but also the confusing plethora of other sidearms that the Department of Defense had purchased over the various wars, police actions, and other combative social engagements we had been in. (Just as an aside, when we went into Iraq and needed sidearms pronto, we found lots more unissued 1911s sitting in depots and warehouses, ready for issue.) The inventory books were apparently littered with batches of revolvers and pistols other than 1911s dating back to WWII, and the supply of ammunition, magazines, holsters, cleaning supplies and storage racks for all the various models was just getting to be too much. So we bought one pistol to rule them all.

But not all branches and units of the Armed Forces were happy with the M9 (as the Beretta was to be called) so we bought a bunch of SIG 226s. And SIG 228s. And yet more 1911s. And now, the government recently bought a bunch of Rugers.

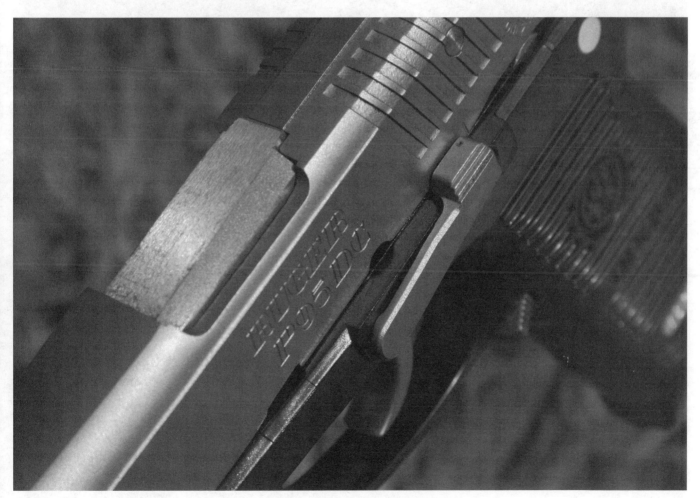

The ejection port is the locking lug area, a design so many modern pistols use.

The Ruger extractor is external, huge, rugged and as "delicate" as a crowbar.

Actually, the U.S. Army Tank and Automotive Command (TACOM) bought 5,000 Ruger P95DC pistols, in contract W52H09-05-C-0058, the fifteen pages of which mostly are concerned with the mundane details of how the pistols are to be packed, labeled, shipped, where they are shipped to (Anniston Arsenal) and what the shipping containers must be made of. Usually on a government contract, there are all kinds of additional documents: contractors submissions, solicitation amendments, attachments, addenda, item descriptions, etc. Curiously, the contract paperwork for this pistol is sparse.

Ruger supplied the government 5,000 pistols, with two magazines each, for $254.34 each. A big movement in procurement circles is the COTS approach: Commercial Off The Shelf items. If

something fills the bill and meets the needs of the end-users, there is no need to develop, publish and then inspect items to rigid mil-spec standards. If the troops like the cookies as-is, there's no need to publish five pages of chocolate chip distribution and cookies weights standards. Same thing with pistols. As an off-the-shelf item, the P95D didn't require volumes of technical descriptions, manufacturing tolerances, inspection protocols and all the other minutia that government procurement is enveloped in – just a promise that Ruger wouldn't change anything during the life of the contract. Still, Tank and Automotive Command? Looking over other purchases by TACOM, we see all the usual suspects: automotive parts such as engine and suspension parts, vehicle maintenance items. And two thousand M240H machineguns, at $3,500 each. I guess if it goes on or in a vehicle, TACOM buys it.

By the way, $254.34 with two magazines is a damned good price for the P95. With an MSRP of $425 to $480 (stainless is more), and an actual, in-the-store price of around $375, getting one at just over $250 is a deal. Then again, you'd have to buy 5,000 of them to get the volume discount.

But still, what is a vehicle depot/armory doing buying weapons? Sidearms, at that? The M240H machineguns I can understand: if you're suppling the Army with vehicles, many are now considered fully-equipped only with weapons on board. But sidearms? Why? Heck if I know, and no one will explain. But what I do have is one of the pistols in question.

When the Ruger P-85 first arrived, we all marveled at how Bill Ruger could make such a

durable and relatively inexpensive 9mm pistol. And how much like a brick it was. The early Rugers were tough, but they were bulky. Later designs have improved the shape, and the P95 is now about as sleek as anyone can make the basic P-85 derivative

The Ruger pistol design holds the rounds high and in a straight line to the chamber.

The magazine button is ambidextrous.

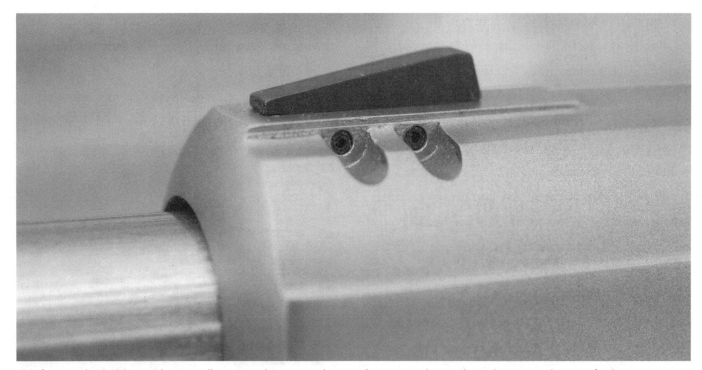

The front sight, held in with two roll pins. Perhaps not elegant, but certainly tough and easy to change if it becomes damaged.

pistols: a nicely shaped if still somewhat chunky hi-cap 9mm.

The "D" in the contract and the "DC" on the slide means the decocker version, where the slide-mounted safety lever drops the hammer without firing it, but pops back up in place when you let go. (The safety, not the hammer.) The DC allows you to get the gun on "Safe," i.e, lower the hammer, so you can resume the double action process at a later time. For those who cannot abide a cocked-and-locked

The captured recoil spring system, with its fluted guide rod.

pistol, and fear having the safety "on" on their double action pistol when they need it most, the DC version is the way to go. The DAO version is your basic "box-fed revolver" mode pistol, while the plain old designation P95 means a traditional SA/DA trigger mechanism.

The P95DC comes in the standard Ruger plastic hard case (which on the pistol sent to me bears a remarkable resemblance to the Browning hard case of the 1990s) with all the usual accoutrements: a pair of magazines, a magazine loading tool, owners manual, lock, and the now ubiquitous sealed envelope with a fired case.

The Ruger double action is long but does not stage or change the pressure needed during the trigger stroke. The single action is a bit heavy, and this particular P95 sent me had a slight step in the trigger pull. Once I had taken up the slack, the trigger then would move at about two and a half pounds, then stop again, and not move again until I had gotten to the five pounds needed to drop the hammer. It was a little more work when shooting for groups, but at speed I never noticed it.

The frame is slimmed down and nicely shaped as compared to the earlier era of Ruger pistols but still a bit larger than some others. The length of the trigger reach might be a bit much for shooters with small hands, but anyone with medium or larger will not have a problem. The safety and magazine catch are ambidextrous, but the slide stop is not. Ruger magazines use a latching hole on the front center of the tube, and pressing the magazine catch forward from either side will drop the magazine. While the Ruger does not have a magazine disconnector, the magazine latch spring is strong. If you go to drop the empty magazine by only momentarily pressing the mag catch, the empty may not fall clear before the spring-loaded catch comes back and traps it in the frame. Press and hold for a moment, and the magazine will drop clear.

Takedown and cleaning on a Ruger can be a bit odd for those not used to it. As this was the first Ruger pistol to arrive on my doorstep, and it had been a few years since I last shot one, it took me

The safety decocks only on the DC version. It is spring-loaded and won't stay down.

All the usual warnings.

The serial number is on a metal plate bound in the moulded frame, left side, down near the magazine well.

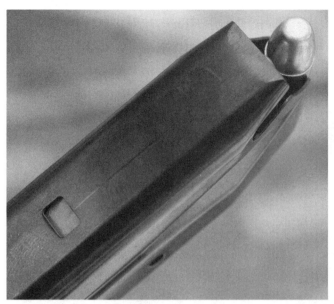

Magazines are held in place via the centrally-located latch on the front of the tube.

While not a target pistol, the Ruger was utterly dependable in delivering average-sized groups all day long, regardless of the ammo I used.

a moment to recall the peculiarities of the Ruger system. The earliest slide stops did not detach from the frame. The P95 does. To dismount for cleaning, make sure it is empty. Pull the slide back until you have aligned the small notch on the frame and the tinier notch on the slide. Then press the slide stop out to the left. The slide will not come off of the frame. Press the slide all the way back, and press the hinged ejector down into the magazine well. You can now remove the slide. The recoil spring is a captured unit, and to remove it you simply pull it down from the barrel.

Now notice the built-in barrel cam and locking angles, manufactured as part of the recoil spring guide rod. The barrel comes out by pulling it down and back. As I mentioned before, the Ruger frame does not have steel inserts in the rails. Ruger makes the rails large enough, and tough enough, that steel isn't needed. To reassemble, install the barrel, then the recoil spring assembly. Start the slide on the frame, and before it gets to the ejector, press the ejector down again, out of the way. Press the slide back until you have the frame and slide notches aligned, and press the slide stop through. If the ejector hasn't popped back up, it will the first time you put a magazine in the frame.

As for durability, all Ruger handguns are legendary. The P95 should not change that. Rated for +P ammo, the P95 would have no problem feeding whatever over-the-counter 9mm ammo you've got

The Ruger P95 is a fun gun, and one you can depend on to work any and every time you ever needed it to.

The Ruger (upper left) isn't the largest, nor the smallest 9mm. It doesn't hold the most, but if what you want is a good gun, at a good price, that holds a lot of bullets, you can't go wrong.

on hand: standard, +P, +P+, surplus; the gun should (and in my case did) gobble them all. I would not count on the stainless barrel resisting the corrosive effects of some older primers, but only because there is no such thing as truly stainless steel. If it is hard enough to be useable as steel, it will rust if you work at it. But the Ruger certainly will give you a fair chance at getting the bore clean before it rusts, should you find a "deal" on surplus corrosive ammo.

The P95's large frame transmits recoil to the hand without a problem. You won't find abrasions on your hand after a day at the range, or strange sore spots the next day from recoil, after using the Ruger. In all, it's a solid choice for the military, who often need a sidearm in places where maintenance is not

omnipresent and corrosion a constant risk. As for durability, the ability of enlisted personnel to break things is legendary regardless of which service you're talking about.

I conducted some accuracy testing, nothing definitive, but while better than average, the remarkable uniformity was interesting. While there were no loads that shot tack-driving groups, there weren't any appalling ones, either. Usually in the course of testing I'll shoot a few good groups, or find some ammo a handgun really likes. That's the bragging group (and often the one many gun writers use to burnish their image as great shooters). And a given handgun will also usually shoot wretched with something, groups that are six, eight or ten inches wide at twenty-five yards. The Ruger didn't do either. I couldn't find "the secret ammo" for best groups with this particular pistol, and it didn't care what I fed it, it shot three inches at twenty-five yards. In the course of testing, I tried it with everything I could lay hands on, and could not find any ammo it refused to function with. At least not with factory ammo. I know some reloaders whose ammunition reloading efforts can choke anything, which is not exactly a fair test. As for accuracy, as I mentioned, the P95 is not a stealth PPC pistol. You aren't going to amaze your friends with super-tight groups shot with it. What

you will get are groups small enough for plinking and defense, with any ammo you care to feed it, and all working without fail.

I guess that's reason enough for the government to consider, and buy, it.

I think, of all the Ruger pistols that aren't .45 or .22LR, the P95 would be the one for me. It is the best looking of the 9mm and .40 pistols. Don't kid yourself, looks count. Unless I'm trying to make a statement with an ugly gun, I want something that looks good, and I suspect a lot of you do also. The grip feels good in my hand, and the sights line up

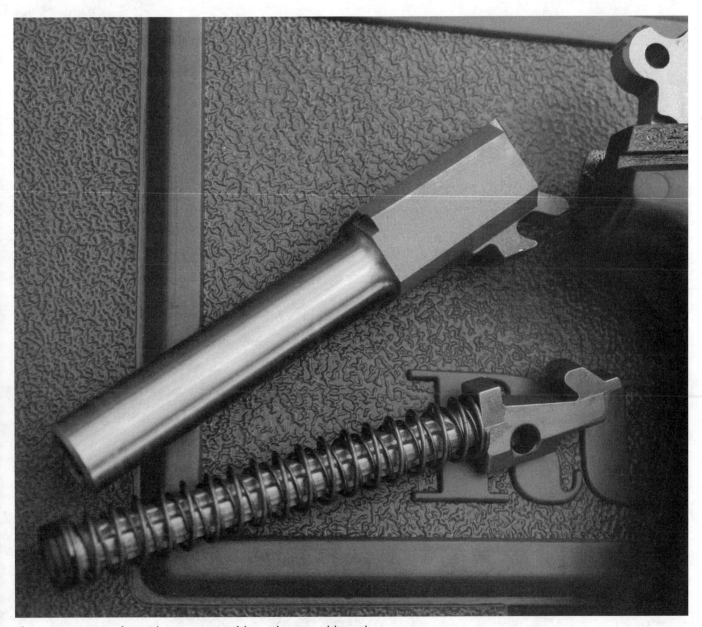

The Ruger captured recoil spring assembly, with integral barrel cams.

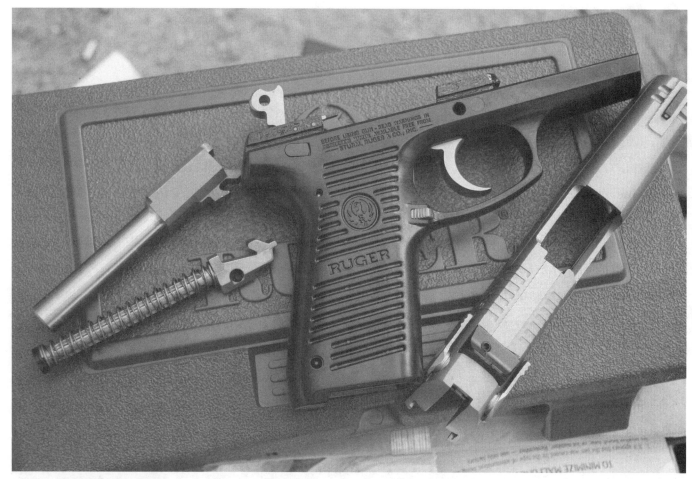

This is all you'll ever need to do in order to clean it.

You have to remember to push the ejector down out of the way in order to put the slide on or off.

without work. I would have to resist the temptation to do some heavy-duty custom work to a P95, but even if I did and ended up with scrap for my efforts, it isn't like I'd be breaking the bank. I think a little work spent on cleaning up the clunky sights could bear some attractive fruit. The polymer frame would no doubt resist any efforts at making it more attractive, but it could be made "grippier" with some skateboard tape or some heat-stippling. I might just have to give in to the temptation.

— PART SIX —
The P345

T he P345 is both the continuation of the Ruger pistol series, and the pistol that Ruger fans always wanted from Ruger. Unlike the earlier Ruger pistols, when the P345 was announced at the 2004 SHOT show we all instantly recognized it as a "nice looking gun." Gone were the blocky, whittled-from-a-chunk-of-lumber lines of the P85 series. Gone was the industrial design grip shape and texture. They were replaced with a pistol that actually had pleasing lines, and a grip that was, well both comfortable and easy on the eyes. It was good enough to be selected as the 2004 *Guns & Ammo* gun of the year.

With a serial number prefix starting at 664, including both the standard safety and the decocker models, the P345 is a .45 ACP pistol that comes out of the box as a DA/SA pistol not much larger than a Commander. In fact, the barrel is a smidgen shorter (4-1/16") and uses magazines the same size as but not interchangeable with the 1911. And those magazines hold eight rounds.

The P345 is a single-stack .45 ACP pistol with a lot going for it. Not only is it sleek, but it is compact as well.

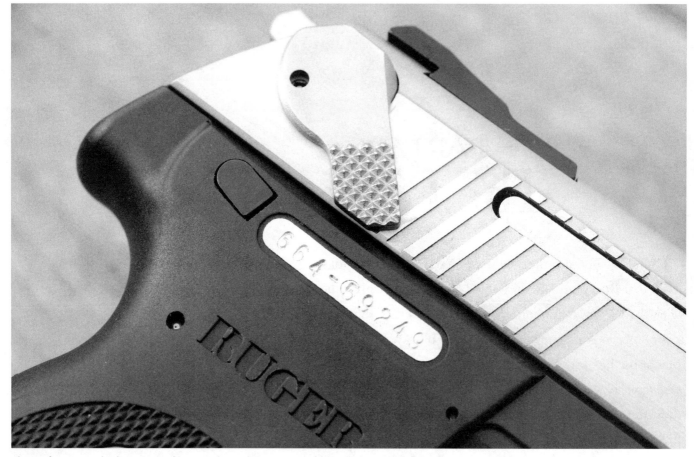

The safety is ambidextrous. The serial number is in a plate on the right side.

The safety is a flat-profile one. It is as large as it needs to be to be a safety, and no more.

The frame is a compact grip, holding the single-stack magazines. The sides are relatively flat, so you can get a good index from the flat sides. The front-to-back reach is a bit more than a 1911 with a long trigger installed, but not nearly the "how can I reach it?" trigger distance of a hi-cap 9mm. And in that Ruger is not alone. A lot of the older designs have

such a long reach that you need big hands to reach the trigger. Not so the P345.

The mag catch is where you'd expect one made by an American manufacturer, and the bottom of the mainspring housing is extended slightly. The extension acts as a funnel on reloads, stopping the magazine from going too far rearward and thus speeding up your reloads. It isn't big, but it doesn't have to be to do its job. The checkering is nicely done (done in the mold, before the frame polymer is injected) and offers a good non-slip grip on the frame.

On the right side of the frame, above where you grasp it, is the serial number plate, inset into and moulded into the polymer frame of the P345. The slide stop lever is on the left, just where you'd expect it, and it and the safety are both low-profile and well shaped. Out in front, the frame has an integral

The rear sight of the 345 is a lot better looking than Ruger sights have been until now.

accessory rail. You can have yours with or without, but if you want it without you'll have to forego other options.

Up above the chamber, there is a small lever inset in the top of the slide. That is the loaded chamber indicator. Such things are more and more required by nosy politicians who have learned all they know about guns from their staff and bad mystery novels. The Ruger's loaded chamber indicator is an unobtrusive design, and if it breaks or falls off (like that ever happens to a Ruger firearm) you won't miss it. Nor will its lack keep the pistol from working. I guess my main objection to it is I really dislike other people telling me what is I must have or do, for my own good.

As you've come to expect from Ruger, the options are not large. You can have blued or stainless finish. You can have a standard DA/SA safety or a decocker.

The front sight blade is in a dovetail in the slide. Look forward to night-sight options on the 345, as the sight makers can now make them for the Ruger dovetail.

No DAO at present. One barrel length. Fixed sights, but they are large and easy to see. Also, the rear sight is additionally secured in its dovetail by means of a large allen-head locking screw. Unlike the earlier Ruger pistols, the P345's front sight is not held in by roll pins but by a dovetail. The front and rear are of

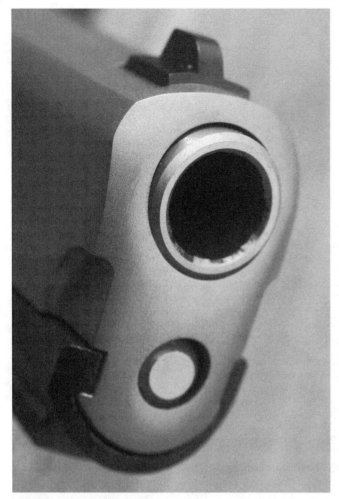

The front of the 345 slide is as sleek as the rest of the pistol.

The mag catch is reversible, not ambidextrous. The checkering is a nice upgrade from the usual utilitarian grooves.

The loaded chamber indicator, large enough to be felt, small enough to be unobtrusive for those who don't need it.

the popular three-dot sight type. The magazines are listed as having different stock numbers, between the P345 and the P90/P97.

At 29 ounces, the P345 comes in a bit lighter than a steel-frame Commander, although not as light as an alloy-frame Commander. The weight is not a problem in recoil. I managed to fire a goodly amount

The mainspring housing sticks below the butt, acting as a funnel on speed reloads.

of ammo through the P345 before having to send it back, and my hands were none the worse for the experience. As the P345 came at the end of the pistol test fire session, it was almost anti-climactic. I had long since given up expecting any malfunctions, and the P345 did not let me down on that score.

What did surprise me was the accuracy. I had been shooting various Ruger pistols for weeks by that time and not getting much more than plinking/defense accuracy out of them. Compared to the others, the P345 was a tack driver. Two inches at twenty five yards was the norm. I know, I know, the Bullseye and PPC shooters are reading this in horror: "Two inches at twenty five yards, and he's happy?" Well, yes. With a standard gun, with an untuned factory trigger, using plain old Black Hills blue

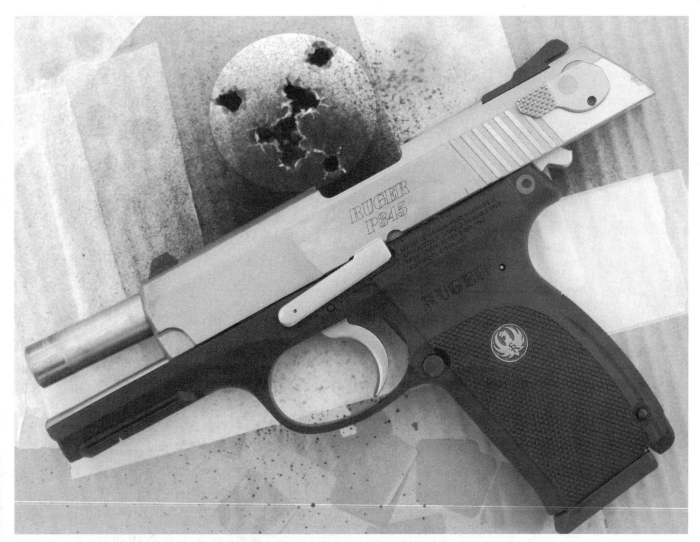

The 345 is plenty accurate. Here is a sub-three inch group at twenty-five yards, over sandbags.

right out of the box 230-grain FMJ, I'm shooting two inches. I've shot expensive custom guns that struggled to do that.

The barrel uses the new Ruger cam-on-the-guide-rod system, which could explain the relatively soft felt recoil. Also, the takedown is the same method used in every Ruger pistol since P-85 #300-00001 rolled out of the factory.

It would be pleasant to see all the Ruger pistols evolve to the looks of the P345. After all, if you could have the reliability and durability of the existing Ruger pistols, along with the looks of the P345, at the typical Ruger cost (MSRP on the P345 is $513 to $548) you'd have a really good-selling line of guns to stock your gun shop with. Or stuff your safe with.

RUGER

— PART SEVEN —
The Ruger SR9

When I was asked if I wanted to come out to the Prescott plant to see the newest Ruger offering, I had some ideas about what it might be. (Oh, I said "Yes" right away. No hesitation there.) After all, the Ruger plant makes pistols, so it probably wasn't a revolver or rifle. Had I been a betting man, I would have lost. My thoughts were along the lines of a further-improved P-345, with better looks, maybe more than just 8 rounds of .45 ACP or perhaps a blend of the P-345 and the 9mm/40 pistols, so there would be commonality and better looks across the Ruger pistol line.

At least I had the "better looks" part down.

By the time you have this book in your hands the news will have been splashed all over the Internet, but when the initial paperwork was done and Bob Stutler, VP of Operations at the Prescott plant, pulled the SR9 out of his desk drawer, there were only two gun writers there: me and Dick Metcalf. Dick's guess was a lot closer than mine. He had correctly projected the Ruger design and

The clean lines and checkering of the SR9 are clearly evident.
Also note the external safety at the rear of the slide.

manufacturing intent: "A polymer-frame, striker-fired pistol."

Richard seemed just a tiny bit disappointed that Ruger hadn't leapt ahead of the pack, producing something truly revolutionary. Me, I was happy to be wrong. As impressed as I am by the Glock pistol, and the engineering that went into it, I do have some shortcomings about the Austrian design. I thought it would be very interesting in the least to see how Ruger went about it, as they have an entirely different approach to pistols.

First, let's take a tour around the outside of it. On top is a stainless slide, underneath a polymer frame. The slide has the now-obligatory front dovetail sight, a good thing. As cost-effective as the

VP Bob Stutler, with one of the first-production SR9s in hand.

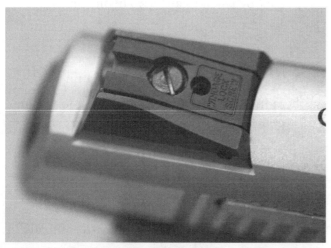

The rear sight is compact, adjustable and unlikely to get hooked or snagged on anything.

The front sight, in a dovetail. No more pinned and un-handsome front sights.

Ruger approach is, of pinned blades, they aren't attractively done, and they offer no option for adjustment except vertically. The new front is in a cleanly-installed dovetail, and no one can complain about the aesthetics of it. On the rear we have not only a solid pyramidal-shaped sight, but also it is adjustable, too. At last, adjustable sights on a centerfire Ruger pistol, and they look good, appear durable, and there aren't any edges to catch on gear.

The barrel locks into the slide by means of the ejection port opening. As much as I love the 1911, locking lugs in the underside of the slide are a royal pain to machine, fit and inspect. The modern, lock the barrel into the ejection port design is much faster, easier to manufacture and control dimensionally, and also makes for a lower

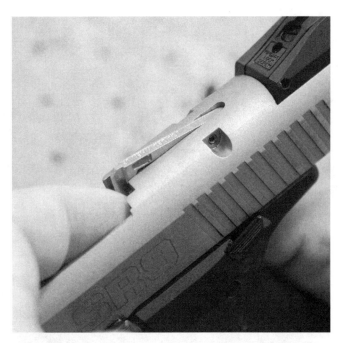

The loaded chamber indicator on the SR9 is unobtrusive but easy to figure out.

My thumb rides higher, but the thinner frame still feels good.

slide top to the bore centerline. At the rear of the ejection port is the loaded chamber indicator. Me, I'm old school. If I need to check the chamber I just find a way to prop the slide back a smidgen. But a mechanical loaded chamber indicator is something some legislators are enamored of, and they will have their way. So it is a prudent manufacturer who makes sure a new design has it. In Ruger's defense the design is hard to miss, and if it falls out the pistol still operates. On the right side of the slide is the extractor, another honking big Ruger part. However, its size is hidden by being flush with the slide, and looking like a simple flat bar. You could practically use the extractor as a tow hook. If it were any larger it would be a lethal weapon all by itself. I can't see anyone breaking one, ever.

The frame is quite an improvement over previous Ruger pistols. Yes, I've been a bit hard on them in this book. And it has been a long time since the P-85 was the apex of Ruger pistol design. The P-345 was the vanguard on the Ruger aesthetic front, and the SR9 carries on with that. Instead of pebbly gripping areas or grooves milled into the mould, we have actual checkering patterns made in the mould. As an added bonus, the shape is subtly sculpted so your hand (at least mine and the Ruger engineers so far) finds the frame comfortable, compact, and shaped for a solid hold even if it were smooth and not checkered. What's more, they made it compact and sculpted while still making it a hi-cap pistol. You can expect to get as many 9mm cartridges into a Ruger magazine as you can anyone else's.

The magazine itself came in for a lot of work. When Ruger was first working on the prototypes they made their own magazines. The pistols were

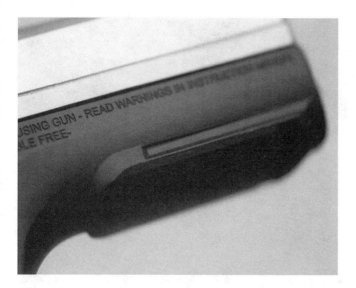

All pistols need a light rail, and the SR9 has one.

The magazines are sturdy, Me-Gar (and thus reliable) and hi-cap. There will be ten-shot mags for those who need them.

simply not as reliable as Ruger desired. So they dropped back and punted. They called in Mec-Gar, the Italian magazine company who makes so many magazines for just about everyone. Ruger told Mec-Gar what they wanted, how small it had to be and how many rounds they wanted it to hold. (I'm sure there were all kinds of other, technical details, like the angle of attack, the distance from magazine tube to feed ramp, the over-travel of the slide, etc.); the results were magazines that fed flawlessly.

Curiously enough, when we were first looking over the pistol in Bob Stutler's office, I mentioned to the videographer from Guns & Ammo TV that "this magazine looks just like a Mec-Gar magazine." When we were later told about the trip to Italy, the videographer looked at me with a "How'd you know that?" look. Simple, I've seen a lot of Mec-Gar mags. At seventeen rounds of 9mm Parabellum, and not overly long, the Ruger mags hold as many as anyone's do.

The additional features of the frame don't stop there. On the backstrap is a removable panel, sort of the mainspring housing of the SR9. There's no spring there, but we all know what it means; the backstrap. The Ruger is changeable too. However,

instead of a box with pistol and a fistful of inserts that you're sure to lose, the Ruger is two-sided. Drift out the pin, pull out the insert, turn it over, re-install it and drive the pin in. You have two choices, and you can't lose them. The pin is also the lanyard loop attachment point. The panel is

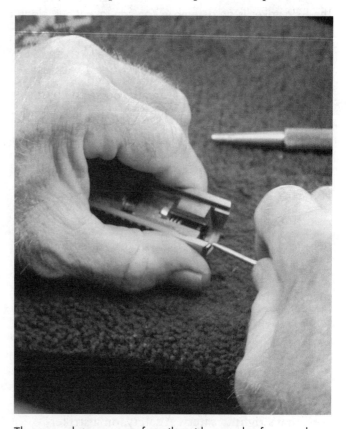

The rear plate comes of easily with a push of a punch, and then you can take the striker and magazine disconnector out.

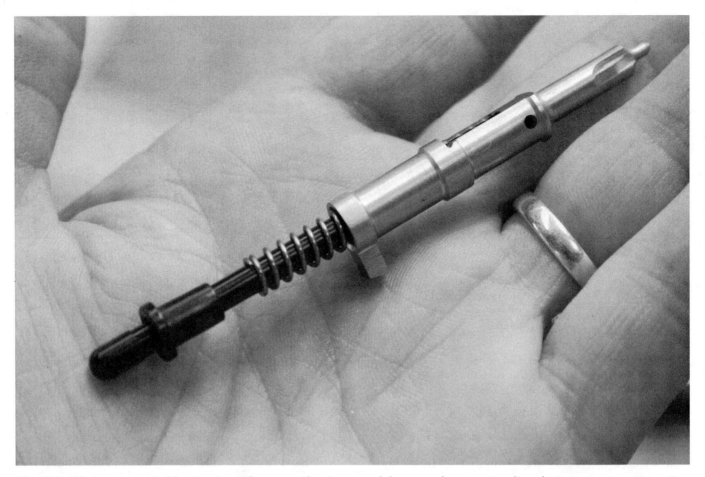

The SR9 striker is an assembly. You can take it out, clean it, even lube it, and not worry about losing parts or getting it wrong when you put it back in.

held in by means of a drift pin. At first I was just a bit grumpy about that. I mean, tools? To change a backstrap? But the more I thought about it, the more sense it made. I mean, no one is going to be changing backstraps in the field, right? And you can't lose the part, right? So I will get over it. Additionally, the rear of the frame projects down behind where the magazine will seat, creating a small but effective "parking block." Not a real magazine funnel, but enough of an aid to fast reloads that it noticeably helps. Out front, the SR9 has an accessory rail, where you can park lights, lasers, a bayonet, or whatever your heart desires.

Look above the grip area, and what do you see? That's right, a safety. A safety, on a striker-fired pistol! Hoo-boy! That is going to create some problems. One of the biggest complaints about

the various striker-fired pistols (at least in some quarters) is the lack of an external safety. So much so that there is at least one gunsmith who offers to retrofit your plastic pistol with an external safety. Now you can have one from the factory that way. The SR9 has a trigger-mounted safety; it just doesn't look like one. Where the Glock has its trigger safety as a bar on the inside of the trigger face, the Ruger has its as a cover around the trigger bar. The initial "take-up" you feel in the trigger movement is the cover pivoting out of the frame block, and allowing you to then compress the trigger itself. The thumb safety is ambidextrous.

Above the trigger is the takedown plate. It covers and is attached to the cam pin and disassembly pin, that both cams the barrel in and out of engagement, and keeps the slide on the frame.

The cam block holds the trigger parts, slide stop and various springs all in one unit.

Takedown is pure Ruger: You remove the magazine and lock the slide back. Reach in and push the ejector down. (The other option is you can push the ejector down after you remove the takedown pin, if you wish) Push the takedown pin from the right side, out the left, and remove it. Now control the slide and release the slide stop. The slide, barrel and recoil spring assembly will come off the frame. When you pivot the ejector down, not only does it remove the ejector from the path of the slide, but a cam punched/machined into the ejector decocks the striker assembly. No need to dry-fire the SR9 before you take it apart.

After that, it gets involved. Once aspect of the Ruger design universe is the use of roll pins. So, if you're expecting a Ruger armorers course to be like a Glock course, where you can wrestle the whole thing apart with your bare hands (pretty much) that won't be the case. The SR9 requires a drift punch to push pins out. They aren't there hard enough to require a hammer, but you can't get them out with your bare hands, either.

The striker assembly is a self-contained unit. Use the same punch to depress the rear plate retainer, and slide the plate off. The striker assembly comes out as a unit. You also do that to gain access to another interesting feature of the SR9; the magazine disconnector. Most designs that call for a magazine disconnector put parts in the trigger assembly path. Adding parts makes the trigger pull less crisp, enjoyable, controllable, whatever. The SR9 magazine disconnector is different: it works off the magazine, but it blocks the striker. If there is no magazine, the blocker bar keeps the striker from going forward. Insert a magazine, and the striker can now go fully forward when you pull the trigger. The bottom leg of the bar touches the feed lip of the magazine, and the magazine pushes the bar clear of the striker. No extra parts in the trigger mechanism, no trigger problems. What if you don't want a magazine disconnector? Simple: remove the back plate, remove the striker assembly, you then lift the magazine disconnector out of the slide, and install the striker assembly and back plate.

It is also simple to see if the magazine disconnector is installed. Lock the slide back and turn the pistol over. You can see the bar (if it is there) or the gap it let behind. In law enforcement, that is what is called "a clue."

Internally, Ruger has done a mix of design features. The rear slide rails in the frame are molded in place, as is the serial number plate. The front rails are in the cam block that does several jobs. The cam block has a hole for the takedown pin, which keeps the block in place. It provides an impact surface for the barrel as it unlocks, and supports it when it is locked to the slide. The front block also holds the trigger parts, the trigger bar, springs, etc. The cam block, slide and barrel are all stainless steel and through-hardened. No case-hardened parts for Ruger. They, along with the extractor and frame, are cast.

Once cast, all those parts get machining attention. Yes, the polymer frame is machined. There are a few critical dimensions that Ruger is

The cam block is another assembly, and once the trigger and slide stop are on it you simply shove the whole thing into the frame.

too fussy to leave, as cast. So the frames come in and spend a very short time in the CNC machines, to be ready for marking and assembly. The slide gets machined and then has a session with various belt sanders, and then the SR9 and Ruger markings are laser-burned into the slide. The barrel is drilled, reamed, rifled, has the outside finish-machined, and is sent off for assembly. The extractor gets a small amount of machining, and then bins of them are stacked for the assembler's attention.

The trigger mechanism of the SR9 will be no surprise to someone familiar with the Glock. In fact, and no disrespect to the Ruger engineers, when I first saw the interior of the SR9, the question I asked myself was "Have the patents on the Glock trigger expired? They must have, the S&W Sigma has been using it for years." Simple; the trigger bar gets pressed back by your finger, compressing the striker spring. Once the trigger bar safety tab passes the Ruger equivalent of the drop safety, the end of the bar cams down, releasing the striker. While that is going on, the upper tab of the trigger bar is pushing the striker safety out of the striker path, allowing it to impact the primer as you wish it to. The slide cam pushes

Here a machined polymer frame is being checked for cam-block fit.

the trigger cam out of the way, disconnecting the trigger bar from the striker, and allowing the striker to reset when the slide cycles. If you've spent any time with the Glock system, this is all immediately and intimately familiar. Ruger obviously did not feel compelled to re-invent the wheel, nor should they have.

The entire SR9 design was obviously drawn from the outset for quick assembly, and when we

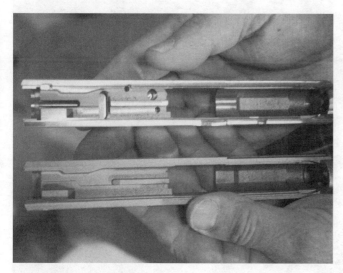

A machined slide, showing the access slot for the magazine disconnector.

A machined slide and machined frame, being checked for fit. Of course they fit. If they didn't, heads would roll.

The SR9 in full recoil, as I test it at high speed on the Ruger range.

were there new assemblers were getting taught the drill. I watched a few steps, and then asked the instructor to show me how to take it apart and pout it back together "So I would know the process." I could tell from the look he gave me that

Racks of SR9 slides getting their casting marks removed via belt-sander and experienced operators.

he wasn't' sure it was that easy, but he did. Two minutes later I gave him the step-by-step recital of the whole process. (Hey, I've been taking guns apart for a living since Jimmy Carter was President. I learn quickly.)

So, Ruger has a product that we can all quickly tell is aimed for a particular market: they anticipate taking sales directly away from Glock. It is polymer, striker-fired, hi-capacity and appears to be as durable as a granite boulder. As advantages, it also has things a Glock does not have, features that some users have expressed a desire for: an external safety, a magazine disconnector, changeable backstraps, and it is made in the USA. But none of that will be of any advantage for Ruger without the real test: how does it shoot?

To answer that, we ambled the next morning out to a range Ruger uses for testing, and sent a whole lot of Ruger ammunition down range. The ammo we were using was the hottest 9mm in common use: NATO-spec 9mm ball, which if it is as hot as past lots I've tried, launches a 124-grain

A rolling rack that holds 500 pistols. One of half a dozen in the ïfinishedî side of the room, with lots more on the way. And this more than a month before the SR9 would even be seen in public.

FMJ out the muzzle at something like 1250 fps. It did not feel sharp in recoil. The slim, sculpted grip gave me a good grip, and the frame soaked up the recoil. Frankly, the location and shape of the external safety had me a bit worried. In handling guns in the factory the safety hit my hand right at the base of the thumb. But in shooting, it was no big deal. I could tell where it hit me, but after a while that simply became part of the "Ruger feel" of shooting that pistol. One particular pistol has two light strikes in several cases of ammo (we started with enough ammo to stuff a small SUV full) and the assembled engineers fussed over it and offered conjectures as to the cause. Last I saw, they were in a small group, muttering to themselves

as engineers do when faced with a new problem, albeit a small one. The rest of the SR9s on hand shot all the ammo we had to feed them, even when they were too hot to handle anything but the polymer.

After a short break, I came back to the first shooting point to find Bob Stutler and other top Ruger brass doing a bit of plinking There was a favorite rock of theirs they like to shoot at, far beyond the backstop and up the "mountain." I took one look and pegged it at about 200 yards, maybe a smidge more. When it came my turn, I held a bit over, got the range, and proceeded to smack the rock for most of the magazine. The misses splashed Arizona sand onto the rock. Yes, the SR9 is an accurate pistol.

Some have complained in the past about unavailability of new Ruger products. That subject came up while we were in the plant getting the lowdown and going on tour. To make sure we knew how serious Ruger was about changing that perception, we got to see the full panoply of SR9s in assembly. At one point I was standing in a sea of racks, where I could see on the order of four thousand finished SR9 pistols, frames on other rack ready to be assembled, cartons of more frames and bins of parts to go on those frames. If when you read this, you can't lay hands on an SR9 to fondle and buy, it isn't because Ruger isn't making them. It is because Ruger is selling them faster than they can make them. I anticipate a hot time in the law enforcement market. To name names, where

Glock had the market to themselves, and S&W with their M&P was the hot new guy on the block, add Ruger. The features will make it very attractive to many defensive-carry, non-LEO (I refuse to use the word "civilian" in that context) and to police departments as well.

The size makes it a soft shooter, so competition shooters will be very interested. If your gunsmith knows how to tune a Glock trigger, he will find the Ruger so similar as to be a piece of cake to figure out. The external safety just adds to the attractiveness, as will the accuracy. No need to hunt for an aftermarket match barrel, if the regular production guns shoot like the one I shot at the Ruger event. As for looks, Ruger finally has a handle on making a pistol that looks good. Which was one of the design imperatives laid down when

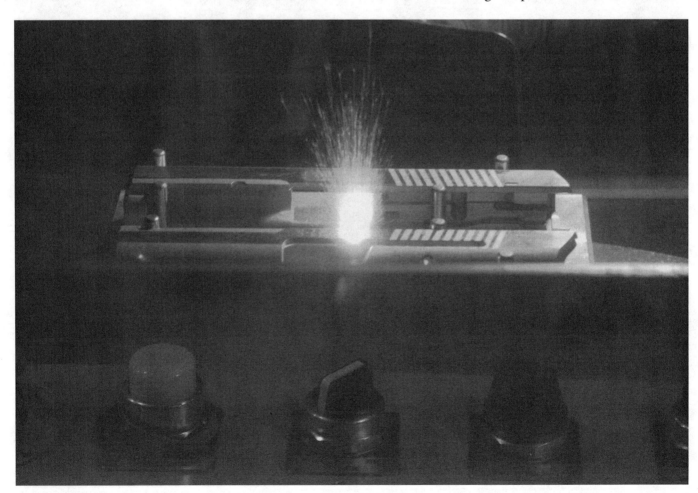

The SR9 slides being laser-etched. No roll markings that need cosmetic improvements, but clean laser cuts.

They held an impromptu competition for us, and of course I had to go at it full-throttle.

they started the project. I can't say it was because of me, as I haven't been grumping in print all that long about Ruger looks. But others have been. When they undertook the project that would be the SR9, the Ruger designers were told it had to look good. And last, we come to the real question: cost. I cannot give you a definite answer, as I have to send the manuscript in before Ruger unveils the MSRP of the SR9. But Ruger has a long reputation of offering its products at prices lower than anyone else. They've figured out the cost-reduction methods that work for them, and they design their products to go towards their strengths in production and price reduction. The features make

it attractive, but my prediction is that the price will make it a must-buy.

And we, the shooters all benefit. Not just the Ruger owners, but those who buy other handguns as well. If someone comes out with a "better mousetrap" then all the other makers of mousetraps have to figure a better rodent-catching system of their own. That is the beauty of the capitalist, market-driven system we have.

Me, I just plan to take the loaner they send me, put tens of thousands of rounds through it to test it, and then send Ruger a check for it. No way is an early-production SR9 leaving this location.

— PART ONE —
The Bearcat

The Bearcat is a neat little gun and thought by many to be the second-oldest model in the Ruger line. Not so. The Single Six holds that distinction, appearing in 1953 and making Ruger a firearms manufacturer on the move. The Mark I had been quite a success, but many shooters in the very early 1950s were still wedded to revolvers. Pistols were something that target shooters shot, and real hunters, outdoorsmen and plinkers shot with revolvers. Back then there were no glitzy ad campaigns (one might argue that there still aren't, as the firearms business simply isn't big enough to support glitz) and the few gun magazines and "men's magazines" were the only sources of info. The story goes that the late Pete Kuhloff wrote a small piece about the new Single Six. Kuhloff wasn't the only gun writer to have knowledge of it, he was just the first to get it into print.

The Southport, Connecticut post office was swamped with mail. So much so that they placed daily calls to Ruger to please pick up the mail, as they hadn't

Like all other Rugers, the Bearcat (named in honor of the old-time Stutz Bearcat car) comes in a solidly built plastic case with all the accessories.

The Bearcat grip is so compact that it is a different experience for me to shoot one. Not that my hands are huge, but my fingers wrap around the frame.

room for it all. And a lot of that mail had checks in the envelopes, asking for a Single Six. Yes, back in those days you could not only send and receive firearms by mail (something that is allowed for only a few today) but you could order one through the mail, send a check and have it shipped right to your door. Ruger had lots of money flowing in.

The Single Six was the first cast-frame firearm Ruger made. They had been using cast parts, but the parts were smaller and less critical. The Single Six frame caused a number of headaches, but the learning was worth it. It was also the intro to the western market (as in "western movie-influenced shooters") and another step that made Ruger the known name among shooters.

After the Single Six came the Blackhawk in 1955, and then the Bearcat in 1958. Soon after, the .44 Magnum would find a new home in the Super Blackhawk. So why a little-bitty .22LR revolver, when Ruger already had the Single Six? So they could offer a single action Kit Gun, of course.

The Single Six is a nice gun. At 32 ounces it wasn't much smaller or lighter than the full-size centerfires that came along soon after. While a plinking .22 at 32 ounces is fun, those packing a gun into the backwoods wanted something lighter. Ruger responded with the Lightweight Single Six, with frame and cylinder made of aluminum, but even then it was large-ish, and those packing wanted small and light. They wanted a Kit Gun,

The cylinder is rollmarked. Partly because it looks good, and partly (I think) because the frame is so small there's no other place for the writing.

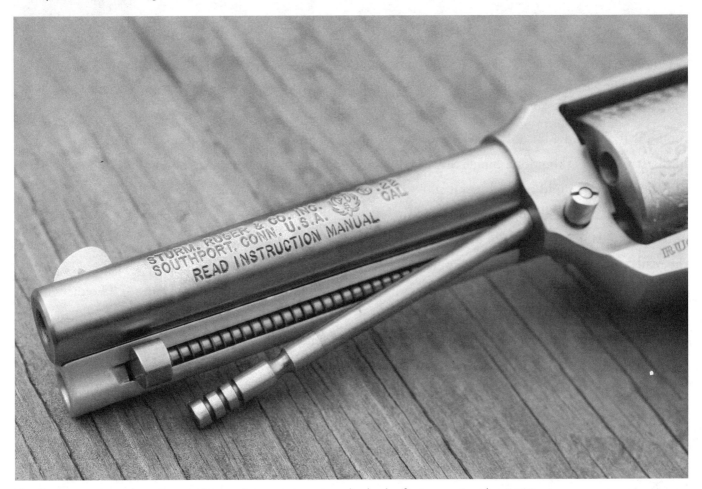

The Bearcat is a single action and as such you remove its cylinder by first removing the center pin.

The Bearcat retains the screws in the frame instead of the pins of the new Model centerfires. On the stainless guns the trigger guard is stainless, not the brass-anodized aluminum found on the early guns.

something that could be put in their packing kit and used when needed.

Unveiled in 1958 (needless to say, with no serial number prefix) the Bearcat, with its aluminum frame only weighed 17 ounces. The aluminum frame was strong due to its being one-piece. No screws holding on the grip assembly, nothing but the aluminum trigger guard anodized to look like brass. The cylinder was chrome-moly steel, unlike the aluminum cylinder of the Lightweight Single Six. It was so small and light you could stuff it in the outside pocket of a rucksack and not notice it until you needed it. The Bearcat revolvers started with serial number 1, and after the 1968 change, they were made with a serial number prefix of "90." The last aluminum-framed Bearcat was made in 1970, with serial number 90-25622. After that they were all made with steel frames, and called the Super Bearcat. Production stopped in 1974, in the "91" prefix serial numbers. The New Model Bearcat is simply called the "New Bearcat" and first arrived in 1993. With a serial number prefix of "93" it has been a steady if not stellar sales item.

The wood on Ruger grips has shown a very nice increase in color and figure in the last decade. On the stainless Bearcat these reddish grips look good.

The Bearcat Ruger sent me was not one of the early ones from the vault. Rather, it was a current production version, the New Bearcat and in stainless steel. Making the frame from stainless adds a bit of weight, bumping it up from the 17 ounces of the original, aluminum-framed one to 24 ounces, but it is still one compact little gun. So small, in fact, that if it were any smaller I'd have a tough time shooting it. My hands aren't the biggest around, but I do wear size Large gloves. When I wrap my hand around the grips, the tips of my fingers are covered by the palm of my hand inside the base of the thumb. I'm basically gripping my own fingers, with the grips of the Bearcat wrapped inside.

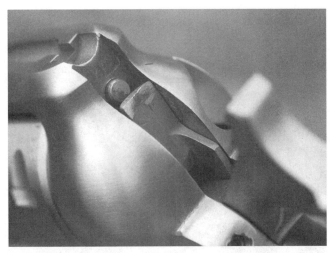

The New Bearcat uses a transfer bar trigger system, like all New Model Ruger revolvers.

The Bearcat's frame is so compact that the hand (pawl, in Ruger parlance) has to be installed by means of an exterior hole, capped with a hex screw.

The barrel is a smidge over four inches – 4-1/16" is the official listing – and that makes it long enough to be accurate and easy to aim, without being un-handy to carry or pack. Yes, a longer barrel would be easier to shoot, but hell to carry. A shorter barrel would be a lot easier, but hard to shoot. It is frustrating to plink with a 2" barrel, but if you really need to whack some furry little critter in an emergency to cook it and eat, "frustrating" hardly describes the stress level.

The Bearcat is a single action revolver. As with all the Ruger single actions, you have to know if yours is an Old Model or a New. The New Model Bearcats have a transfer bar. With an old model you cannot carry it with the hammer down on a loaded chamber. With a New Model you can. To load, pull the hammer back one click. Open the loading gate, and turn the cylinder to insert a cartridge. To unload, do the same thing but use the ejector to push each empty case or loaded round out of the chambers.

Shooting the Bearcat is a blast. .22LR ammo is cheap, plentiful and has no real recoil. At any reasonable distance you simply line up the sights, cock the hammer, press the trigger, and watch whatever you aimed at get hit. You can go through a lot of ammo, even considering that the Bearcat might be a bit slow to load and unload.

In the change to the New Model lockwork, the Bearcat did not get, as the Blackhawks did, pins in place of screws. The right side of the frame still has a pair of screw heads, the hammer and trigger pivot pins. The Bearcat does have the coil spring over a strut mainspring design that all the other Ruger revolvers have, that wasn't anything that needed to be changed. Due to its small size, and the lack of a separate grip frame, the hand spring of the Bearcat is retained in place by a hex screw on the back of the frame next to the hammer. If not for that, you'd never know the Ruger Bearcat wasn't a little doll of a traditional single action revolver, done up in stainless steel.

— PART TWO —
The Blackhawk

W hen the Blackhawk debuted in 1955, Ruger hit the big time. While the Mark I was a runaway financial success, and the Single Six was every would-be cowboy's plinking gun, they were back then not considered "real guns." A Real Gun was something in a centerfire, preferably in one of the big, standard cartridges of the time: .38 Special/.357 Magnum, .45 Colt, and for the real cognoscenti, .44 Special or .45 ACP. But most definitely .38/.357 at a minimum.

When wartime production became obvious on Monday morning, December 8, 1941, Colt set aside all the tooling for the Single Action Army. The military, the country, needed machine guns. Also sidearms, in the form of 1911A1 pistols and .38 revolvers. Any tooling meant for anything else was pulled off the shop floor, stuffed into storage and left "for later." Colt then went on to produce huge volumes of what was needed. (While this isn't a history of Colt, the condition of Colt bears heavily on our story).

Blackhawk revolvers have a reputation for durability and ruggedness in the field. They are some of the most advanced single action revolvers ever made.

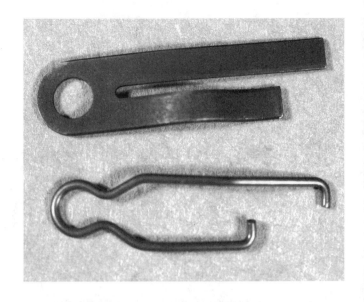

The Colt SAA leaf spring that powers the trigger return and the cylinder stop bolt is fragile. Any gunsmith who works on them either has a drawer full of replacements, or talks his customers into used the Wolff wire spring seen below it.

After the war was over, Colt and S&W had a number of problems: they had huge plants, with many trained personnel, but no guarantee that there would be a post-war market for all their output. The government had huge stockpiles of surplus arms. If the government simply dumped the excess, not only would there probably be no market for them but by the time there was, both companies would be long out of business. Congress, in a momentary fit of rational thought, recognized this situation and forbade the War Department from dumping surplus small arms on the civilian market.

After the war, the two big players in the firearms market got to work in their own way. Both had large numbers of machine tools on hand. Those in the S&W plant were relatively new and in good shape. Those in Colt were not. Colt had not gotten any new machines or tooling for a couple of decades at that point. While S&W started making old models again, and coming up with new ones, Colt simply continued the old guns, with a few notable exceptions such as the New Service (dropped, never to be seen again). Colt was also hammered by a flood in New Haven that left their plant floor under water for nearly a week. As if all that wasn't enough, they made two decisions that had long-term

consequences: first, they jumped on the US Army proposal for a lightweight new sidearm.

The Colt was the Lightweight Commander, a 9mm 1911 with a shortened slide and barrel and an aluminum frame. The Army ended up looking at the huge stocks of 1911s, .38 revolvers and other small arms and decided they really didn't need a new sidearm. Colt desultorily offered the LWC to the market, but never really pushed its benefits. S&W, with their M-39, kept at it. While Colt simply withdrew from any R&D, market testing or new product introduction, S&W persisted. (To jump forward three decades, by the late 1970s S&W had a relatively perfected high-capacity 9mm pistol that was positioned to take advantage of the ammunition advances. New hollow points and new powders both lifted the 9mm from a modest 125-grain FMJ poking along at 1100 fps to a high-performance 115-grain JHP screaming along at 1250. With a magazine capacity of 14 rounds, the S&W M-59 offered a police officer with two spare magazines on his belt, 43 rounds. Compared to a revolver, with six in the gun and twelve more in loops on his belt, the 9mm was very attractive. Colt had nothing to compare to the M-59, and their meager R&D efforts came to naught.)

The second decision Colt made was to not put the SAA back into production after the war. Just before the war it had not been selling well. The new double action revolvers had put a crimp in its sales. The Depression hadn't helped any, either. What really put the hurt to Colt as far as SAA sales were concerned was the lack of R&D and marketing efforts. Did Colt improve the design to make it stronger, smoother, more accurate or more durable? No. Did Colt refine production and adopt manufacturing processes that would bring the cost down? Again, no. What did Colt do? Not much. After the war, Colt announced that SAA production was not going to be resumed, as there simply wasn't enough demand for it.

What happened next was neither predictable nor avoidable: Westerns took off in a big way. While movies set in the west had been big before the war, after WWII they became even bigger. Adding to the consumer frenzy was TV. By the mid 1950s, you could see all westerns all the time. You could see a western at the movie theater every weekend, and watch westerns on TV just about every night. The viewing had the effect of inventing new competitions: Quick Draw and Fast Draw. The idea was to draw and shoot as fast as possible, while hitting a (size and shape varied over time) target faster than anyone else. The difference between them is that Fast Draw shooters fire blanks driving the coarse shotgun powder, or wax bullets, to break balloons. Quick Draw is done with real ammunition. (Not that the Fast Draw ammo wouldn't hurt if you were too close to it.) Such shooting either done thumb-cocking, or by fanning the hammer which is hard on guns. Colt SAA revolvers are not strong in the areas worked hardest by such shooting. A regular practitioner would have to have a battery of guns in play, all tuned, with spares when the inevitable

The Blackhawk could withstand steady use of loads that would quickly throw a Colt out of time. And still be accurate.

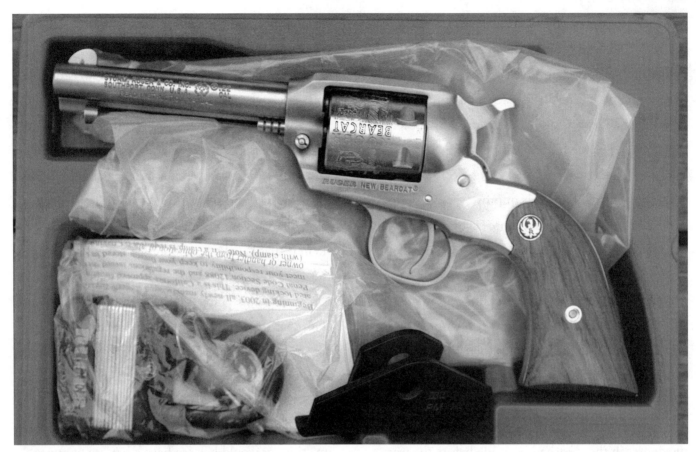

The Bearcat was a nice little gun (as was the Mark I) but neither were what the hordes of cowboy shooters wanted in the 1950s. For that, Ruger had to make a centerfire single action.

breakage occurred.

With lots of shooters, and no more Colts coming out, prices went up. So much so that there was even a new crop of makers showing up, making Colt revolvers. One was the Great Western Arms company. One of the owners of the company was Audie Murphy, the most decorated WWII vet. The company was savvy enough to present John Wayne with a matched pair of engraved Great Western revolvers, and use his photo in their ad campaign. So great was the demand that European manufacturers entered the market, with guns coming from Germany and Italy. By the time Colt re-entered the SAA market in 1956, it was too late. Yes, they made a lot of guns, but they didn't own the market any more. By 1956, two things had happened that made the SAA from Colt slip from "essential item" to

"boutique firearm": the Ruger Blackhawk and the .44 Magnum.

As with his previous designs (and the later ones, too) Bill Ruger did not simply copy an existing design. No "me too" marketing efforts, then or later. While the Blackhawk was intended to fit in with, and compete well against, the cowboy offerings, it was to be more. To that end Bill Ruger addressed and eliminated the shortcomings of the Colt SAA.

When I was relatively new working in gun shops, I had a crusty old-timer dismissively describe the Blackhawk as "A Colt with coil springs." Now, if that was all Bill Ruger had done he'd have sold a lot of them. But such a Blackhawk would not have been the amazingly rugged canvas that later gunsmiths, hunters and cartridge experimenters could work on. No, they would have been left empty-handed by the limitations of the Colt SAA, which were many and obvious. To many, it will seem that I am about to be off on an extended Colt-bashing episode. Not so. In order to know how much of an improvement the Ruger Blackhawk was in 1955 (and even today) you have to have a sense of what things were like back then and how the Colt was made and is still made, as the SAA design is still the same, even though Colt and its copiers have made some minor improvements in materials or methods.

I'm also spending a lot of time on the Blackhawk for other reasons: as the first big centerfire handgun, it was the one that put Ruger on the map. Not just for the money it made them, nor for the status a successful product brings, but also for the experience of mass-production of a big handgun and the marketing experience it brought them for later firearms. Last, looking at the Blackhawk gives you a glimpse into the mind of Bill Ruger, how he solved problems, how he made his manufacturing processes work for him instead of against him, and why there are so many Blackhawk revolvers extant.

First, the frame or receiver. The Colt was (and still is) made by forging and machining a chunk of low-carbon steel. Once shaped and polished, the receiver is then carefully hand-packed in bone charcoal and leather strips. It is then heated in an air-tight furnace. The heating drives carbon into the surface of the frame, hardening it. When removed from the packing, the frames are quenched in cold water. This rapid cooling prevents annealing, a slow cooling that softens carbon steel or alloys. Cooled

After the war, Colt decided here was no longer a market for the Single Action Army. As a result, they saw Ruger taking the power-guns part of the market, and imports like this Uberti taking the nostalgia part. By the time others were done, there was no room left for Colt.

When the .41 Magnum came out you could have the Ruger Blackhawk, an S&W M-57 or M-58 in that new caliber. Of the three the Ruger was much less expensive.

quickly, the parts stay hard. They also, in the case of the Colt, end up with the colors you see on the frames. That is the color of "color case-hardening." The process has drawbacks: for one, a certain percentage of frames will warp. The more-skilled and experienced the operator, the fewer warped frames. But you'll lose a certain number of them regardless of how good he is. Many of them can be salvaged. (I'm convinced that a certain number of the nickel-plated Colt SAAs were salvaged warped frames, polished and plated.)

The Ruger Blackhawk, with its investment cast frame, did not suffer from warpage. It needed no salvage operation. It could not be color case-hardened, as its alloy steel prohibited the operation. But not all shooters wanted color case-hardening anyway.

The Colt frame did not come out of the manufacturing operation with an absolute internal dimension for the cylinder. The cylinder as a result was designed for, and fitted with, a bushing or sleeve. The sleeve is the rotational axis of the cylinder on the centerpin, i.e., the cylinder does not rotate directly on the centerpin; the sleeve does. With a separate sleeve, assemblers could hand-fit the sleeve to the cylinder and to the frame. As a manufacturing method of the 1870s, it makes sense. Assemblers were cheaper than the technology required to make every frame dimensionally perfect.

The sleeve was a simple hand-fit step. However, by the 1950s, time had caught up with Colt. First, hand-assembly was becoming more-and-more expensive. Anything that required hand assembly meant higher costs. Second, the sleeve is relatively fragile. Every shot pounds the sleeve, as the frame and cylinder jolt back and forth. With enough shooting, the sleeve peens and wears, and the cylinder enters a physical state known as "endshake." A revolver with endshake has a cylinder that moves forward and back on the centerpin. With enough movement the cylinder can rub against the rear of the barrel, or significantly change headspace. Yes, it can be corrected on the Colt SAA with a new (or the old one stretched) sleeve. But that takes time or money and the skill to fit a new one or re-fit a stretched one. And the fast draw shooters of the 1950s were working their guns hard. The beginnings of a handgun hunting cadre were forming, and they also shot the guns hard.

Ruger figured out how to make revolvers and make them quickly. The investment casting process sped things up considerably.

When the Colt SAA was new, no one shot much. In the last quarter of the nineteenth century, shooters who shot a lot shot the .22LR or other rimfire calibers. A shooter who went through a couple of thousand rounds a year with a large-bore centerfire handgun would have been a very active shooter indeed. By the 1950s, a couple of thousand was a good average if you wanted to get better.

The Blackhawk's cylinder does not use a sleeve. The thrust collar (the portion of the cylinder that takes the impact of recoil as the cylinder recoils) is an integral part of the cylinder. And it is much larger on the Blackhawk than it is on the SAA. You can shoot a Ruger a whole lot more than you can a Colt before it starts to show endshake.

The Colt's grip frame is two pieces of steel, bolted together. In total, the grips of the Colt require seven screws, all of which must be tight for the revolver to work properly. The lower half, the trigger guard and frontstrap, need three screws to bolt them to the bottom of the frame. The backstrap takes another two, going through the upper part of the backstrap on either side of the hammer. Then, there is a screw that secures the two halves to each other. Finally, the hammer spring is held in place with yet another screw, inside the grip halves. They comprise nearly half of the fourteen screws in the Colt SAA – fifteen, if you use two-piece grips instead of the one-piece some are fond of. The Old Model Blackhawk takes ten screws and uses five of them in the grips. The New Model Blackhawk uses eight screws. Now, a few screws here and there are not a big deal. However, the screws on the Colt grip frames matter. If any are loose, the whole suffers. Also, with the frame made in two pieces, the two halves do not offer each other nearly as much support as they would if it were made in one piece. It is possible to break off the screws of

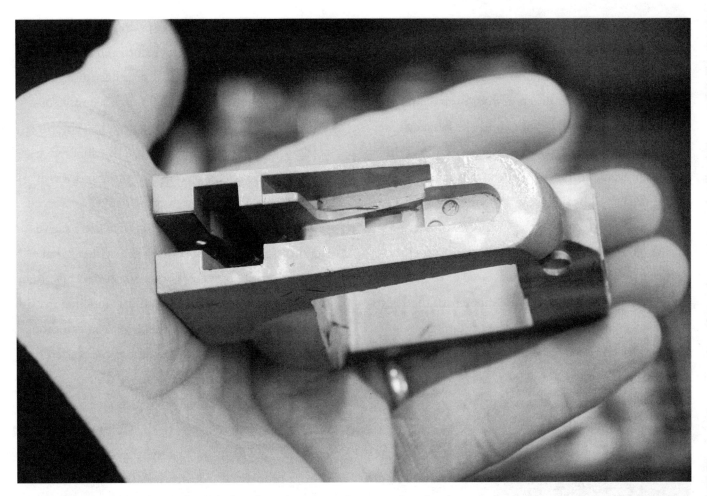

Investment-cast parts only need a little bit of machine or surface grinding finishing, at least when properly designed.

the frame parts if you drop a Colt. Dropping a Ruger simply bends things. Sometimes the bend matters, but usually it is simply cosmetic.

Inside the grip, the Colt uses a simple leaf spring, bolted down at one end with one of those many screws. The Ruger uses a coil spring on a strut. Coil springs are more durable, last longer, and less likely to quit from less than perfect manufacture. One additional advantage of a coil spring is adaptability. For decades, gunsmiths fussed over SAA mainsprings, learning just where and by how much you needed to shave the spring to ease trigger pull. The original spring/hammer combination was designed for use in extreme conditions, and with ammunition of sometimes dubious quality. Wandering the frontier, a cowboy or soldier could not always count on up-to-date and perfect maintenance. The revolver might be

frozen in ice, caked with dust or soaked in a holster in the rain. The ammunition might have been sitting in a dusty shack for decades before being loaded and called on. Colt wanted no chance of a failure. So the spring is strong and the hammerfall just short of a ball-peen hammer in impact. If you still need that, you can have it. But most of us want something a little more civilized. Thinning the SAA spring is an art. Shortening a coil spring, or using one with thinner steel wire, is simply a matter of counting. By mounting the coiled spring around a shaft (stamped, and easy to make) Ruger is able to control the spring without elaborate measures.

Also, polishing the bearing surfaces of the Colt mainspring/hammer interface, to smooth out the cocking and hammerfall, is another art. On the Ruger, it's a relatively easy task to knock any sharp edges off the stamped shaft, and polish the rounded head of the shaft where it bears against the hammer.

Instead of needing yet another screwdriver (the Colt needs three or four sizes, depending on screw slot variations) to take the mainspring out, on the Ruger you do it easily: cock the hammer. Stick a wire through the hole in the bottom of the strut. Ease the hammer forward. The spring is now caught, and can be removed when you take the grip frame off.

Inside is where the Blackhawk really differs from the Colt. Inside the Colt we see two more leaf springs, both quite troublesome. The hand on a revolver advances the cylinder each time the hammer is cocked (single action or double action revolvers) or the trigger is pulled (double action revolvers). The nose of the hand engages a ratchet on the rear of the cylinder. Each time the trigger is pulled, the hand not only pushes the cylinder, rotating it, but it then also has to fall back to

its original position, awaiting the next trigger pull. In order to stay engaged to the ratchet, but free to slide back down, it has to be pressed against the ratchet by a spring. On the Colt SAA, the spring that does the pushing is a little bitty leaf spring that is staked to the hand. If that spring breaks you have two choices: replace the hand, which means re-timing it (not an easy task, and one usually reserved for the experienced gunsmiths in a shop), or replace the spring.

Re-timing is a hassle. If the hand is too short, the cylinder is said to fail to "carry up." That is, it doesn't rotate fully to line up with the barrel. Quite often you can count on rotational momentum to bring the cylinder fully up, in line with the barrel and locking in place. But depending on momentum is a poor gunsmithing practice. If the hand is too long, it will try to over-rotate the cylinder, bind, wedge, and generally make for a miserable shooting experience. Fitting a new

Compared to the extensively hand-fitted Colt SAA, these Vaqueros are a breeze to assemble, comparatively speaking, and are much stronger and more durable.

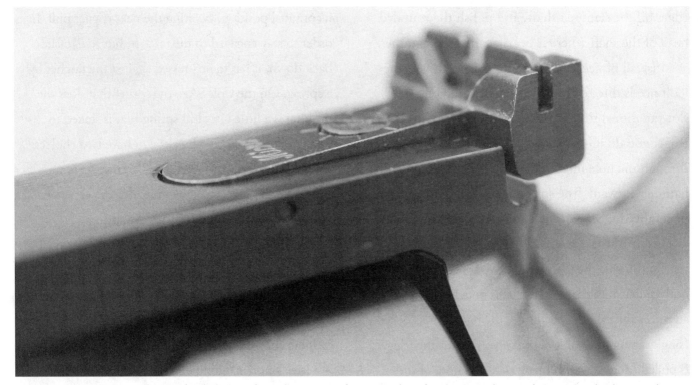

Investment-cast parts only need a little bit of machine or surface grinding finishing, at least when properly designed.

spring? The old one is staked in place. First you have to remove the busted off stub of the old one, without damaging the hand. Then you get to fit and stake the new one.

If you thought hand work is enough to drive a gunsmith to drink, the cylinder stop and its spring are worse. Underneath the frame, the cylinder stop rides on one of the three side screws of the Colt. (The smaller, forward and slightly higher of the three.) The leaf spring there has two legs on it. One works the cylinder stop; the other is the trigger return spring. Those legs, despite the small amount of work they have to do, break with maddening regularity. When they do break, you have to remove five screws to replace them. The three lower grip frame screws, the one holding the front and rear grip frames together, and the spring screw itself. Luckily, the screw does not often need fitting. However, when it does, there is no getting around it. Usually, a spring too long will bind against the trigger, and make it impossible to shoot the SAA. You (if you ever do this) have to

shorten the spring without using a grinder. If you get lazy and try to grind the tip shorter, you risk either taking the temper out of the spring due to heat, or shortening it too much. Now, as a gunsmith I had a fondness for the Colt. Anyone rash enough to work on one without experience, training or luck soon found themselves overmatched. Most would simply shove the parts into a box or bag and bring them in. Those who couldn't help themselves did the same, but with parts missing or obviously filed/stoned/ ground/knarfed.

I'd put things back together, replace parts, fit and time, and write up the bill. But there was one aspect that even made me crazy at times.

The cylinder stop has to be pulled down to allow the cylinder to rotate. It has to come back up in time to lock the cylinder as it comes to the next round. The rear of the cylinder stop is split, with the legs heat-treated to spring tempter, and one leg has a hook on it. The hook bears on a beveled stud set in the hammer. The hammer pivot lifts the leg (pivoting the cylinder stop down) until the cylinder is moving, whereupon the hammer lets go of the leg. The cylinder stop snaps back in place. As the hammer falls, the beveled edge of the stud flexes the cylinder stop leg out of the way. Down, the mechanism is at rest, ready to go again.

The fit of the leg to stud is critical. The engagement surfaces have to be polished smooth, or the action is rough. The leg cannot be bent, nor can the stud surface be "lifted." Fitting a new cylinder stop (you guessed it, the fragile little leg would break from time to time) made all the other work look easy.

How is the Blackhawk different? First, the springs that push the same parts are coil springs or torsion springs. Second, the springs usually push a plunger that bears on the part involved, not the part itself. So there is a neat surface to polish if

you need to. The hand on the Blackhawk is pushed by a plunger and spring that work on them from directly behind; the frame is drilled through where the gripstrap covers it, beside the hammer pivot, and the plunger and spring work on the hand in the most-efficient angle possible. Coil springs break so rarely that even considering such an eventuality is borrowing trouble. However, if it does break (more likely you lose it or bend/kink it while reassembling after cleaning) you simply poke another one into the frame in its place. Unlike the hand slot in the Colt frame, you can easily polish the bearing surfaces of the hand and plunger of the Blackhawk. You can pull them out and look at the part as you polish it. On the Colt, you can only gauge your progress by the feel of the stone or crocus cloth you're using, as it rides in the slot.

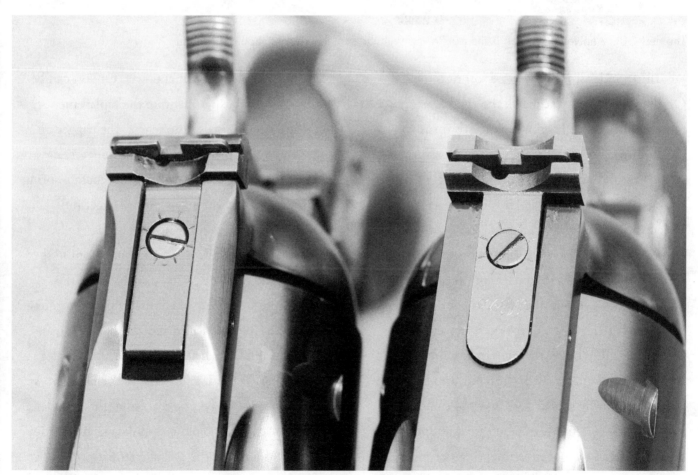

The rear sight was changed early on to one with protective shoulders so it could be raised for long-range shooting and not be at risk of getting broken.

The new 50th Anniversary frame is the old flat-top with the protective sight shoulders left off.

The cylinder stop is the same sort of thing. On the Old Model Blackhawk the cylinder stop is powered by a torsion spring that winds up as you lock it into place in the frame. The torsion spring seems tiny and weak compared to the larger Colt spring, but it is actually far, far tougher. While I replaced Colt springs on a regular basis, springs that had broken, I never replaced a broken Ruger spring, only those that had been lost or bent due to ham-handed assembly. The New Model Blackhawks went one better: the cylinder stop is powered by a coil spring and plunger that ride in a tunnel drilled into the grip frame. As with the hand, you can easily polish the bearing surfaces because you can see them as you work on them. You can swap springs, cut coils, do all sorts of experimenting, secure in the knowledge that all you need do is replace the springs with new ones to return the spring forces to their original and normal power. Or you can be really smart and experiment on the replacements and leave the originals untouched. The trigger on the New Model Blackhawk is even more amenable to experimentation, as it has its own separate spring for its return force. You can adjust trigger pull by working on that spring, as well as (carefully, deliberately, and while using a fixture) stoning the sear surfaces.

And the worst part of all, the cylinder stop reset? Unlike the Colt, the Ruger has another spring and plunger. The Blackhawk does not have a split-leg rear. The rear is solid, and bears on the plunger. As the hammer is cocked, the rear leg of the cylinder stop bears against the plunger and cams on it from the side. As a result, the cylinder stop cannot move the plunger, and is instead moved by it. When the hammer falls, the plunger is now pushing on the cylinder stop leg along its axis. As a result, the plunger is compressed back into the hammer, and the cylinder stop does not move. Not only does it not move, but the impact of the plunger actually adds to the locking force, as the cylinder stop is pushed harder against the cylinder.

The Colt hammer has the firing pin pinned to it. The pin has to be fitted precisely, or it will be too large, or too small, too short or too long. Fitting a new firing pin was rarely needed, which was a good thing for it was a bit of work. On the Blackhawk, the firing pin was contained in the frame. The flat-faced hammer had only to hit the firing pin to drive it into the primer. As a small part the Blackhawk firing pin was extremely unlikely to become damaged, worn, or the subject of experimentation. If it was it could be easily changed.

Almost as minor afterthoughts, Ruger fitted the Blackhawk with an adjustable rear sight and a front sight that was a blade with an integral base, silver-soldered to the barrel. Before the Blackhawk, only target guns had adjustable sights. And the Colt SAA front sight is a blade soldered into a shallow slot cut into the barrel. It was relatively easy to bend it or break it off the barrel. Underneath the barrel, the Blackhawk and Colt were almost identical: there was a spring-loaded ejection rod. To unload, or eject empty, fired cases, you lined up the chamber of the cylinder with the ejection rod, and pushed the rod back. When the round or case had been poked free, you let go and the rod sprang forward again, awaiting a repetition. On the front of the frame, both had a cylinder pin retaining assembly. The

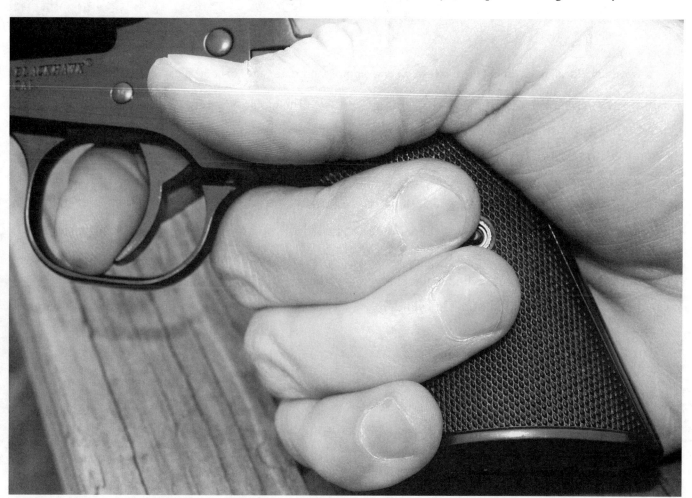

The 50th Anniversary grip is the old, small grip. Comfortable to shoot until the loads get up to the top end of power, and then it can become objectionable. Still, keep the power level appropriate and you'll have a fun time shooting.

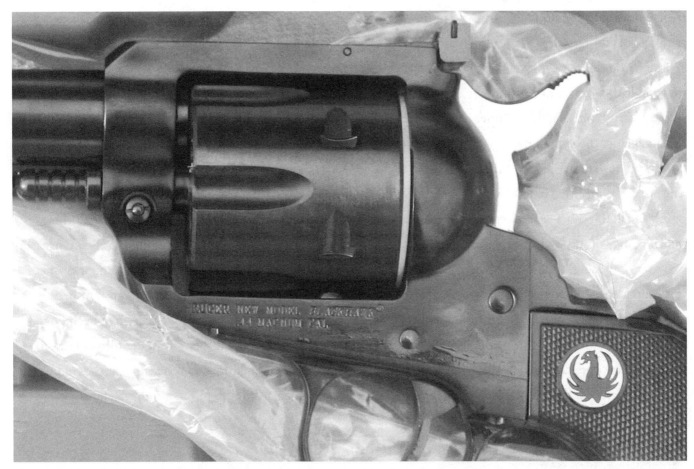

The New Model Blackhawks do not have screws on the side of the frame, just flat-head pins.

assembly is spring-loaded (one of the few coil springs in the Colt) latch. Push the latch to the side (into the frame) and it released the centerpin, which you could pull forward. With the centerpin out (or fully-forward under the ejection rod housing) you then opened the loading gate and pulled the cylinder out. From there it was easy enough to do a field-cleaning. You could scrub the frame, bore, cylinder and charge holes, and get oil into the action from the cylinder stop slot and hammer slot.

Still, all was not perfect with the Blackhawk. The action of the Blackhawk was the same in the way it worked as the Colt. That is, the action had four clicks: cylinder stop unlock, trigger past the "safety notch," trigger past the load/unload notch, and last the full-cock notch and cylinder stop locking at once. The safety notch was the problem. Not in 1955, but later.

The Colt SAA, as well as early Blackhawks that have not had the safety upgrade, can be carried safely with only five rounds; the hammer MUST be down on an empty chamber. If it is not, and you carry those with the hammer down and all six chambers loaded, you can easily shoot yourself in the leg or foot. At rest, the Colt SAA and the early Old Model Blackhawks have the firing pin resting directly against the primer. Anything that strikes the hammer can set off the chambered round.

The "load five" method arose in the days when people rode horses all the time. Here's why: to saddle up a horse you place the blanket on the horse's back. You throw the saddle up on the horse and place it correctly on the horse's back. You put the near-side stirrup on the saddlehorn, or tossed over the seat of the saddle, so you can loop and tighten the bellyband. If the stirrup falls off the horn or saddle seat while you are working on the band, it will fall pretty much right onto the hammer of your holstered Colt SAA. If you have the hammer down on a round, the force will set it off, shooting the ground or your leg, and scaring the horse.

When everyone rode, and those who carried a single action, everyone knew these facts. By the 1950s and 1960s, few rode horses. Those who carried a single action revolver did so for shooting in various fast-draw or quick draw competitions. Or hunted. Enough people hurt themselves that the lawsuits were a problem. So Ruger designed the safety upgrade, and advertised it heavily. Unveiled in 1973 and a fixture ever after, the upgrade was simple: send in your Old Model Blackhawk and Ruger would, free of charge, install the new parts that made it safe to carry all six loaded safely. And you'd get your old parts back. But I'm getting ahead of myself.

The first Blackhawks, introduced in 1955, were available in .357 Magnum, and with your choice of 4-5/8- or 6-1/2-inch barrels. You could have any finish you wanted, as long as it was blue. The first Blackhawks had the top of the frame flat, with the rear sight pivoting up out of it. For most shooters and shooting, that was just fine. Traditional target shooting then and now is done at 25 and 50 yards. For those distances the sight settings didn't make much difference. But Elmer Keith, the acknowledged dean of handgun shooting, was famous (or infamous) for having shot an antelope at 600 yards. Anyone who wanted to be anyone wanted to know what his handgun could do at distances beyond 50 yards. Maybe not 600, but certainly out to 100 and even out to 200. When the Blackhawk rear sight was cranked up past the 50 yard setting, it looked odd and wasn't well-protected. So in a few years Ruger added bolsters, or shoulders, to the rear sight slot, to give it better protection. Collectors now refer to those early guns as "Flat-Tops" and will pay a premium for them.

The grip castings of the Blackhawks were made of aluminum. They were lighter, easier to finish and fit, and probably easier for Ruger to cast, but critics hated them. Over the years Ruger has made Blackhawks with brass and steel grip castings and you

The Ruger Hawkeye was a single-shot in .256 Winchester Magnum that never caught on.

can retrofit one of them to your Blackhawk if you so wish. Shortly after production commenced, Ruger also changed the ejector rod housing from steel to aluminum.

The 1955 Blackhawk was a fine bit of engineering, a great revolver for the market at the time, and would be in the Ruger production schedule and catalog from then until now. But things were about to change.

After decades of advocating his big-bore loadings in print, and harassing the manufacturers at the only trade show of the time, the NRA Show, Elmer Keith finally hit paydirt in 1955. He cornered the President of Remington, and got him to promise to make the ammo if S&W would make the gun. Elmer then promptly marched over to the S&W booth and cornered the president of S&W, eliciting the same promise: S&W would make the gun if Remington

would make the ammo. Those two companies then followed through. Bill Ruger heard of the R&D, was handed a few empty cases, and managed through his contacts to lay hands on a paper sack with a fistful of loaded ammunition. He almost beat S&W to the punch, offering his .44 Magnum Blackhawk almost before S&W could ship their own .44 magnum revolver.

Part of Ruger's problem was making it fit. The Blackhawk had been designed for the .357 Magnum cartridge. Frame and cylinder both had to be made about .150" longer to accommodate the bigger cartridge. Barrels of the first guns were 6-1/2 inches, but later a 7-1/2 inch barrel became an option. However, even in the tough-as-nails Blackhawk, the .44 Magnum was just too much. Not just for the gun, which wasn't designed for it, but also the shooter. Shooters of the time, accustomed to the

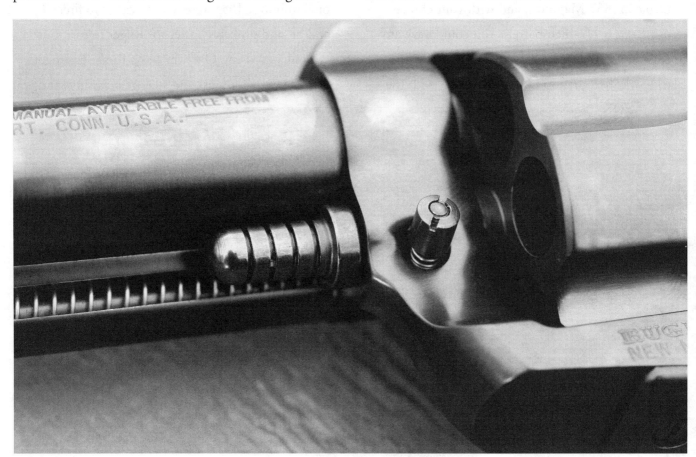

Both the Colt and the Ruger use a spring-loaded plunger to keep the centerpin in place.

Press the plunger and draw the centerpin out. Of course, recoil batters the plunger, and on Rugers used with heavy-recoiling .44 Magnum hunting loads you'll have to replace the plunger now and then.

recoil of a 35-ounce gun in .38 Special, found the 41-ounce Blackhawk in .357 Magnum a handful. Chambered in .44 Magnum, it was just too much. So in 1959 Ruger unveiled the Super Blackhawk, in its full 48-ounce glory, and dimensioned for the .44 Magnum cartridge. But the Super Blackhawk is for another chapter.

The Blackhawk in .44 Magnum was dropped from the catalog when the Super Blackhawk was announced, and collectors were all over it. Now, finding a Blackhawk in .44 is akin to finding a winning lottery ticket. But that didn't hurt sales of the .357, for it was still a great gun at a great bargain. That it could be shot with .38 Special ammunition made it all the better.

In 1967, my father walked into Acme Sporting Goods in Royal Oak, Michigan, and bought a Ruger. He and the rest of the neighborhood gang were going to go off "bear hunting" that Fall. The .44 (no doubt a Super Blackhawk) was too big. The .357 was the right size. Through the years to follow, my brothers and I shot a literal ton of bullets through that Blackhawk.

Each summer we'd go to the cabin up north and shoot to our hearts' content. I learned to reload so I could feed that gun, and my shooting habit, even more. We got pretty good at it. Our typical shooting session was chasing a tin can on the ground out around the target frames, taking turns shooting. "Shoot until you miss" is a great way to learn to shoot. Little did I know, but I was plinking up north but also learning to handle the pressure of competition. After all, bragging rights matter. As long as either of us was hitting, we kept shooting. Miss, and you'd have to hand it to the other guy, who shot until he missed.

What made it fun was that we were shooting at large tin cans at 100 yards. Dad made us lay off that shooting game whenever any of the other club members came out to sight in their deer rifles. It was bad enough that a couple of kids were shooting with handguns at absurd ranges, but they were doing better than grown men with rifles. We continued that game even after getting other guns of our own.

As an aside, Colt tried to add the .44 Magnum to its lineup. What they found had to be most discouraging. Not only was the recoil truly fierce in an SAA but the gun couldn't stand up to it for much shooting. They quickly went out of time, or battered into severe endshake, with even just a small (even by the standards back then) amount of shooting. No, Colt wasn't going to have a .44 Magnum, not even in a big double-action revolvers, for quite a few years.

In 1964, Remington introduced the .41 Magnum. A subject for another book, the .41 did not receive the accolades expected. It was a case of "neither fish nor fowl" and the .41 didn't fit in anywhere. Except the Blackhawk revolver. I much later happened to buy one. I was working at the gunshop as an apprentice gunsmith, and the owner came back with a pair of guns. The shop was buying a batch of guns, and he wanted to know if I had any interest. This is a common practice of gunshop owners everywhere: they offer guns to the employees, to offset the purchase of a collection. Invariably, any collection has guns that will be slow sellers. If the owner can sell them to his employees at the purchase cost, he saves dead inventory, keeps

Back in the day, cowboy shooters wanted something tougher than the Colt, as many Cowboy Action Shooters do today. The Blackhawk was their choice.

dust magnets out of the display case and keeps the troops happy.

What he had in his hands were a Blackhawk in .41 Magnum and an early S&W M-39-1. Yes, I was interested in both, and bought them for the bargain sum of $100 each. (The Blackhawk probably retailed for that when the .41 Magnum was introduced in 1964.) In due time I learned the lessons that everyone who ever worked in a gunshop learned; one, you can't buy everything. And two, if you sell it, it is sold. I sold the S&W to a friend of my younger brother, with the proviso that if he ever sold it, he'd sell it back to me. He didn't. The Ruger I kept. It is a first-year .41, with a four-digit serial number. Yes, Ruger started the serial number over again when they offered the Blackhawk in .41, a point of contention that the ATFE (then the Revenue Department) brought up some years later. Check that chapter for the messy details.

What I found was old news: the gun is a beast with full-power magnum loads in it. However, as a big-bore plinker, and using medium-power reloads, it is a pussycat and a great learning tool.

Ruger has always been a successful company. That is, they make money at their profession. Which means they attract those desiring money. The design of the Old Model, despite following the Colt SAA, brought lawsuits. Those unknowing about the safety requirements, or who couldn't be bothered to read up on the system, or didn't have existing knowledge, injured themselves. They then brought suits against Ruger. You might ask "How did Ruger and Colt solve this problem?"

The answer is simple: Ruger did, Colt didn't. To be perfectly blunt about it, Colt wasn't worth suing. The American legal system is commonly described as an "adversarial" system. The lawyers, judge, jury and plaintiff and defendant do not sit down, hash out the situation, and come to an agreement. (Well, some do, but that's part of the pre-trial negotiations.) No, it is the legal equivalent of "trial by combat" where both sides bring out their experts, witnesses, evidence and skills, and duke it out in court. No lawyer will take a case unless he thinks he has a chance of both winning, and collecting. That is, if a potential client wants to sue on something that can't be won, no sane lawyer will take the case. (Try suing on the Law of Gravity sometime. A flippant example, perhaps, but it makes the point.) Second, no lawyer will take a case where the defendant has nothing to pay with. Oh, there are lawyers with pet subjects who will sue to make the law recognize or conform to their ideas. But most won't sue if there's nothing to win.

Colt, for a long time, had nothing to win. Ruger, on the other hand, had lots to win. So they bore the brunt of the lawsuits. And won time and again. Rather than keep defending against the same suits over and over (and eventually running into an obstinate jury that would find for the plaintiff) Ruger re-designed the Blackhawk.

The re-design was twofold. First, it allowed for new parts to be installed in old Blackhawks, to bring them into the twentieth century. Along with the re-design, Ruger began the decades-long campaign to upgrade Old Model Blackhawks free of charge. Which you still can do.

The second part was to update the Blackhawk to make it easier to manufacture and stronger and to take some of the quirks out of the design.

Looking at a New Model Blackhawk, the first thing you'll notice is that there are no screws. Well, fewer of them. On the side of the frame are two smooth-headed pins. One is the hammer pivot pin, and the other is the pivot pin for not only the trigger

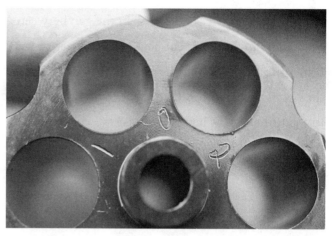

The Ruger does not use a separate centerpin bushing, as does the Colt. As a result, the Ruger is both larger and more durable, and rarely in need of attention.

but the cylinder stop as well. They are held in place by a bent spring made of flat steel. Unlike the usual leaf spring, the pivot pin retaining spring is not stressed each time you work the action. It rests in grooves in each of the pivot pins, which keeps them from walking out of the frame. It takes no real stress, and would have to shear or shatter to move out of the frame. The chances of that happening are slightly less than the chances of the Sun going nova in our lifetimes.

The trigger is much different from that of the Old Model, as it not only releases the hammer when pressed but also lifts the transfer bar. The transfer bar is the heart of the New Model design. Instead of the hammer impacting the firing pin directly, the new Model hammer has a "stopping flat" up near its top. The flat hits the frame. Below the stopping flat, the hammer is cut back so it cannot make contact with the firing pin. At rest, the pin is not touched by the hammer. As the pin is a tiny thing, it lacks mass. So the New Model Blackhawk, even when loaded with six rounds, is safe to carry. Even if you were somehow to quickly and sharply accelerate it (say, by dropping it on the muzzle) the firing pin doesn't have enough mass to set off the primer on its own.

The transfer bar is thicker than the gap between the hammer where it is cut back, and the rear of the firing pin. With the transfer bar up, the hammer hits the bar, which transfers (hence the name) the impact to the firing pin. When you release the trigger, the transfer bar slides down, out of the way. Cool, neat, and elegant as well.

If the transfer bar itself was enough to make the New Model better, and it could be fitted to the Old Model, why the other changes? Simple: it takes time, tooling and effort to both drill holes and thread the holes for screws. It takes time, tooling and effort to make screws instead of pins with relief slots in them. Also, screws loosen over time and when faced with vibration. The new pins in the New Model reduced manufacturing costs. You may fuss about that "I don't care about a few small savings in production costs, I want my old gun the way it was." Fine, be that way. In 1973, you could buy a brand-new New Model Blackhawk in .357 Magnum for a suggested retail of $109. Next to it in the counter was a Colt SAA for $195. In 2007, the MSRP of a new Model Blackhawk in .357 is $482. The Colt? If you can find one, and it doesn't need extra gunsmithing just to make it work, the MSRP is going to be $1,380. Tell me again how you don't want Ruger to be constantly looking at cost-cutting measures in production. If you want the real Colt, but can't stand the Colt price, then you have to go to an Italian import. They are well-made, but they aren't any stronger than the Colt, so you need not look to anything stronger than a .357 Magnum/.44 Special/ .45 Colt. There, nostalgia will cost you about $500.

The "manual of arms," the way you interact with the New Model, is markedly different from that of the Old Model and the SAA. Where the Old Model and the Colt have four clicks when you cock the hammer, the New Model has two (sometimes only one). The two clicks you hear with the New Model are the cylinder stop unlocking (sometimes) or the cylinder stock locking (again, sometimes) and the hammer engaging the sear of the trigger. The unlock is sometimes too faint to be heard, and the lock is often so close in time to the hammer engaging the trigger than you have to cock the New Model very slowly to separate them.

On the Old Model, you could have the hammer in four positions: fully down, on the first click to the "safety" notch, on the click for the loading/unloading notch, and at full-cock. You have to be knowing and careful with each of them. On the New Model, there are only two positions the hammer can stop at: fully down or at full cock. When down, the hammer does not touch the firing pin. At full cock, it is ready to fire. To open the loading gate to load or unload, you simply open the loading gate. That unlocks the cylinder, which spins free and allows you to line up each chamber with the loading trough and the ejector. When the hammer is cocked you can't open the gate. (The last is an old trick revolver makers have used since the waning years of the eighteenth century. The hammer has to be down to load and unload so stupid people don't have accidents.)

When the new Model Rugers were introduced, you couldn't believe the crying, whining and moaning. "Oh my god, they've ruined single actions!" was the general response. Never mind that the new Model now safely carried six instead of five rounds, and was still so indestructible that Colts looked like they were made of paper maché in comparison. No, the shooting world was ruined, the world would come to an end, and we were all going to die.

Instead, the Blackhawk has proven to be quite adaptable over the decades. In 1967 the big surprise came when Ruger offered the Blackhawk in .30 Carbine. As with the other models, it started its own serial number sequence, at least for one year until the 1969 production run where it gained the "50" prefix. Why .30 Carbine? In 1967 .30 Carbine ammo was so common and cheap that it wasn't really worth reloading it. For those who did, it was quite accurate in the Blackhawk, and in the 7-1/2 inch barrel an interesting varmint and small game gun. In 1974 it was switched over to the New Model frames and the prefix changed to "51."

Sales of the .30 Blackhawk have not exactly been brisk, but it has sold well enough to remain in production each and every year since then. If you're thinking of getting a .30 Carbine Blackhawk because it sounds cool, or you think it would make a nice, low-recoil plinking gun, I have to warn you: it is loud. Especially with factory ammunition. Factory .30 Carbine ammo is loaded to run in the carbine with an eighteen-inch barrel. The powders used are in the medium-burn rate for handguns, or quick rifle powders. H-110 is an example. Run in a barrel half the expected length, the muzzle blast is quite impressive and the noise can be overwhelming. If you're using it to teach a new shooter, use mild reloads and not factory ammo. (Unless you're one of those obnoxious guys who hand their girlfriend/wife a loud and hard-kicking gun just so you can laugh at their reaction.)

About the same time Ruger started offering the "Convertibles." Since the bore diameter of some cartridges is the same, a revolver has the advantage of multiple cylinders that launch bullets from different cartridges down that common bore-diameter barrel.

Convertibles have dual cylinders, one for each caliber. Here is a .45 Colt and .45 ACP combo.

The first was a .357/9mm convertible Blackhawk. With both cylinders, you could shoot .38 Special, .357 Magnum and 9mm Parabellum in one session. Not all from the same cylinder, but changing cylinders is easy enough. The nominal groove diameter of the two is close enough: the .38/.357 is supposed to be .357" and the 9mm is supposed to be .355". Given the slight tolerance-wandering that is allowed in modern manufacturing it would be easy to either split the difference (and make all convertible barrels .356" plus-or-minus .001") or just pick one and stick with it. In proper pragmatic fashion, Ruger stuck with .357" and let the 9mm bullets worry about the .002" nominal difference. My experience is that bullets don't care. Yes, if you were to fuss over the details, and narrow things down, you'd see a difference. But you'd have to go to a lot more trouble than most shooters feel is worth it, to see how much accuracy suffers. (Less than an inch at 25 yards, most of the time. Usually less, and this from a machine rest.)

In 1971 the .45 convertibles came out. And there was a slight problem. The first were Old Models, but with a prefix of "45." In 1973, they were made in the New Model, with a prefix of "51" and the serial numbers continued, not started over again. The problem was that the power and bullet weights of the two rounds had a large range where they didn't overlap. The .357/9mm convertible had this problem, but back in the early 1970s no one worried. Anyone using the .357/9mm convertible with 9mm ammunition was using surplus ammo that was cheaper than dirt, and the accuracy could be anything from OK to awful. It was simply plinking ammo.

The .45s were different. First, the .45 ACP was viewed as having great potential accuracy. The .45 Colt could have great power. You could hunt with a .45 Colt. However, accurate .45 ACP ammo, with soft-recoiling 185-grain wadcutter bullets (actually semi-wadcutters, but that was what they were called back then) did not hit to the same point as hunting 255-grain semi-wadcutters in the .45 Colt loaded hot. So when you switched you often had to adjust the sights. However, with a little practice you could quickly determine just how many clicks up or down you had to go, and set the sights accordingly.

Since then, we've had a whole slew of convertibles, as the idea is just too good to let go of. In addition to the previous gun, there have been combos in .32-20 and .32 Magnum, .38-40 and 10mm, and .44-40 and .44 Magnum. If you were willing to sacrifice a good gun, and had a gunsmith capable of the task (say, Hamilton Bowen) you could take a Blackhawk of any given caliber and have it made over into something bigger. I can't imagine why, but if you've always had a burning desire for an 8mm Nambu Blackhawk, you could have a .32 cylinder re-chambered for 8mm Nambu. Or get really silly and have Hamilton Bowen make a cylinder from scratch, which would probably work better anyway. What he does for real is take Blackhawks and work his magic. One example would be to take a .357 Blackhawk and change it to a .41 Magnum. Why? In any production process, tolerances have to be allowed to wander. The lands of a barrel meant for a .41 Magnum can be anything from .4095" to .4105" as an example. The cylinder throats (the portion of the cylinder where the bullet rests, outside of and in front of the cartridge case) might be .4110" to .4130" or anything in between. Someone like Hamilton sets up his machines and makes sure everything is exact. Your .357-turned-into-a-.41 will arrive with lands at .410" and throats at .4110", or as close as a master machinist/gunsmith can make them. You get more accuracy and more consistent results from your ammo.

But convertibles aren't made, or meant, for tack-driving accuracy. Oh, they're plenty accurate enough, but they are for versatility. And there, they deliver.

The next big change for the Blackhawk were the Bisleys, named after the shooting range in England. The change was in the grip design. The shape of the Bisley grip is such that the curve of the rear backstrap is higher, and the front strap is straighter than on the original grips. The result is a shape that more consistently sits in the hand and doesn't roll up as quickly or as high in recoil. Designed over a century ago as a target-shooting grip shape (by Colt) the Bisley grip also makes it possible to shoot heavier loads in a somewhat more comfortable manner. Refined by Ruger and using the shape of Elmer Keith's famous Number Five revolver for input, they made the Bisley grips in recognition that their revolvers were being pushed past previous limits.

I say "somewhat more comfortable" simply because over time the top-end loads of the biggest calibers of the Blackhawk have risen markedly. When the .357 was unveiled we shot factory ammo, which the manufacturers assured us was a lead 158-grain bullet at over 1,400 fps. (When unveiled in the 1930s, the ammo makers unashamedly told shooters then it was going 1,550 fps. Liars.) When chronographs became common, we found that 158s commonly went 1,250 fps and had all along. When the .44 Magnum came out, the ammo makers tried to tell everyone it was a 240-grain bullet going at the dinosaur-killing speed of nearly 1,400 fps. They quickly backed off on that, and settled for a "mere" 1,225 fps or so.

If you ever shoot a 240-grainer going an honest 1,200 fps, you'll remember it. Many loads do not do that well unless they are leaving 7-1/2-inch barrels

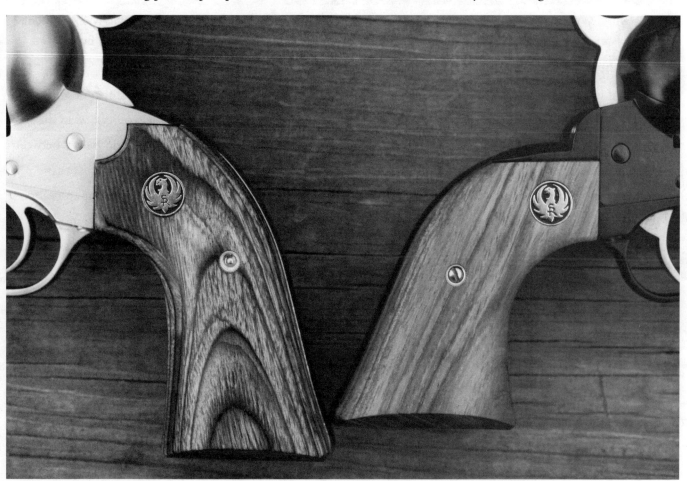

The Bisley grip gives you much more control, and comfort, when used in hard-kicking handguns.

After the war S&W concentrated on the police market and high-quality double action revolvers like this M-27. (Actually a near-duplicate of the pre-war Registered Magnum, but that kind of revolver was what people wanted.) By the time S&W was done, Colt's police share had been reduced to nothing.

and the load is fully up to spec. Well, the Blackhawks (and more often the Super Blackhawks) have been worked over by handgun hunters, who have increased their velocities. Out of a long barrel, a .44 Magnum for the serious hunter can be a 285-grain bullet going on the order of 1,300 fps. For those wishing a bit more weight for a bit more penetration, at the top end are 315-grain bullets cruising out the muzzle at just over 1,200 fps. Ouch. On anything not plated in heavy steel, that will leave a mark. In fact, it will shoot cleanly through just about anything walking the North American continent, from any angle, and regardless of what it hits inside the unfortunate critter.

To handle such recoil you need practice, and the Bisley grips help a lot. Starting in 1985, the Bisley grips were available on Blackhawks and Super Blackhawks. They did not receive a separate prefix,

as they were just Blackhawks with different grips. In fact, if you have them available, you can swap the aluminum, steel, brass and Bisley grip frames between Blackhawk revolvers without any more fuss than keeping track of the screws and not losing the various springs and plungers associated with each model. Old and New Model grip frames cannot be swapped, as they require certain elements to keep the actions working. But within the Old to Old and New to New, they can be swapped.

The next step in the Blackhawk history was one custom gunsmiths had been doing, although not in a big way. Shooters are a notoriously cranky and persnickety lot, and always want what doesn't exist. While the adjustable sights on the Blackhawk were a great advance, some didn't want them. They wanted more durable fixed sights. There were a few gunsmiths willing to undertake the task of removing the adjustable sights and re-contouring the frame to make it look at least presentable. Some did a decent job of it. But the task was always an expensive one. So it was with great pleasure that the Cowboy Action Shooting community greeted the news of the Vaquero. The intial Vaquero was built on the new-size Blackhawk frame meant for fulltime .44 Magnum use. Nice, but not exactly what they wanted. After a few years Ruger came out with the New Vaquero, which is the same frame size as the original Blackhawk, and the same size as the Colt SAA (or close enough, as the Vaqueros I test fit right into holsters meant for the SAA).

So after fifty years the Ruger Blackhawk has come full-circle: from being a durable, inexpensive replacement for the Colt SAA, to an incredibly durable hunting handgun, back to being the durable and inexpensive replacement for the Colt SAA. Back then it was for movie-inspired quick draw. Now it is for movie-inspired action shooting. *Viva Vaquero! Viva Ruger!*

50th Anniversary Blackhawk

Since Sturm, Ruger & Co. began operations in 1949, they have now begun their series of 50th Anniversary firearms, firearms that collectors love and the rest of us often have to have. The one we're working on here is the 50th Anniversary .44 Magnum Blackhawk.

It is almost the same as the original, with a few changes. Some changes are for the good; others, to steal a quote from a short-lived TV series of good popularity, "not so much." The frame is the Blackhawk's, slightly lengthened for the .44 Magnum from the .357 Magnum size, just as was done in 1956 to accommodate that larger cartridge. It has the flat top, adjustable sight, 6-1/2-inch barrel, and it comes blued. Comparing the flat top side-by-side with a later Blackhawk (my .41 Magnum) it is easy to see both why Ruger added the protective shoulders and why some shooters didn't like them.

Where it differs is in the action and the markings. On the barrel, inlaid in gold, is "50 Years of .44 Magnum" and "1956 to 2006." The serial numbers have their own prefix, and here we have a mystery. Ruger tells me that the serial number prefix for the 50th Anniversary .44 Magnum Blackhawks is supposed to be "89" but that doesn't seem to be the case. Fellow gunwriter Sheriff Jim Wilson received a 50th Anniversary .44

The barrel is rollmarked to reflect the anniversary and is gold-inlaid.

with a prefix of "880" and I received one with a prefix of "870." Why, I don't know, and I leave the mystery for future Ruger collectors to ferret out and uncover.

In the original frame the Blackhawk in .44 Magnum is quite handy, well-balanced and a joy to handle. The New Model action is what you'd expect; simple and straightforward to use. The 50th Anniversary guns come in bright red plastic boxes, with an anniversary banner inset in the lid. Inside are all the usual extras, including the odious fired case in an envelope. Those of you who live in states where the politicos have saddled you with empty case requirements will want to make sure that yours stays with your Ruger until it is the appropriate time to hand it over to the authorities. Those of us who don't live in a state where they waste taxpayer's money with such schemes will either toss it, add it to the reloading bin, or save it

in case we ever sell the gun to someone who needs the fired case.

One addition that we all have to live with is the locking mechanism. As many States now require an on-board lock, Ruger has added one in the least-obtrusive manner possible. You have to take the grips off to find it. Then you use a key to turn the lock to either lock it for storage or unlock it for use.

Fussing and grumping aside, the lock is as unobtrusive as possible, and if you never take the grips off you'd never know it was there.

Shooting the 50th Anniversary brought back memories, not all of them good. With .44 Special-level reloads or .44 Special ammo, it is a sedate and well-behaved revolver. With a 240-grain going about 850-900 fps, you could shoot all day long and have a blast doing so. However, when you step up to the full-power .44 Magnum loads you find

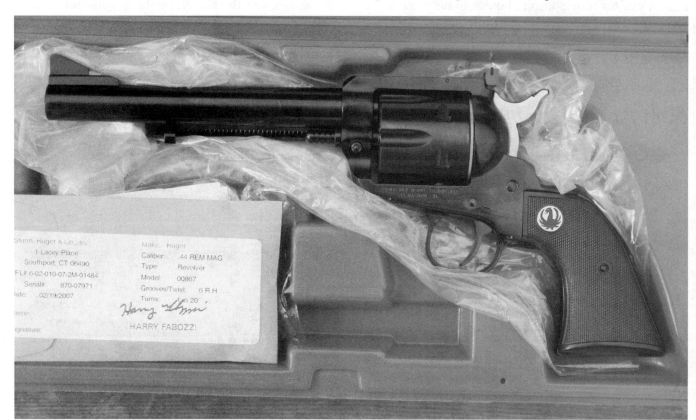

The 50th Anniversary Blackhawk, built like the originals except with the New Model lockwork. Light, handy, affordable (the collectors will change that) and safe to carry with all six chambers loaded.

out why Ruger designed the Super Blackhawk. Recoil becomes stout. One reason the recoil can become objectionable at the upper levels is weight. Where the old Blackhawk is supposed to be 47 ounces, the Super is listed at 49. Two ounces might not seem like much, but it all matters at that recoil level.

Where the Blackhawk really gets me with the full-house load (a 240-grainer going 1250 fps) is in the trigger guard. The grip curve of the Blackhawk is rather tight. When I grasp the Blackhawk, the rear of the trigger guard is tight against my second finger between the knuckle and the first joint. With .44 Special ammo, or in the smaller Blackhawk, .357 Magnums, the trigger guard doesn't thump me that hard. But when I load the full-power stuff it whacks with authority, enough so that after the first box shooting isn't much fun any more. Such is the lesson I learned a couple of decades ago with my .41 Magnum Blackhawk. Recoil can be a real downer.

Still, for those who want a lighter .44 Magnum, or one a bit more compact than a Super Blackhawk, here it is. Also, you needn't pay the sometimes startling prices collectors have bid originals up to. After all, the original .44 Magnum Blackhawk, made from 1956 to 1962, had a production run of only just over 28,500 guns. When you consider attrition, conversions (Hamilton Bowen will make a cracking-good bigger bore on one if you so wish) and all the originals sucked into collections, never to see the

The 50th Anniversary Blackhawk box is red and has a 50th Anniversary logo inset into the lid.

range again, those left can be pricey. If you want one of your own, here they are.

If the lock is something you find really objectionable, you can always remove or disable it. Not that I'm advising you remove or defeat some "vital safety equipment" (vital perhaps in the fevered imagination of a bureaucrat) but if you store all your guns in a locked steel safe, you may not have need of extra locks. Or, you can just leave it nestled in the grips, ignored and untouched.

I'm sure more than one shooter will take their .44 Magnum 50th Anniversary Blackhawk, a semi-collector's piece, and have the barrel shortened to something handier, 5-1/2 or 4-5/8 inches. Hey, why not? Ruger may make them that way, and they may not. If you want it, do it.

— PART THREE —
The Super Blackhawk

"The Super Blackhawk came about for two reasons: shooters of the time were wussies, and the Blackhawk wasn't tough enough to withstand the .44 Magnum." Now you know why I stopped going to gun shows for quite a few years. I was standing at a table, looking over the stuff, when two guys walked by, decrying the fact that they couldn't find any more flat-top .44 Magnum Blackhawks. Forget that they were a couple of decades late to the party, they wanted a lightweight single action .44 Magnum, and they wanted it at the prices they recalled when they could still find such a beast.

The original Blackhawk, as we discussed in the Blackhawk chapter, was designed for the .357 Magnum. It was just possible to shoehorn the .44 Magnum into it, but no one was happy with the arrangement. The sidewalls of the cylinder are a bit thin in those models. The cylinder is just barely long enough for standard-length factory ammo. And if you are a "wussie" for not wanting to shoot

Yes, it is a big gun. You want big, when the ammo you're feeding it starts at factory .44 Magnum power and go up from there.

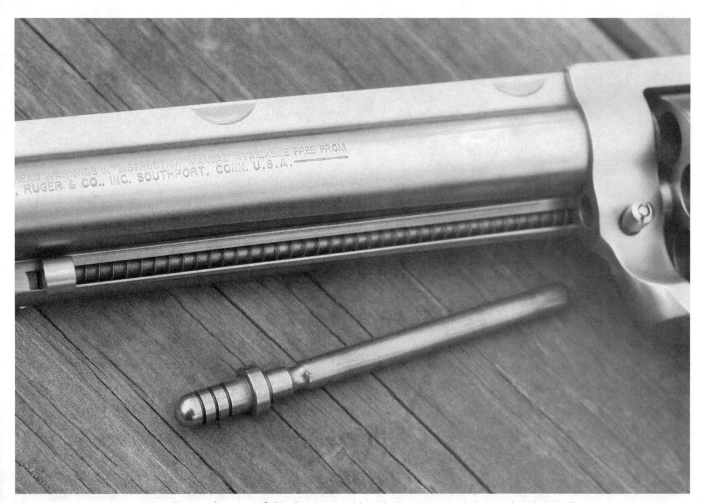

The centerpin is the only really weak point of the Super Blackhawk. With enough heavy loads it will start jumping its retention latch and require some ministrations to correct.

a lot of 240-grain bullets at 1250 fps out of a 36-ounce single action revolver, then where's my sign?

The Super Blackhawk had the basic dimensions of the frame and cylinder increased. The trigger guard was changed from a rounded back to a "dragoon" style back, with a greater distance between the frontstrap of the grips and the rear of the trigger guard. The result was to bump the weight up from 36 to 44 ounces. The extra weight made the Super Blackhawk much less of a bear to shoot. The greater distance between the frontstrap and the trigger guard took most of the pain out of shooting. On the Blackhawk, the tight gap between the frontstrap and the trigger guard means your second finger gets hit every time you shoot. The recoil drives the gun back, your hand leaves the

To see if your center pin is in need of care, look at the groove (not the shoulder thingie) and see if the edges of it are battered.

frontstrap just a bit, and you get rapped in the knuckle by the trigger guard. On a .357 Magnum or a .41 or .44 with mild loads, the rap is no big

The Super Blackhawk Hunter frame is marked, and the barrel is ribbed with scope mount recesses milled into it.

deal. If you spend a whole day shooting, you might be a bit sore, but the overall sensation of a numb hand (try shooting three to four hundred .357s in a day) causes the rapped second finger to recede from the overall "I need a cold drink" feeling.

Shoot a box of full-power .41s or .44s through

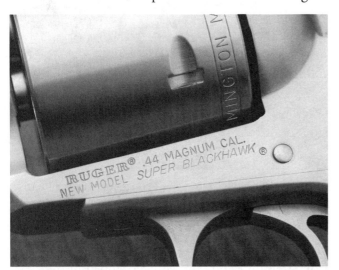

"New Model" indicates it is safe to carry with all six chambers loaded. The flush-headed pins on the right are another indication.

an old model Blackhawk, and your second finger is crying out in pain which the overall numbing effect won't diminish. It hurts to shoot. Back in the mid-1950s, it had to have been traumatic. Back then the .357 was just beginning to be accepted as a level of recoil that "average" shooters could deal with. And most shooting back then would have been with one hand, making the effect of recoil even more apparent.

No, the super Blackhawk needed to be invented, and so it was. Unveiled in 1959, only three years after the Blackhawk came out, the Super Blackhawk has gone on to legendary status. You can take a normal Super Blackhawk and by fitting a stronger than usual cylinder retention pin, load it up to power levels that the 1950s shooters would only have dreamt of. In fact, at the top end, a Super Blackhawk with a 10-1/2" barrel can hurl a 355-grain bullet at 1250 fps. Such ballistics back in

The Hunter can be had with the Bisley grip. Get it; you want it to deal with the recoil you'll have dished out every time you shoot it.

1959 would have been possible only from a .45-70 carbine, not a handgun.

The Super Blackhawk started as a blued gun that you could have in any barrel length you wanted, provided what you wanted was a 7-1/2" barrel. The sights were adjustable. For a handgun that didn't have many (any) options, it sold quite well. Quite a few buyers bought it with the intention of making it handier. The firm of Mag-Na-Port (half an hour drive form the old gun shop I worked at) did a land-office business of taking Super Blackhawks and cutting the barrels back. They'd shorten them to 5-1/2" or 4-3/4", re-crown the muzzle and reinstall the sight. The result was a belt gun that was a lot handier than the 7-1/2" tube Ruger had shipped it with. Or they would drill and tap the receiver (which must have been a real chore) and install a scope on it for the burgeoning sport of handgun hunting, which Larry Kelly (then owner

of Mag-Na-Port) was promoting. His son Ken still does all that work and more on Super Blackhawks. In fact, pretty much anything you want done to a Ruger he can do it.

What Ken can't do, Hamilton Bowen can. Hamilton takes a Super Blackhawk and converts it

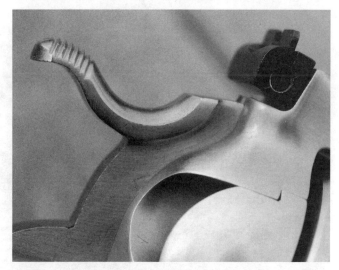

The Bisley hammer spur is just the coolest-looking thing designed in the last century. If you don't like it, don't get one, but I do.

The rings in place. They are precisely machined and need little lapping, and then only if you're going to fire the real heavyweights for hunting ammo.

The rings, showing how they fit the slots milled into the barrel rib.

With a bit of machining, some belt-sanding of the finish, there is a finished frame ready for assembly.

to a five-shot big bore in things like .45 Colt (which you can really boost if you're a careful reloader), .480 Ruger, .475 Linebaugh or .50 Special or .50 Bowen Express. There you're talking real recoil,

A Super Blackhawk frame, fresh (but cool) out of the casting house.

not the "mere" recoil of a .44 Magnum – and performance to punch a hole through anything that walks. The .480 tops out at a hard-cast lead bullet of 420 grains going 1250 fps. The .475 Linebaugh adds 100 fps to that. The .50s are even more intense. There, you have your choice of "light" and fast, or heavy and "slow." The light-bullet loads are 410 grains and leave the muzzle at 1450 fps, while the heavy bullets are 468 grains, and leave your immediate vicinity at 1350 fps. The Power Factor in the first load is 595, the second, 631.

All of which I describe only so you can then appreciate the "moderate" recoil of a factory .44 Magnum load in our test revolver here: the Super Blackhawk Hunter.

The Super Blackhawk Hunter is a new model, both in that it is a New Model action (and thus safe to carry all six chambers loaded) and that it first

If this isn't accurate enough for you, with iron sights and factory ammo, then you're a lot pickier than I am. You can kill a lot of deer with this level of accuracy.

appeared in 1992, which is a relatively short time for the gun industry. I mean, there are shooters still wailing about how Winchester "cheapened" the Model 70 and Model 94 back in 1964. For those of us who have been in the gun biz, the Hunter is an old favorite. The Hunter serial number prefix started out as "88" and has been all along. As the prefix block is good for 100,000 guns, and they show just under 30,000 in fifteen years, I can confidently predict that "88" will be the Hunter prefix for another half-century or so.

The big difference in the Hunter from the regular Super Blackhawk is the barrel. First, the whole gun as well as the barrel is currently stainless, and stainless only. I vaguely recall seeing blued Hunter models in the past, but then they could have been gunsmith-modified. I don't really recall. (In 1992 I wasn't looking to become a gun writer,

so I didn't take copious notes on everything I saw. That came later.) Also, all the literature I could find on the Hunter only mentioned it having been made in stainless. The barrel is 7-1/2" long, and the top rib is wider and taller than the normal ribbed Ruger barrel. Well, the normal ribbed Ruger barrel on the double-action revolvers. Neither the Blackhawk nor the Super Blackhawk had ribbed barrels before the Hunter Models appeared. The rib is machined to accept the Ruger scope rings, so you can mount a scope to your handgun without having to drill and tap the receiver.

The grip is where your options appear. You can have the standard or the Bisley. They both come with black laminate grips. The Bisley option also includes a re-sculpted hammer spur, which looks good and gives your thumb a better purchase for cocking. As the Hunter is a single-action revolver,

Assemblers fussing over the triggers.

you'll have to cock it each time you want to fire it.

The scope rings are included in the box, along with the owner's manual, fired case and lock. One addition is a card good for a year's membership in the NRA. All the firearms manufacturers are doing this, as the NRA is one of the few groups you can count onto fight the good fight for your firearms rights. If you expect to be hunting with your Hunter, you should be an NRA member.

I tested the rings by installing them, but I didn't put a scope in place. Recalling the hassles I had in mounting scopes at the gun shop (it was a big part of the seasonal business, it brought in a bunch of money, and it nearly drove us all to drink each year) I bolted them on and test-fitted a scope. Perfectly aligned, and no apparent need to lap the rings. However, were I mounting a scope I would lap the rings just because you should. After all, the time and work spent lapping is a small price to pay to ensure nothing goes wrong on your hunting trip.

I took the rings off and tested the Hunter with iron sights and a wide variety of ammo. I first tested it for accuracy using Magtech ammo. As I've mentioned before, they have impressed me with their accuracy and reliability. I spent an afternoon beating fellow gun writer Dave Fortier in a 200-

A rack of non-Hunter Super Blackhawks, ready for test-firing and shipping.

meter shooting contest. We were using Magtech .44 Magnum ammo, and those watching us weren't really sure at first they could see the steel La Rue target we were hammering. After that I had them send me some so I could test-fire it here and in other projects.

The results were as expected: the Ruger Super Blackhawk Hunter shot about three-inch groups at fifty yards with iron sights. That's with Magtech 240-grain jacketed soft point ammo, which is well-suited for deer hunting. So, if you will be shooting at 50 yards and in and have practiced, irons will do. Otherwise, mount a good low-power handgun scope on your Hunter and get to it. Even then I think I'd limit myself to 100 yards, simply due to a limited ability to judge distance. A little deer might look to be at 100 when it is only 75 yards away, and a monster buck might look to be 100 yards out when he's more like 130-140. With the little one at 70, your shot will be almost two and a half inches high. The monster at 130 will have the bullet just about five inches low. If he's at 140, you bullet will be over seven inches low. If you're deer hunting, you should either have a laser rangefinder, or pace off the distances to various landmarks around your blind, so you know exact distances.

The Hunter worked just fine with all the factory ammo I had to feed it. I didn't bother dipping into my stash of reloaded ammunition, as none of it was as stout as the factory stuff. And I certainly didn't have any "monstah-recoil bull killer" loads on the shelf. However, there have been enough shooters for a long-enough time who have abused their Super Blackhawks to let us know how that goes: pretty well for a long time. How will you know? You'll see the center pin got battered in the retention notch, the retention plunger will get beaten up even more. When the center pin jumps free from the recoil of shooting, you'll have to replace at least the retention plunger and maybe even the center pin as well. Considering how much lead you will have sent downrange the cost of those parts is negligible.

Who needs a Super Blackhawk Hunter? Well, none of us, really. But as my brother Mike has been known to say, "There you go, confusing wants and needs again." OK, so who wants one? Anyone who is looking to go handgun hunting, wants a scope, and doesn't need a double action gun. If the .44 Magnum will serve your needs, there is no need to even consider jumping up in caliber. You can find lots of suitable ammo right over the counter, too. If reloading is your game, then you can either pump it up, or throttle it back, to suit your needs. Reloaders should look into .44 Special-level and mid-range loads, to build up shooting skills without risking the learned flinch we all dread.

The Hunter is also a great "trump gun." You know, the range session where you and your buddies show off the new guns and your skills at shooting. You can hit things farther out with a Hunter than you can with an iron-sighted handgun.

Go ahead, give in to temptation.

RUGER

— PART FOUR —
The GP100

The idea of fighting with handguns is a mainly American custom. For most of the world, combat is divided into two arenas: the personal and the organized. (The latter of which, in some places, isn't very organized at all.) In the personal, quite often the weapon of choice is the knife. In "knife cultures" a personal knife or dagger is an article of clothing. Fights are either brief, ad-hoc affairs in the local bar, tavern or other such place, where tempers flare and the blades come out. Or they are ambushes, where someone coming home drunk from the bar is waylaid. (Thus following the alcohol dicta of John Farnam: 80 percent of all the trouble you can experience in life is found in, entering or leaving bars. Don't go to bars.) Fighting in groups is done with rifles. The idea of packing a handgun for defense is viewed in many places as just downright strange or paranoid. Or, solely a police function. After all, if you get in a fight in a bar, you need a knife, right? And if the village/collective/whatever goes out to fight, you need a rifle, right? Only officers, police and military, carry handguns.

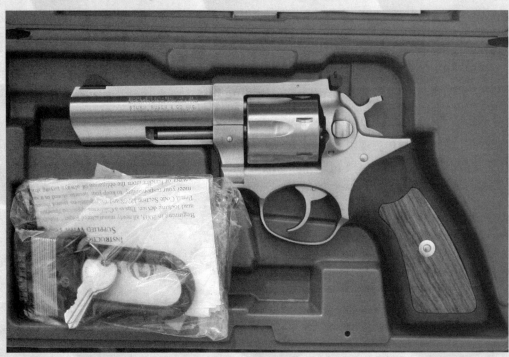

The GP100, in all its glory, resting in the Ruger plastic box.

Not only should you buy a GP100, but you should join the NRA. The GP100 is a heck of a deal, and the NRA will be working to make sure you get to keep your Ruger for a long time.

The American idea of fighting with handguns comes, to no great surprise, from the Old West. There, the law could be far away, and a man had to take care of himself and his family. Since it is really hard to get a lot of work done while carrying a rifle, holstered handguns were relatively common. Not as common, perhaps, as the movies might lead you to believe, but still common. In the 19th century the holstered handgun was often as not a single action. From the beginning of the 20th century, the double-action revolver became the more-common handgun. Oh, there were the owners who had to be different, and pistols (self-loaders, as they were called back then) could be found in holsters, pockets and luggage across the country. But by far the most-common

handgun to be seen in a police officers holster was a double action revolver.

By 1972, the revolver wars had been won: Colt lost. While the Colt Official Police was a good firearm, it was not up to the task of unseating the S&W Model 10. They were both accurate. The S&W had a bit more durability, due to the lockup fore-and-aft its ejector rod lock provided. But what really got Colt was a double-whammy. They had a design that required lots of hand-fitting, a design they did not update. Thus, training assemblers was long, expensive and something Colt wanted to keep in-house. The S&W design, while taking some hand work, was simple and precise enough that you could train people to do it relatively quickly. At least the basics of keeping a batch of guns going through even hard service. So S&W spent a lot of time, money and effort to get every police department in sight to send one of its officers to the S&W Armorer School. The decision for police administrators became easier and easier: Not only was the S&W design easier to assemble, tune and keep in proper function than the Colt, S&W would teach one or more of your own officers to do all that for you.

When Ruger unveiled the Security Six in 1972, revolvers were still the norm. Pistols had not yet taken a solid hold on the market, and wouldn't for another ten years. Ruger made the Security Six pretty much like the existing revolvers of the time. The ejector rod had a front locking latch/plunger. The grip frame was the outline of the grips. It was in .357 Magnum. It was, however, only a step on the Ruger

journey. A very profitable step, as Ruger sold over a million of them before the Security Six was replaced in 1985 by the GP100.

Just in case you run into the Security Six, and are thinking "This is a solid-looking wheelgun for $200." Be aware of one detail: the grip frame was changed

The GP100 barrel shape echoes the Colt Python without all the extras that made it so expensive to fabricate.

The GP100 did not use the traditional ejector rod lock to secure the front of the cylinder. Instead, it used a new latch pivoting on the crane, that latched into the frame.

The GP100 ejector rod is not long enough to fully eject the cases. You'll have to learn (as we did in the old days) to push it sharply to get them clear.

in shape partway through production. The original design, the pistols with the "150" prefix, which were made in the first three years, has a grip that is at more of an angle to the norm. The grip sticks out more on the bottom, and thus the angle of the barrel to your hand is less-conducive to fast shooting. It may not matter, and it may even be that you prefer the old grip shape. Just be aware that this difference exists between the 150- and the 151- and later Security Six models.

In 1985, the GP100 swept all the Security Six's shortcomings away. Too bad it was too late for revolvers at that point. Yes, they'd hang on for a while, but the handwriting was on the wall. The common perception is that the GP100, when it came out,

replaced the Security Six and that Ruger made no more of them. Not true. Production of the Security Six continued through 1988. But it was clear, despite the continued slow (and slowing) sales of the Security Six, that the GP100 was the new gun, and the old would have to go. Starting with a "170" prefix, the GP100 sold like gangbusters for five years, then slowed a bit, and now "enjoys" sales that make it an occasional participant in the production line. In the early years Ruger was making 25,000 to 50,000 of them a year. Now, 20,000 would be a boom year. Such is the dominance of pistols in the current market.

Were you to obtain a GP100, what would you be getting? One heck of a revolver. First, the design took advantage of the design elements of the Redhawk,

The cylinder locking bolt is off the centerline of the frame. As a result, it is not directly in line with the chamber and will not create a thin spot.

while building on the pioneering en-bloc trigger mechanism of the Security Six. The trigger assembly is a single assembly that comes out by pressing a plunger. No sideplate, and the ejector is of the

The GP100 front sight is solid, simple, and easily changed.

Redhawk type. That is, there is no lockup in the end of the ejector, so there is no need to make it anything more than a solid rod to whack out the empties with. In its one shortcoming, the GP100 ejector does not travel far enough to get the empties clear of the chambers. If you don't give it a brisk push, the empties might not clear. (Back when we all shot and carried revolvers, that was something everyone understood: not all ejector rods got the empties out. Nowadays it comes as a surprise to some.) The front sight is held in with a spring-loaded plunger, so you can change your sight any time you want. The rear sight is solid, protected by strong shoulders, and click-adjustable. The Ruger DA action uses a transfer bar, so you can safely carry it hammer down on a live round. (Yes, Virginia, some people still worry about that in double action revolvers. It has been

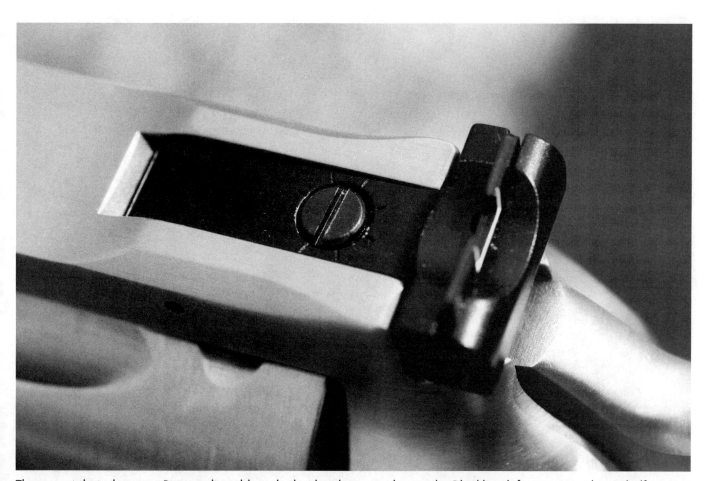

The rear sight is the same Ruger adjustable style that has been used since the Blackhawk first appeared over half a century ago.

safe to carry double-action revolvers with all six chambers loaded since before the Titanic sank. And no, Leonardo DiCaprio wasn't on board.) The lockup is by means of a rear centerpin in the frame, and as with the Redhawk, a locking tab in the crane that latched into a slot on the front of the frame.

The cylinder latch was different from that of both the S&W and the Colt. On the S&W you push the latch towards the muzzle to unlock the cylinder and hen swing out the cylinder to load, unload, clean, whatever. On the Colt, you pulled the latch back towards the grips. To unlock the GP100, you push the latch down into the frame, as if you were pushing it towards the hammer. The shape of the recoil shield helps you there, as its curves translate an attempted push-forward or pull-back into a "frameward" movement of the button.

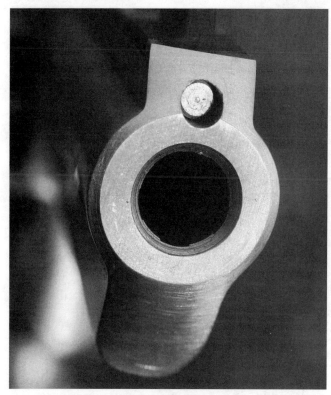

The front plunger is spring-loaded. Press it in and you can remove and replace the front sight.

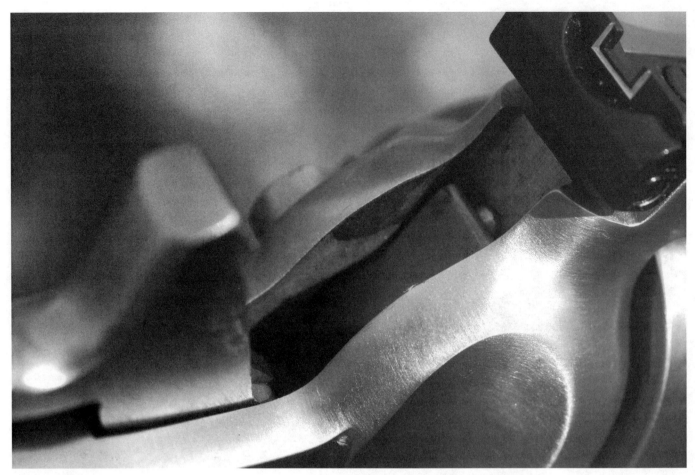

The GP100 uses a transfer bar to deliver the slap of the hammer to the firing pin. It is perfectly safe to carry the hammer down on a loaded chamber.

The really big deal of the GP100 was the grip frame. It didn't have one. The coiled mainspring worked down a shaft that rode in a tang. There, it was much like the earliest Ruger centerfire revolver, the Blackhawk. The grips completely enclosed the tang, which didn't come anywhere near the edges of the grip fore-and-aft. As long as you could secure it to the tang, you could make the grips on your GP100 any size, shape angle or material you wanted to. That was revolutionary. Since the designs of Samuel Colt, back in 1836, revolver grips had been secured to a frame that defined their outer edges. Not so anymore.

Coming onto the market with Ruger's already sterling reputation for durability, made of stainless steel, and in .357 Magnum, the new grip concept was enough to make it a big seller. They were always

in short supply, and shooters who couldn't wait for the Ruger would often "settle" for something else. Life in gunshops then was not bad, if you had any source for Rugers at all.

One thing Ruger had an advantage over S&W at the time was that they knew what shooters were doing. Well, S&W did too, but they had to make a "work-around" and not a clean sheet of paper. What was the big deal? When the .357 Magnum was invented, it was chambered in full-size guns. The classic S&W N frame, the .44 frame, was the first home of the .357. However, a lot of people found the big .44 frame too big for a mere .38 Special, and while the weight was nice when shooting .357 Magnums, you carried a gun a lot more than you shot one, especially back then. The grip of the N frame was also larger than that of the K, and those with average hands might struggle. Those with smaller than average hands could not use an N frame comfortably.

When the S&W Combat Magnum came about (later to be known as the M-19) shooters were still not shooting a whole lot. Someone who shot a couple of thousand rounds a year was a high-volume shooter. Bullseye and the beginnings of PPC were the events you could shoot, and you shot a lot of that with a .22LR pistol. Someone who shot a huge volume, say 5,000 rounds a year, would be splitting that evenly between .22LR, .38 Special wadcutters and .45 hardball. (Bullseye is a three-handgun affair.) Police officers who shot a lot might shoot a thousand or two a year, mostly .38 Special. It was common for police officers to shoot a lot of .38s, and then fire a cylinder or two of magnums before going back "on the job."

With that kind of firing schedule, guns lasted a long time. Also, the recoil of the .357 Magnum wasn't pleasant in the lighter guns, but it was endurable, as you were shooting less than a box a year of the stuff. The first change came from the Newhall Incident in 1970. In summary: California Highway patrol officers encounter bad guys, get in a shootout, at the end of which four CHPs end up dead. Training is the culprit, as in training not relevant to the street. Law enforcement starts an accelerating pace of shifting to full-power ammunition for qualification. Result: If you carry magnums, you practice and shoot magnums for the qualifying course.

When I arrived at the first of the gun shops I'd work at, in 1977, the Detroit Police Department had already made the change. They probably had done so

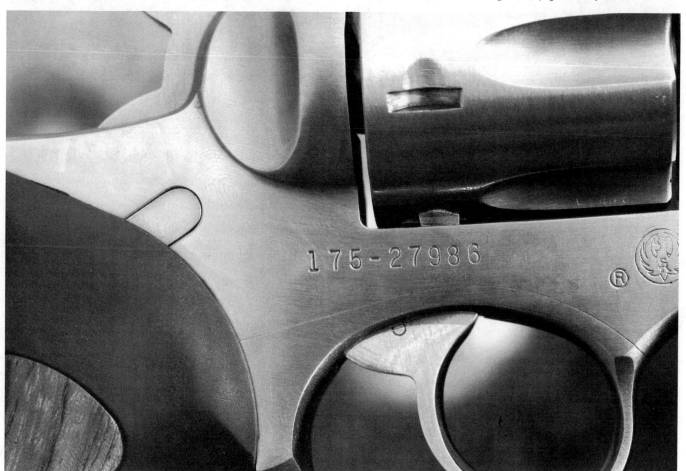

Starting with a "170" prefix, the GP100 is already up to the "175" prefix. Going by serial numbers, this is obviously a 2007 gun, and came off the assembly line only days before it was shipped to me.

Here you see the result of simply pushing the ejector rod back. The example case has not cleared the chamber, and will not fall free of its own weight. Rap that rod!

even before Newhall, as things happened slowly back then. On the DPD you could carry pretty much anything you wanted, but first you had to qualify with it. We had officers arriving before each quarterly qualifications (that was another change many departments made: from annual to much-more-often) to find the ammo they needed.

After those changes had gotten underway, ammunition designers also started making improvements in bullets. (The two changes were not unrelated.) To make the "inconsequential" .38 Special more effective, ammo makers experimented with high speed hollowpoints. The old 158-grain lead round nose which often barely broke 800 fps out of a service revolver was exchanged for a 125-grain JHP that did over 1,000. By the early 1980s,

the change had overcome much of the market: the lead 158-grain bullet in .38 and .357 revolvers was not the norm. Instead, the much more effective 125-grain jacketed hollow point became the gold standard. However, the toll became too much. Where the .38 Special might be doing just over 1,000 fps, ammo makers were staying up late at night to get the .357 over 1,400 fps and keep it there. From medium-size revolvers shooting a mix of mostly .38s, and a few .357s, and shooting a few hundred a year on average, in twenty years the mix was mostly full-house 125-grain .357 magnum loads, and a thousand or two. Some shooters shot a lot more.

As a result, guns went out of time faster (it is relatively easy to re-time a revolver, however), but more importantly the forcing cones eroded and even cracked. Basically, we were wearing out guns.

I've had people ask me just how big a deal the difference is. We can see by consulting loading data. A 158-grain bullet uses 5.7 grains of powder to push the bullet just under 1,200 fps, for a pressure of 31,200 PSI. With a 125-grain bullet, we use 7.5 grains of powder to push that bullet out the muzzle at a more-or-less velocity of 1,400 fps. The peak pressure is 33,800 psi. The pressures and powder charges don't seem out of line. But on every shot the bullet gets squirted out of the cylinder and into the forcing cone. The hot, abrasive gases slam into the forcing cone like a blowtorch. The 125-grain bullet is a bit less noticeable in recoil than a 158-grain load, so shooters would shoot more of it. Lots of fast, double action shooting and the forcing cone would

be eroded, the edges rounded. And the surface would be heat-cracked like a dry lakebed. It would happen with any load at magnum pressures, it just happened faster with the 125s than the 158s. The S&W M-19 was particularly troubled by this load. The bottom of the barrel shank had to be filed/broached flat to clear the cylinder and crane. That made the forcing cone thinner still at that area. That is where most of the cracked barrels would be found to have failed. The GP100 barrel is larger in the shank, and is not filed/broached flat, so it has a full diameter of support.

S&W responded by offering the 586-series guns. Basically, it was a revolver where the rear half was a K frame (the .357 models) for the smaller grip and the front half was the N frame (the .44 models) for the larger barrel shank diameter. The heavier frame,

The GP100 is plenty strong enough to take a steady diet of .357 Magnum ammo. Probably better-suited to it than many shooters are.

Fighting with handguns is an American preference, and using a DA handgun is a peculiar American trait.

thicker barrel and stouter threads and forcing cone stood up to magnums better.

Ruger, not stuck with the legacy that S&W had (a K frame revolver in 1985 was not markedly different from one made in 1905) could start fresh. And the GP100 was fresh. Rather than beef up the Security Six, Ruger simply replaced it with a better gun, and let sales tail off as the new gun took over.

One detail that might be overlooked, unless you've managed to break a revolver, is the location

of the locking stop. On S&W revolvers the locking stop (or locking block) is in the center of the bottom of the frame opening. That means that on a revolver with an even number of holes in the cylinder, the locking slot in the cylinder is directly next to a chamber in the cylinder. The thinnest part of the cylinder now has a slot milled in it. Worse yet, that slot is milled where the chamber pressure is going to be greatest. I have several cylinders in my scrap/ photo demo box that had to be replaced due to bulged slots. The owner got a little too optimistic in reloading, and ended up with a round whose pressure was great enough to bulge the chamber into the locking slot, where the steel was thinnest. Ooops. I have never seen a Ruger damaged that way. I'm sure there is at least one out there, as the optimism of reloaders seems to know no bounds.

For as long as the Colt Python had been around, shooters valued it for the barrel shape. Oh, the action was praised for its long smooth DA that could be tuned to a beautiful pull. But it was the barrel that gunsmiths worked on. There were even some who made "Smolts." They would take a Colt Python

barrel (God only knows where they got them, as Colt parts were always fabulously expensive, and no one ever junked a Colt barrel that didn't have to) and, re-threading a Smith & Wesson M-19 frame to take it, installed the Colt barrel into the S&W frame. The extra weight of the underlug, and the rib, were just part of the bonus. Colt Python barrels were said to be more accurate than other factory barrels.

The Pythons I've shot seemed to be nicely accurate, but nothing magical. However, Ruger copied the Python barrel in that they used a barrel on the GP100 that had a full underlug. The extra weight was nice when shooting the rapid-fire portion

Your GP100, like all Ruger handguns, has the barrel torqued-up just enough and not too much.

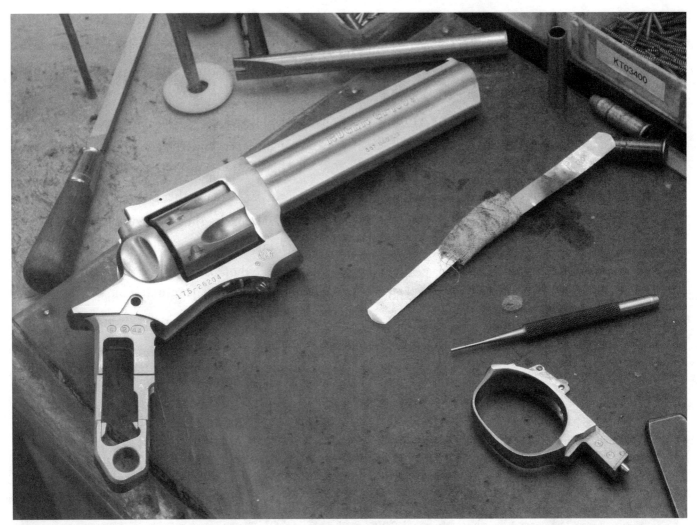

The frame of the GP100 does not follow the contour of the grips. It is merely a tang to hold the hammer strut and mainspring, and to give you a place to clamp on the grips.

of PPC courses, or shooting the qual courses in law enforcement.

The grips that come with a GP100 (the same grips that have come since 1986) are relatively soft rubber, with wood inserts in them. They wrap around the frame stem, and are comfortable enough that I've never looked into the market of replacement grips to find new ones. I know, it is heresy for a gun writer not to be searching for something better. Well, I've never felt the need to with the GP100 grips. The grip panels also cover the disassembly tool, a short section of steel rod. You remove the grips (and don't lose the rod.) Cock the hammer (make sure it is unloaded first) and then poke the rod through the hole in the end of

the hammer strut. Then when you pull the trigger and ease the hammer down, the spring is captured. Most used GP100s have the rod missing, as it is easy to lose when taking the grips off, especially if you have no idea it is there.

When the GP100 was announced in 1985, it was part of a family. It was to be the middle of a three-revolver lineup, the smaller being the SP101 and the larger the Super Redhawk. The Super Redhawk appeared two years later, and the SP101 didn't appear until 1988.

I hauled the GP100 of to the range with a case of ammo, mostly various Black Hills loads, but also some reloads of mine and factory ammo from Hornady and Magtech. Can I tell you how unsuspenseful reliability testing is with a GP100? A couple of club members asked what I was up to, and when I remarked that I was "reliability testing a Ruger handgun" they looked at me like I'd been out in the sun too long. Of course, when I offered them a chance to shoot it, they stepped right up. Free ammo, and someone else's gun? Why not? They too, found the utter reliability of Ruger handguns as something to simply accept as a feature of the GP100. We'd have to do something a lot more involved than just shoot, to find out what it takes to make a GP100 cry "uncle." Which Ruger would not have been too happy about. I'm sure if I had subjected the GP100 to mud and dust tests, or the vastly popular (at least to readers) underwater shooting, Ruger would have insisted that I either pay for the gun or pay for polishing the stainless

With bins of parts, an assembler can put one together quickly. With a few spares, a trained armorer can keep Rugers running for a long, long time.

surface. After all, they can't have a scratched gun going off to the next gunwriter, can they?

I shot groups until I produced one that seemed a bit more photogenic than the rest. The accuracy was as boringly high-class as the reliability. Six shots

If you want to shoot lots and lots of .357 Magnum, you might want the 6" barrel instead of the 4". It will offer more weight, and soak up recoil better.

Accurate and reliable; there is not much to complain about here.

Every single GP100 is proof-tested before it leaves. Perhaps yours is one of the ones in the plant when I visited.

into two inches at twenty-five yards, over sandbags, was the norm. You can win a lot of matches, or bets, with accuracy that good and reliability that the GP100 demonstrates. You can, if you stalk close enough to ensure of your point of impact, bring home a lot of game with a .357 Magnum that shoots that well. And if you depend on it for defense, then the reliability and durability of the GP100 will serve you well.

I don't anticipate Ruger dropping the GP100 from the lineup any time soon. From looking at the serial number listings, they are selling enough of them to keep it in the lineup and catalog for quite some time. The only reason I could see there being a shortage is if some new product consumes so much of the available production time that there is none left for the lesser-selling guns. That would have to be one heck of a high-selling firearm, to push the GP100 off the schedule.

But who knows, Ruger may decide to drop it. So be sure and get yours sometimes between now, and say, the next ice age.

— PART FIVE —
The SP101

Pocket guns are nothing new. When gentlemen rode in coaches to and from their estates and the big city or town, or when people had to ride a coach to get anywhere, they were viewed as prey by some. In those genteel times the predators were called "highwaymen" and at times would, and often legally could, be simply shot on sight. For protection, gentlemen carried pocket pistols. Of course, back then a pocket could be large enough to hold today's microwave oven, so a "pocket" pistol could be rather large. Those early pistols were all hand-made (all firearms were back then) and the level of quality, decoration and reliability would depend on the gentleman's means. I'm sure a lot of them were simply short-barreled copies of the dueling pistols said gentleman might already own.

Here in America in the first half of the 1800s, Henry Deringer made short, concealable pistols. Called the Philadelphia Deringer, the name became so commonly used and misspelled that we now call any single or double-barreled

The SP101 nestled in its storage box with owner's manual, lock, etc.

The idea of a snub-nosed (short-barreled) revolver as a constant-defense companion is a uniquely American one.

pocket pistol a "derringer." John Wilkes Booth used a .41-caliber Philadelphia Deringer to assassinate President Lincoln. Later, when self-contained cartridges became available, Remington made a two-barreled derringer. It had the barrels stacked vertically, and cocking the hammer cycled the striker to alternate between the barrels.

Unlike the single-shot percussion cap muzzleloading derringers, the Remington derringer was not very powerful. Indeed, even at the time it was viewed as anemic. However, given the barbaric level and "quality" of trauma surgery, and the lack of antibiotics, someone shot with a .41 Remington was probably going to die. Not soon, not painlessly, and not without a lot of regrets for the actions that led up to his having been shot. Then again,

sometimes power comes with a price. A single-shot muzzle-loading derringer (or deringer) depends on the hammer riding close to, but not touching, the percussion cap. If the hammer rides too high the cap can come off in your pocket. If it rides too low the pistol might go off in your pocket. At least the Remington had some measures to keep the firing pin off of the rims of its rimfire cartridges.

As we've discussed before, the whole idea of fighting with handguns is very much an American invention. As the country became settled, and walking around with a holstered handgun clearly visible became more and more something only police officers did, guns got hidden under suitcoats. I'm sure the idea of a short-barreled revolver was one many gunsmiths explored, but not until 1915 could

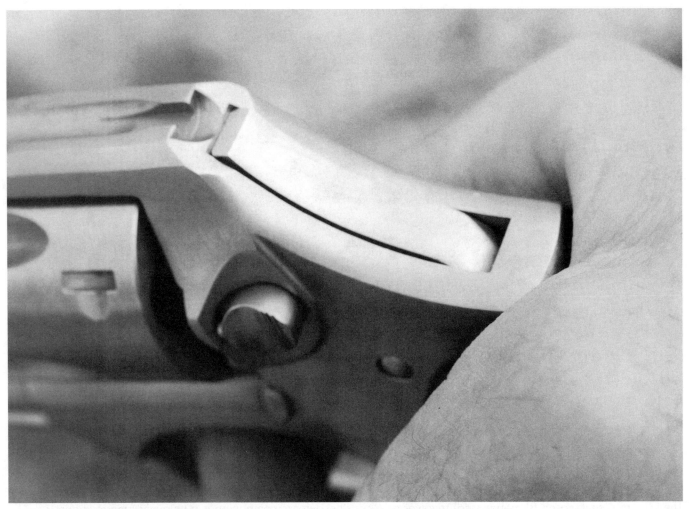

The spurless model is very convenient to carry, and doesn't let lint get into the action.

you get a standard S&W with a barrel shorter than 4 inches. That year the Military & Police, Model 1905 4th Change had a 2" barrel as an option. In 1927, Colt offered a special version of their Official Police, called the Detective Special, with a 2" barrel in place of the 4" of the OP. From then on, you could always find a snub-nosed revolver in catalogs and gun shops across America. Now, if carrying a handgun in case you needed it, with which to fight, was a peculiarly American trait, the choice of a snub-nosed double action revolver as that tool was unheard of elsewhere. In the early part of the 20th century in Europe police carried .32 and .380 pistols, and gentlemen who went discreetly armed might carry a .25 or a .32. But a revolver? They were quaint relics of the 19th century military fixation with stopping cavalry

This one is in .357 Magnum. You can also have a .38 or a .32. Ruger makes 9mm and .22LR from time to time, so keep an eye out for them.

charges. And a short-barreled revolver was beyond odd.

Americans have never had a problem with ignoring advice from Europe. So the "snubbie" took

Five shots. Need more? Carry a speedloader or a backup gun. There is a price to be paid for convenience and compactness, and five shots is one part of it.

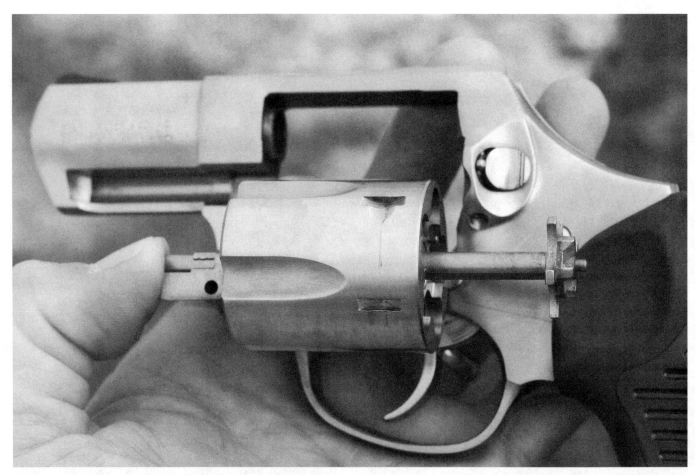

The ejector rod does not go full-length except on the .22LR and 9mm versions. In a pinch, you'll need to develop the habit of smacking that ejector rod to clear the empties.

hold and stuck with us. Now that self-loading pistols are more popular you can probably find the use of a snubbie waning, but it still serves a useful purpose.

The SP101 is one of the rare models of Ruger handguns that you can hear someone describe as "a cute little gun." Well, OK, someone who is really into guns could call it cute. The average person isn't going to describe it as a cute little gun, but they will certainly notice that it isn't the massively overbuilt revolver that we're so accustomed to seeing out of a Ruger box.

The SP101 came out in 1989, long after Ruger had perfected its DA designs, and the result is a compact and very handy little wheelgun. With the serial number prefixes starting at 570 and now having extended into the 573 series, it is obviously a popular model for Ruger. And understandably

so. Available in .22LR and .32 H&R Magnum as six-shot revolvers, and 9mm and .38 Special /.357 Magnum as five-shot, they make great little carry guns. You might ask about the caliber selection. Designed as a five-shot .38/.357 for carry, the design is easy enough to convert to a .22 LR that is would have been negligent of Ruger not to have done so. Considering the volume of .22LR ammunition that is made (and shot) each year, and how many shooters view a "range trip" as an occasion to shoot off a box or three of .22LR ammunition, any firearm that you can make in .22LR you ought to.

Given the compact size of the SP101, and its relatively unthreatening-to-a-new-shooter weight, it makes a great learner gun for new and young shooters. Getting someone to be comfortable and competent at shooting is a lot easier with a .22LR.

The cylinder lock, like all Ruger revolvers, is set off the centerline. Not that the five-shot SP101 needs it, but it is a good design habit to have gotten into and to keep.

There is also the economic argument: you save a lot of money. Let's say you spend the full MSRP of $530. (You could have gotten a much better price by shopping around, of course.) Let's also lowball the price of .38 ammo and shoot full-price .22LR, just to make the payback as long as possible. At $2 per 50 rounds of .22LR, and $12 per box of 50 .38 Specials, you save $10 per box. You'll have to shoot 530 boxes to recover your investment. But 5,300 rounds of .22LR isn't that much in cost, gives almost no recoil, and is one heck of a lot of fun. It is easy to shoot of 200-300 rounds of .22LR in a single range session. And done right, it is fun. Fun and cheap: in those roles a .22LR is perfect. At 300 rounds a range trip, you'll have to go to the range 17.5 times to break even. (Oh, don't throw me in dat dere briar patch, mistah!)

Moving up, the .32 is an underrated cartridge. With older .32 short and .32 Long ammunition it is a pussycat to shoot. You might be surprised at how much ammunition in those calibers is still floating around. At the gun shop we bought used guns (all gun shops do) and we quite often got a lot of ammo

The SP101's cylinder latch, like its big brothers', goes into the frame to unlock the cylinder.

The serial number, in the current location. The sharp-eyed among you will note that the serial number is applied before the surface is belt-sanded to its satin finish.

with each gun bought. As the ammunition wasn't in the normal procurement stream we couldn't re-sell it. (Although I have heard of shops that did. Some even sold ammunition by the bullet or magazine-full.) So the ammo we bought would go on the test-fire shelf in the back. One whole shelf was nothing but .32 Short, Long and some boxes of Magnums.

Granted, we didn't have as many occasions to test-fire .32 revolvers, but we still ended up with a great deal of ammo. In the .32 Magnum loading, you can have either low-recoil ammo from the Cowboy Action Shooters (Black Hills is great for that) or you can have full-power defensive ammo from Black Hills or Federal. In the lead bullets, Black Hills is softer, with Federal offering a lead bullet as well. From Black Hills the lead bullet is a 90-grain bullet listed as going 750 fps. The Federal is a 95-grainer listed at 1020 fps. Out of the short barrel like the 2" or 3" of the SP101, you aren't going to get either.

However, if you need a soft-recoil load for a new shooter, the Black Hills is great. The realistic velocity of 675 fps is going to be not much more than what a .22LR hi-speed would feel like. Then step up to the Federal, which will be more like the high 800s to low 900s.

I'm not being evasive on velocities. The velocity differences between individual firearms and individual production lots of ammunition can cause swings of over 50 fps. You could be shooting your SP101 in .32 Magnum (or any other caliber or pistol) with the same brand but a different lot of ammo while your buddy is shooting his (or her) SP101 with the same brand but another lot of ammo. And you could easily have a 50+ fps difference in the velocities you two shoot.

Once your new shooter (or you) has gotten accustomed to that recoil, then the defensive ammo is next. There, Black Hills and Federal show their

85-grain JHP bullets at 1100+ fps. While it may not seem as much, the performance difference between a .32 Magnum and a .38 Special is not as great as other compact cartridges. Compared to a .32 ACP or a .380 Auto, the .32 Magnum is a pretty stout little number. If we use the manufacturers' specs you'll see. A Federal .32 Magnum load of an 85-grain bullet going 1120 fps, compared to a .32 ACP which is a 65-grain bullet at 925 fps, makes it pretty clear which is bigger. Using the bigger pocket pistol caliber, the .380 Auto with a 90-grain bullet at 925 fps, again gives the nod to the revolver.

But what about the bigger bore? How does it stack up to the .38? The .38 Special standard-pressure load is a 110-grain bullet at 980 fps. Yes, that is more, but you pay for it. And there are a lot of people who are recoil-sensitive and might find the .38 just too much to shoot well. After all, only hits count, and if you have the bigger cartridge but your "practice" session simply reinforces your flinch, how much hitting will you be doing?

So if you want a defensive handgun that doesn't have the recoil of a .38 Special and gives you the option of a selection of even softer practice loads, the .32 Magnum has a lot to recommend it. The .32s are also the only SP101s in the catalog that you can get with a 4" barrel. The .38 and the .357 you can get with either 2-1/4" or 3-1/16" barrels.

The 9mm? It is a bit of a niche caliber. Some people don't like the fact that you need to use the Ruger full-moon clips to load your ammo into the revolver. Hey, you get ten of them when you buy the

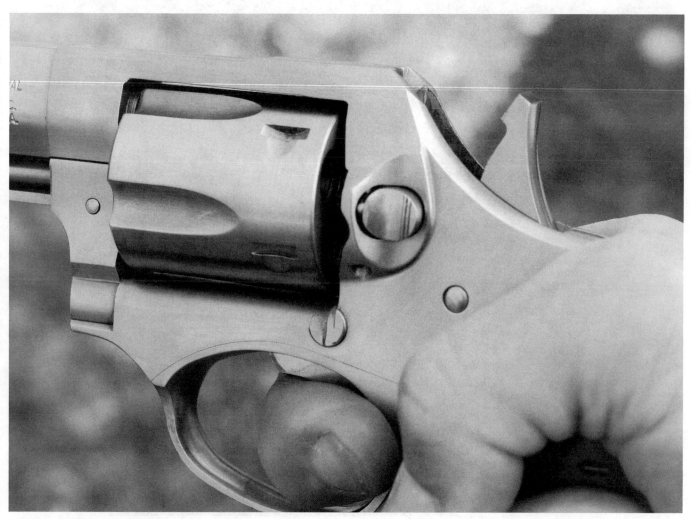

The SP101 is a very easy revolver to trigger-cock. Also, dry-firing is very easy and the cheapest practice you can get.

Five shots, DA, twenty five yards with .38 Special ammo from Black Hills. Not bad, not bad at all.

The SP101 is a great little carry gun, either as a backup to a bigger gun or as your main gun. If you carry it as your main gun, be sure and have reloads on hand (or in pocket) just in case.

gun, and they aren't expensive anyway. And revolver competitors will gladly tell you that reloading the gun with a moon-clip is much faster than with speedloaders or loose ammo. The availability of 9mm ammo, and the interoperability of ammo between a 9mm SP101 and a 9mm pistol, works great. Ruger produces the 9mm version as demand calls for it, which is about every other year.

One advantage the 9mm has over the .38 is case efficiency. In a given barrel length, the small case of the 9mm, running at a higher pressure, ends up delivering as much or more velocity than the .38 Special. And as a little bit of icing to that particular cake, the 9mm has in effect a longer

barrel. The shorter-cased 9mm has its bullet starting further from the muzzle. Longer distance until pressure drops to atmospheric as the bullet leaves the muzzle generally means a higher velocity.

And it adds a bit of panache to your plinking sessions with your buddies to simply drop in another moon-clip of nines and keep shooting.

The big cases are the .38 Special and the .357 Magnum. Why both? Why not just one that chambers both? After all, if it were chambered for .357 Magnum, any .38 Special ammunition would work in it, right? Yes it would, but that is beside the point in some cases. It may be law that you have to use ammunition marked as to the caliber of the firearm itself. (Usually a result of legislators who have gotten too much of their firearms "knowledge" from bad mystery novels.) Or it may be departmental regulations that so restrict you. One example would be Detroit before they switched to Glocks. The departmental weapons policy was pretty simple: if it was a Colt or S&W (this before Ruger revolvers were available.) and double action, and if you could shoot a passing score on the qualification course with it, you could carry it.

There were a few caveats, of course. You had to shoot the ammunition the weapon was marked for. So, if you wanted to carry an S&W M-29 as your duty weapon, you had to shoot ammunition (factory ammunition, no reloads) that was marked ".44 Magnum." As a result, we sold lots and lots of medium-power .44 Magnum ammunition,

.41 Magnum ammo, and for those officers lucky enough to have a revolver in other calibers, .44 Special, .45 Colt and .45 Auto Rim. Were that still the policy, an officer who showed up with an SP101 in .357 Magnum would have to shoot magnums in it. But with an SP101 marked ".38 Special" they could shoot the softer loads in it.

Fed .38 Special ammunition, the SP101 is a great little gun. Fed .357 Magnum ammo it is a beast. After all, despite its stainless steel construction, it only weighs 25.5 ounces.

The assembly/disassembly of the SP101 is like that of the GP-100, with the grips covering the frame stem, and the trigger assembly coming out of the frame as a complete package when you depress the spring-loaded retaining plunger.

In my shooting with the SP101, I discovered a few interesting things. One is the "trigger-cocking"

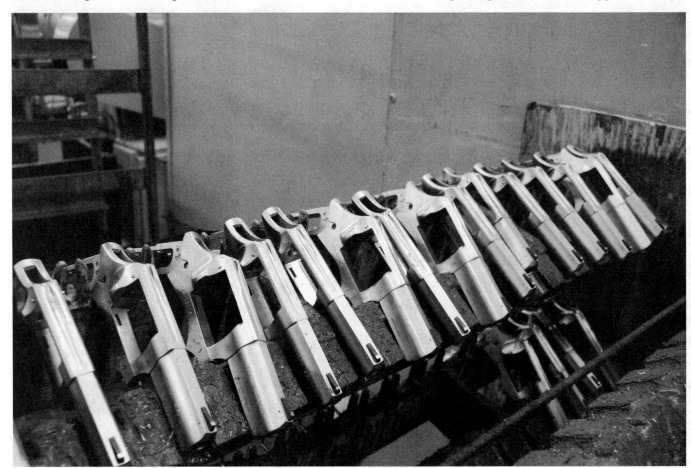

A rack of 3-1/16" barreled SP101s works its way through the factory.

Here you see the modular trigger housing, each fitted to a frame and hung on the rack beneath it. All the trigger parts go in there, and come out as a self-contained unit when you go to clean your SP101.

ability of the SP. When I was early working at gun shops, the boss of one of them was in the habit of dry-firing and trigger-cocking revolvers when things got slow. Mike was the only one I've ever seen who broke the floating firing pin of a Colt Python. Dry-firing should be self-explanatory. You stroke the trigger while keeping the sights aligned, as if you were shooting, but with the handgun unloaded. Done correctly, it is safe and the least-expensive way to get used to proper trigger control. Trigger-cocking is where you stroke through the double-action trigger cycle only far enough to rotate the cylinder and have it lock up, but not far enough to drop the hammer as if you were dry-firing. It was a popular technique of PPC shooting for a time, where you'd trigger cock the gun and

then fire as if you were simply squeezing off the shot from an already-cocked-to-single-action revolver. When rubber-backed trigger stops became available it fell out of favor. Also, as IPSC shooting progressed we learned that it had limited use, and you really wanted to "pull straight through" on the shot. I haven't practiced trigger-cocking for a couple of decades, but when I picked up this SP101 I could do it pretty quickly.

I also re-learned that a snubbie revolver requires you to do your follow-through correctly or pay the price. Follow-through is where you keep the sights aligned all the way through the shot, and keep them there until recoil lifts the sight off the target. If you get sloppy and relax a bit, you can see it with a long-barreled revolver but still get your hits.

But with a snubbie sometimes only the target will tell you. The unforgiving requirement of follow-through is what makes a snubbie "hard to shoot" for some people, or for those less willing to accept the blame, it makes snubbies "not very accurate." I've won a few bets shooting snub-nosed revolvers though the years, taking loot from those who haven't learned about follow-through.

In the beginning of this chapter I mentioned that a snubbie has certain advantages over a pistol. The reader who is following closely might ask "What are they?" Basically, they are these: ease of use, dependability and long-term storage reliability.

When it comes time to use a double-action revolver (and speaking here of snub-nose carry guns) there isn't a decision tree you need negotiate. You simply get your sights on the target and stroke back through the trigger. No safeties to deal with, no worries about lint, dust, etc. Is there a round in the chamber? If there isn't, stroke the trigger again. If there's only one round in there you'll get to it in a second. On pistols, you may or may not have safeties. There may be a magazine disconnector (politicians love them) and if there is and the magazine button has been bumped you may have a non-working pistol as a result. Is the safety on or off? And which direction does it go, anyway?

Dependability is more than just "How many rounds can you fire before it malfunctions?" How well does it work after having been in your pocket for weeks? Or under a suit coat in a muggy June or July? Modern springs are marvels of design and material. But springs can be quirky things. Yes, we now expect pistol magazines to work even after

Here we see 2-1/4" .38s awaiting grips and a trip to the test-fire room.

years of storage while loaded, but there is a one in a million chance otherwise. And magazine springs can only do so much when choked with lint. You may think I make too much of the "lint problem" but I spent many years as a gunsmith in an area with a lot of concealed carry customers. I saw dust bunnies large enough to have names and lint collections that were working on union organizing and asking for health care benefits. Petrified oil on the surface of guns that looked like Jackson Pollock paintings.

Long-term storage is a different aspect of spring design. I've shot magazines that had remained loaded for nearly twenty years (as far as we knew, they might have been loaded longer) but those were full-size pistols. Not compact carry guns. A revolvers mainspring is not stressed at rest. Yes, it is tensioned, but not nearly to its design limit. If you consider how much a spring is worked when cycling to fire, at rest if is sitting there under perhaps 5-10 percent of the strain it is expected to withstand for tens of thousands of cycles. Resting, is well, resting, for a revolver. The pistol magazine spring, however, is sitting there under the maximum workload it is expected to deal with. I've carried pistols for defense, but there is a comforting extra margin of function available from a revolver.

Now, factor that into the SP101. The mainspring is a coil spring, made from music wire. The strain it rests under is again, 5 percent or so if the work it is going to be asked to do. And a music wire spring is much more durable than a flat leaf spring. At rest the hammer covers the firing pin and fills the slot in the frame. Lint can't pack into the slot and block the hammer, not unless you are in the habit of holstering it while it is cocked. (If you are in the habit of doing that, please don't tell me, and do it someplace else!)

There is a reason every gun shop I was ever in had loaded double-action revolvers scattered behind the counters as defensive guns.

The SP101 comes from Ruger in not only all the calibers listed, but you have your choices of barrel lengths of 2-1/4" and 3-1/16" but not all combinations are available. Also, not all calibers are always available. The 9mm, for instance, is a now and then production item, as well as the .22LR. Some models come with the hammer spur gone, and others with it present. If you don't need the hammer spur, don't sweat it. Taking the spur off is one of the simplest gunsmithing tasks you can do, or pay a gunsmith to do. One interesting variant I've seen is the Target Gray Stainless. It looks a lot like the Low Glare Stainless, and was made for one particular distributor. You'll have to search for it, but it (the one I saw) is a neat little gun. Or, you could get a plain satin stainless one, and send it to a custom gunsmith for a careful bead-blasting to matte the finish.

You can do a lot worse than to have a pair of SP101s: a .22LR for cheap, low-recoil practice, and a .38 or a .357 for carry and to keep on the nightstand.

RUGER

— PART SIX —
The Redhawk

The Redhawk, announced in 1979 and available in 1980, was a big advance for Sturm, Ruger & Co. While at that time they had been making the .44 Magnum Blackhawk and Super Blackhawks for nearly fifteen years, and producing double-action revolvers for eight years (the first was the Security Six in 1972), they had not combined the two to make a .44 Magnum double-action revolver. And for good reason. The .44 Magnum is a lot to ask of a double-action revolver. It is high pressure, and with a heavy recoil. Asking a double-action revolver, which is basically a late 19th-century invention, to operate at nearly three times the pressures that DA guns had to face when originally designed is asking a lot.

So, Ruger updated the design of the DA revolver. The main method of securing the cylinder in place had been laid down in the late 19th century, using one of two methods: either a single latch at the rear of the centerpin, or a latch at the front and rear. Colt DA revolvers used a single latch at the rear. To add strength to the system,

The standard Redhawk, with its 5-1/2" barrel, used to be thought of as a big gun. Now it's almost a backup gun to the Super Redhawk.

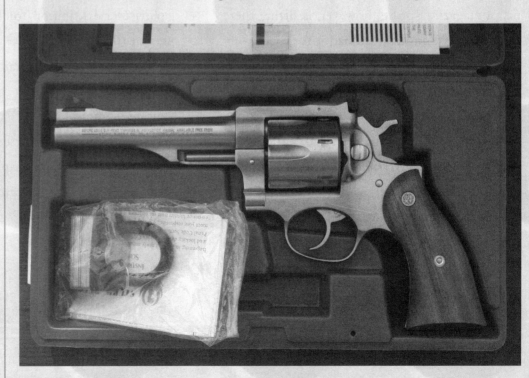

The grips at first were not something I looked forward to. But the shape is good, and your second finger is not hammered by the trigger guard like on other DA revolvers.

The barrel of each Redhawk is clearly marked as to caliber. Only some have the larger ribs cut for the scope mounts.

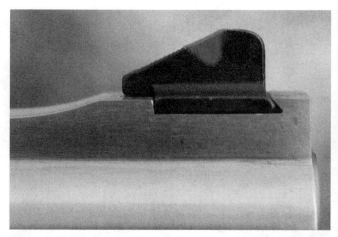

The front sight is a dovetail slot, with an axially-aligned spring loaded plunger keeping the blade in place. You can change it yourself if you want to.

the Colt cylinder rotated clockwise, and the hand thus kept the cylinder closed by being in the path of its opening. S&W used a centerpin latch in the rear, and a spring-loaded plunger in front of the ejector rod. Ruger, In typical "get to the heart of things" over-engineering, improved upon the S&W method.

Ruger had used the front-and-rear method for the Security Six, but that was only a .357 Magnum revolver.

For the Redhawk, they removed the latch at the front of the ejector rod, and instead put that latch on the crane. There, it moved laterally to lock into

The cylinder stop is located off the centerline, so the cylinder slots are not lined up directly next to each chamber. That avoids a potential weak spot in each chamber.

The front latch is a tab that slides into a slot in the frame, forward of the cylinder. Very strong, secure and resistant to recoil.

a slot in the frame. Locking there was much more effective. The unlocking forces of recoil work on the crane and the cylinder at the crane. That's where the potentially-moving mass is. To have the mass/force at one spot and the lock at another spot several inches away, is not the most solid locking system possible. Elegant, simple, good looking and traditional, but not efficient. The change had the additional effect of making the ejector rod smaller. With the need for a spring-loaded centerpin extending the length of the ejector rod removed, the ejector could be a simple solid rod. A small rod means less room through the crane, and a smaller chunk taken out of the frame and barrel for clearance. Both the crane and frame could thus be stronger in that area.

As he typically did with all firearms, Bill Ruger and the design team made things bigger and stronger. The topstrap of the Redhawk is over a quarter-inch thick, and nearly three-quarters of an inch wide. S&W had an advertising campaign going for a while in the early 1980s making fun of the thick topstrap. It said that you wanted your milkshakes thick, but you wanted your topstraps forged. S&W and Ruger went back and forth for a while, but the market pretty much did what markets do: settled on each for different reasons.

The frame was made as the Security Six was, without a sideplate. Such a design is much stronger than the traditional method and has the virtue of being less machine-tool intensive: no need to machine out the insides, then fill it with parts and bolt down a sideplate. The Ruger trigger mechanism came out in one piece, and the parts could easily be taken out, polished, put back and then the whole assembly slapped back into place (once you figured out how they fit).

The Redhawk has its name on the side of the frame. Some shooters object to the serial number on other models being so visible. Me, I don't care, but this does look classy.

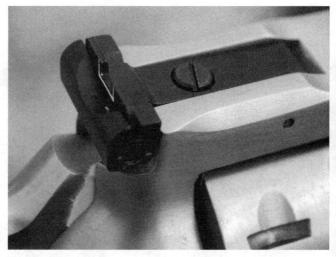

The standard Ruger rear sight, tough as nails, common as dirt, and a classic design.

The cylinder release is in the normal location, but unlike the Colt/S&W latches, it is pressed into the frame to releaser the cylinder. (Colts go back, S&W go forward, Ruger goes in.)

Ruger took advantage of the compact ejector rod design to add steel all around the frame and to install a thicker barrel with a longer and larger-diameter threaded shank than is found on other revolvers. Combined with a larger-diameter cylinder, the Redhawk was a "scaled-up" DA revolver in .44 Magnum in more than just size. As we've discussed before, using investment casting as the fabrication process allows for the use of tougher alloys than in the forged-and-machined process. The lack of a sideplate adds strength. Compared to an S&W M-29 (the up-to-then standard) at 48 ounces, the 54-ounce Redhawk was heavier, dampening felt recoil. So a heavier, tougher, .44 Magnum would allow the burgeoning handgun hunting movement to reach greater power.

When it appeared, the Redhawk sold like hotcakes. Hmm . . . that doesn't quite do it justice. They sold like hotcakes on the buffet table of an Antarctic expedition before the passengers were to go out and photograph the scenery. Why? Well, partly it was because it was a hell-for-tough Ruger gun. Ruger had sold plenty of handguns by that time, and everyone knew that whatever Ruger made and offered was something you couldn't hurt with a ball-peen hammer. But also, we were still in the throes of the "Dirty Harry" sales explosion of .44 Magnum revolvers. After that movie, S&W couldn't keep up in production, Model 29s were selling at a premium, and you could even in some gun shops move up the list by greasing a palm or two. At the time the MSRP of S&W N frames was on the order of $300. It was easy to find buyers willing to pay twice that. My brother picked up his .41 Magnum because it wasn't a .44 and was not such a hot seller. He paid only retail for it, no premium and no bribes.

The Redhawk was a double action .44 Magnum, and it had an MSRP in the same ballpark as the S&W M-29. So Ruger (and gun shops) sold a lot of them.

One aspect that put me off when I first saw the Redhawk was the grips. Having shot quite a bit of .44 and .41 Magnum ammunition through S&W revolvers with factory grips, I wasn't happy with the thought of using standard wood grips to deal with the recoil. The first time I handled one, however, my impression changed. The traditional grip shape of a double action revolver has the curve of the frontstrap coming up high behind the trigger guard. In essence, your second finger is forced to ride up behind your trigger finger. There it can be pounded by the trigger guard during recoil, and you hand is in an awkward potion to do anything about it. Custom grips fill that gap. Well, the Redhawk frame curve didn't go nearly as high, and was a low enough curve that it matched the curve of some custom grips. My hand was still taking the thump from wood grips and a steel backstrap, but at least my second finger knuckle wasn't getting hammered on each shot.

The late 1970s was a time of flux for me, and soon after I learned about IPSC and bowling pin shooting I stopped shooting metallic silhouette. So my time with the early Redhawks was limited. I only fired factory-standard ammo through it and didn't have a chance to try the hunting sledgehammer loads that soon after became en vogue.

The early guns were available at first in 7-1/2-inch barrels and later a shorter 5-1/2-inch barrel. When I was touring the factory in Newport, New Hampshire, they were in the middle of assembling the new 4-inch model Redhawks.

The early guns also lacked a feature that came along in a few years: scope mounts. The Redhawk barrel is ribbed, with a rail on the top

The double action Redhawk has all-chamber ejection, and the rod is a bit short (a common situation on Rugers) but if you really need a speed reload with hunting loads and a Redhawk, shame on you. You should have either learned to shoot better, or learned to count better.

Iron sights, fifty yards, full-power .44 Magnum ammo. 2-1/4" is a pretty good group, and with some practice I could do better. (That, and laying off the coffee drinks before shooting.)

With full-power ammo the Redhawk is almost fun to shoot. Step back on the throttle with reloads and it is lots of fun. A lead 240-grain bullet going 1050 to 1100 fps is a killer long-range plinking load. Steel gongs at 100 yards do not stand a chance.

that is grooved for looks and ease of sighting, and the front sight rides in a raised shoulder near the muzzle. The front sight is held in via a spring-loaded plunger, so you can swap out front sight blades to your hearts' content. While early handgun hunting pioneers used scoped handguns, putting scopes on handguns took a while to catch on. When it did, Ruger realized that their then-premier hunting handgun had no such provision. And gunsmiths rash enough to attempt drilling and tapping the topstrap of a Redhawk soon found out just how earnestly Ruger took the idea of using investment castings to improve strength. The job is near-impossible. If you were to try it, you'd dull or break drills (solid carbide works best) and use a whole can of tapping fluid getting your taps to cut threads. You'd get one-hole's use out of a tap, by

which time it would be too dull to continue, and if you managed to drill and tap four holes without breaking anything (muttering prayers and curses the whole time) you would have proved you are an accomplished machinist. If you really had to do it, the only way would be to both burn the holes with a precision EDM machine, and then EDM the threads. (Can you say "expensive?")

Ruger, rather than try the same on a production line, went with another method: notching the barrel. The barrel rib on the scope-mount Redhawks have four semi-circular recesses. On the top of the rib are a pair of slots. The special Ruger scope rings (developed for Ruger's rifles) clamp into the recesses and are kept from moving during recoil by tabs on the rings that fit the slots on top of the barrel. The end result is heretical to purists; it makes the

Here's a batch of the new 4" Redhawks going through the plant. I'm going to have to get one of them.

gun too front-heavy, it spoils the clean lines of the barrel, and it "just doesn't look right." It also is something that gunsmiths can't do afterwards. The rib of the non-scope barrels are not proportioned properly to let you machine them for the rings. Even if they were, machining them would be only slightly less of a hassle than drilling and tapping the frames. No, if you really have to have a scope-mount barrel on your Redhawk, it will have to go back to the factory.

In the fullness of time, Ruger offered the Redhawk in a few additional calibers: the .41 Magnum, back when the .41 was still viewed as a competitive cartridge in the marketplace; the .45 Colt, because of the interest in big-bore handgun hunting; and what has to be the softest-shooting magnum extant, the .357 Magnum. A 54+ ounce

.357 Magnum? How hard can that kick? You'd be surprised. Taking advantage of the same strengths that the .45 Colt shooters did, and the longer cylinder, reloaders have taken hard-cast bullets meant for .35-caliber rifles, and fit them into the Redhawk. Where a standard loading for the .357 Magnum uses 158-grain bullets and produces nearly 1,600 fps (in the right handgun, as in Ruger), handgun hunters went with hard-cast bullets of 180 (low end) to 205-210 grains, and pushed them over 1,400 fps. While the frontal area isn't nearly that of the .44 Magnum or .45 Colt, the penetration is quite impressive, and you aren't subject to nearly as much recoil. It is still stout, as a .357 with those specs produces a Power Factor of 250 or so, which is in the ballpark of factory .44 Magnums Power Factor.

Early Redhawks were blued, then you could have stainless. Today, the stainless version is available in 4-, 5-1/2- and 7-1/2-inch barrel lengths, while the blued is 5-1/2 inches only. And in the current production guns you can have any caliber you want, provided you want a .44 Magnum.

The Redhawk that Ruger sent me was a stainless version, 5-1/2-inch barrel length, in .44 Magnum. The obligatory lock, fired case, owners manual and warranty card were all in the gray plastic case. My first heft brought back memories of the then-radical grip shape of the Ruger. Firing it brought back other memories. The shape is good, but you'll need practice to get used to the recoil. You may want to look into Hogue grips of rubber to soften the impact to your hand, or wear a shooting glove.

I shot the Redhawk with Magtech ammunition. I have been favorably impressed by the accuracy of their ammo. I won a shooting contest with fellow gunwriter Dave Fortier at a writers' get-together a few years ago. We were shooting at a steel plate at 200 yards, offhand, with Henry Big Boy lever-action rifles. I found my zero with the Magtech ammo, and proceeded to hammer the plate more often than Dave did. Since then, I use Magtech quite a bit in testing .44 Magnum firearms. In the Redhawk, the Magtech continued the impression I had of it. At 50 yards, over sandbags and using iron sights, I was able to regularly punch 2-1/2- to 3-inch groups. At least until I got tired from the recoil. Anyone who tells you recoil doesn't bother

him is a liar. Even of you don't think it does, it has an effect. Sharp-eyed readers will note that the gun sent me does not have the scope mounting slots. Only the 7-1/2 inch version can be had with the scope mounting features. And if you don't want them, you can get the 7-1/2 inch barrel Redhawk without them.

For additional hunting loads, Black Hills (among many) makes a 300-grain jacketed hollow point bullet. Now that load kicks. But if you want hammer-of-Thor hunting ammo for your .44 Magnum handgun, and aren't into reloading, then the Black Hills ammo is a very good choice.

A very nice, big gun without being too big. If you think you need a .44 Magnum you should look into it. The Redhawk is a particular favorite of those looking to have custom work done by Hamilton Bowen. If you take a Redhawk to him, he can slick it up, even re-chamber it to .45 Colt for heavy handloads, and make the barrel whatever length you need (shorter than factory, obviously) for the envy of your Alaska hunting party. As a constant companion in case of Alaska hazards, a 4-inch Redhawk in .44 Magnum or in .45 Colt loaded as stoutly as you can stand will serve you well.

There must be a whole lot of shooters who want such a gun. As the Redhawk prefix started as "500" in 1980, and now is past the 50,000 mark in the "503" series prefixes. That's a lot of big, sturdy, hard-hitting guns. Me, I'm thinking a 4" might be just the thing to have around for testing really heavy .44 Magnum reloads in.

RUGER

— PART SEVEN —
The Super Redhawk

When the Super Redhawk came out, in 1987, we at the gun shop were agog. The already tough-as-nails Super Blackhawk and Redhawk were now "the little guns?" I mean, it was tough finding holsters for hunters that were large enough to take the other guns, but now this? And what's with the funny-looking frame?

The Super Redhawk was simply a reaction on the part of Ruger to the apparent shortcomings of the Blackhawk and Redhawk. Shortcomings, you ask? What "shortcomings?" Well, for one, recoil. In the time since the introduction of the Super Blackhawk in the early 1960s, and the Redhawk in 1979, through to the late 1980s, handgun hunters had made great strides in recoil. When the .44 Magnum was first introduced, it was more than a lot of shooters could stand. Even when I started working in gun shops in the late 1970s, it was still common to see used .44 Magnum handguns for sale: with a box of 44 rounds left of the 50 originals. One cylinderful and the previous owner had had enough.

The Super Redhawk is big, and needs a big case. (And big holster.)

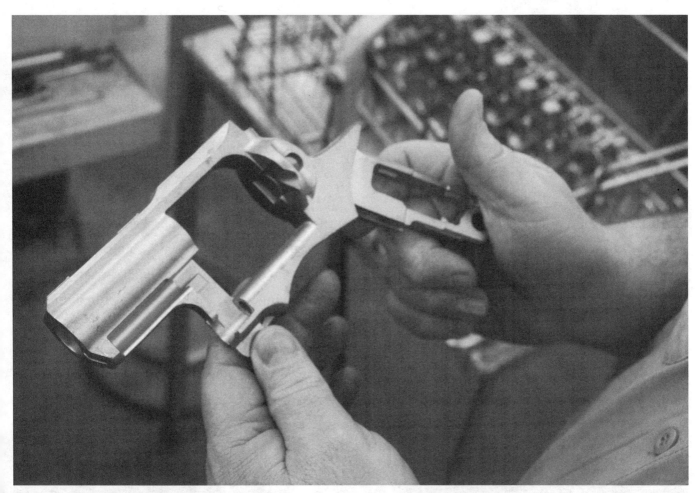

Alaskans start as Super Redhawks do, as investment-cast frames ready to be machined.

That didn't keep .44 Magnum handguns from selling for a premium, they just got six rounds per owner sometimes. But there were experimenters who persisted, and with practice and good grips you can learn to handle the .44 Magnum. And more. The printed ballistics of the .44 Magnum in the 1950s had shooters back then believing it actually delivered a 240-grain bullet at nearly 1,400 fps. The actual performance was more likely 1,200 fps. Even today, getting much more than 1,300 fps out of factory loads is not common. Hunters, by the late 1980s, had gone well past that. The development of heavier bullets made recoil even stouter. From those first few experimenters who jumped up to a slight increase in bullet weight to 260 grains, dedicated handgun hunters had soon after gone up to heavyweights in the 305-315 grains of weight range. The only reason

to not do more was the inability of the case to hold enough powder, and the limits of rifling twist rates to stabilize yet-heavier bullets.

Those heavier bullets were not launched at much less velocity than the .44 Magnum factory rounds actually were: a 280-290 grain bullet at 1,300 fps, and a 315 at 1,200 fps were considered "normal" for a heavy hunting handgun cartridge load. ("Normal" if you thought bone-crunching recoil on the shooters end was what handguns should be doing. The first time I heard of such loads, the speaker referred to them as "killing on one end and crippling on the other." He had stolen the line.)

The effect on everyone; hunter, handgun and game, is impressive. The hunter could end up, like John Taffin, the famous big-bore wheelgun aficionado, with hand problems. John published a copy of his x-rays some years back, showing the bones of his hands almost in a jumble, seriously out of alignment from years of heavy-recoiling handgun shooting and thus explaining the hand problems he was having. Shooters who shoot large numbers of full-power rounds have reported elbow and shoulder complaints, and the only real solutions are rest or heavier guns. The game? There is nothing that walks the surface of North America (or South, come to think of it) that can't be perforated from any angle by a hard-cast 315-grain .430" bullet leaving the muzzle at 1,200 fps. Shoot through a moose? How about shooting through two moose? As a bone-breaker and hole-maker such loads can't be bested short of going to rifle calibers.

The effect on handguns is almost as impressive. My introduction to such loads came when I had to fix my CPA/lawyer's Super Blackhawk. Rob was a handgun hunter (and a rifle and shotgun hunter as well) who had quickly worn his Super Blackhawk out of service. His problem, as so many battered Super Blackhawks evidenced, was that the centerpin of the cylinder was jumping on him. The recoil of firing tries to throw the handgun backwards. The inertia of the centerpin causes it to slam against its retaining lug. Given enough recoil, the lug peens, and the pin begins jumping past the retaining pin. In jumping past, it comes out of the pivot hole in the breechface of the frame. When that happens, the cylinder won't rotate, as the cylinder is no longer supported both

Here are racks of Alaskans with fitted trigger guards, cranes and barrels, awaiting their cylinders and lockwork.

The threaded portion of the Super Redhawk/Alaskan is longer than the diameter of the barrel. Very strong, very rigid, bonus engineering points.

fore and aft. The hand, trying to turn it, simply binds it in the frame. Or, the cylinder spins free, but can't match up with the locking lug and stop in place. The binding is an annoyance, as you can't shoot until you push the centerpin back into place. Spinning free can be dangerous, for if the cylinder should happen to catch on a locking lug it could line up close enough to center to let the firing pin reach the primer. The resulting discharge, with the cylinder more-or-less in line with the barrel, would be, shall we say, exciting?

Long story short, if the centerpin is jumping on you, get it fixed.

Rob's Super Blackhawk was jumping the centerpin. So I miked the centerpin and found it correctly-sized, and free of marrs, burrs or other damage. The retaining lug, however, was toast, so I replaced it with a new, hardened one from an

aftermarket specialty gunsmith. (I don't remember who, after this long span of time.) Once I had fitted it, I test-fired it with the hunting ammo Rob had so kindly provided for me. Hoooo boy! Up until that time I had been shooting what I had thought were hot loads for bowling pins. I had been shooting them for some time by then. I even test-fired customer's otherwise normal .44 Magnums after repairs or for sighting-in before hunting season. They had been the hard-hitting standard to that point. Compared to Rob's load they were not hot, they were barely past "wimpy" on the recoil scale of hunters. A handgun measure of recoil (a general one, anyway) can be gotten from the Power Factor used to measure ammo in practical shooting. Power Factor is the bullet weight in grains, times the bullet velocity in feet per second. To make "Major" in

IPSC or IDPA competition, you have to post a 165. (We customarily drop the last digits or zeros, thus 165,000 becomes 165.) A factory-standard .45 ACP, with a 230-grain bullet going 825 fps, posts a 190. Bowling pin shooters like to use a load between 195 (the minimum many will settle for) up to 215. The honest .44 Magnum load of today, with a 240-grain bullet going a full 1,300 fps, brings us up to a 312 Power factor. Rob's loads? Those hunting loads? A 315-grain bullet trundling along at 1,200 fps delivers a Power Factor of 378. That's right, literally twice the momentum of the .45 ACP load so many think of as "too much recoil."

Those loads are why the Super Redhawk was developed. It was made to be bigger and tougher. Bigger to soak up some of the recoil, and tougher to withstand the hunting-level ammo that more

and more users were shooting. Safety was a small part, but an important one. The design of a double action revolver makes loading and unloading easier. For hunters, after a long day out in the cold, rain, or whatever, unloading a single action is just a bit more hassle than a double action unload would be. A double action revolver just makes it so much easier, you open the cylinder, dump the rounds out, look to make sure any haven't stuck in place, and you're done.

Reloading is as simple, even though it would be a rare hunter who has to do a speed-reload in the field. It strains credulity that someone, somewhere has to deal with so many whitetail deer (or other critters) that he needs to do a quick reload to get the rest of the herd. If he does, I have two suggestions: milder ammunition (you really don't need a 315-grainer

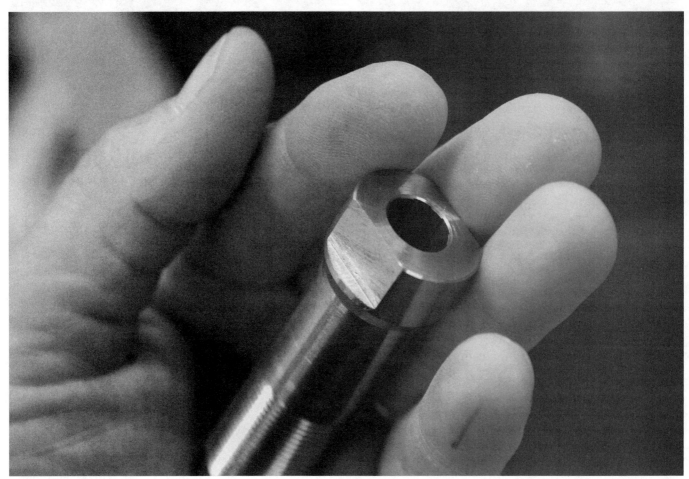

The end of the Alaskan barrel comes out of the lathe with wrench flats on it. Once torqued into place, the flats are cut off and the barrel crowned.

A rack of .45 Colt/.454 Casull Alaskans that are just about done.

at 1,200 to deal with whitetails) and spread the wealth. Call some friends. After a cold, wet day out hunting, some hunters faced with unloading a single action might just skip it: "Ah, we'll just load it up again tomorrow morning, why bother unloading?" Or be so tired that they mis-count and don't get all the rounds out. Either can be the first step to an unfortunate situation, even a tragedy.

It also makes those of us around the hunters more comfortable during the unload. Unloading a double action revolver, you can keep the muzzle pointed at the floor during the entire process. A single action is easiest unloaded by pointing the muzzle up. To go up it has to swing from down. That quite often means bystanders are looking down the muzzle of careless hunters who are unloading their single action revolvers.

As an aside, if you want to learn how to safely load and unload a single action revolver (as well as

This is what Alaskans look like halfway through the assembly line. They're now ready for the internals, then test-fire, then off to your local gun shop.

shoot one quickly) you should attend some Cowboy action Shooting matches.

Recoil

The Super Redhawk in its heaviest configuration weighs 57 ounces. That is, three pounds nine ounces. You wouldn't expect a handgun that weighs that much to kick very hard. And in .44 Magnum, you'd be right. In the .44 Magnum chambering, using factory ammo, it is a pussycat. Even with the heaviest hunting handloads it is reasonable. But when you move up in the world, things get brutal. The .454 Casull (one of the three chamberings of the Super Redhawk) is a step above .44 Magnum hunting handloads. The .454 Casull hunting bullets (hard-cast lead) start at 325 grains each, and go in turn to 335, 360 and 395 grains. Even at the low end, a 335-grain bullet can leave a 9-1/2" Super Redhawk barrel at over 1,500 fps. In recoil terms, that is a Power Factor of 488. The recoil energy and velocity are 31.52 foot-pounds and 23.88 fps. Compared to a normal .44 (12.05ft/lbs and 14.77 fps) or a hunting load .44 (22.84 ft/lbs & 20.33 fps), that is stout. And that's just the start. Up at the extreme end of things, a Super Blackhawk can boot a 395-grain bullet at 1309 fps, and then the recoil number get a bit scary. Power Factor jumps up to 517, recoil energy becomes 32.16 ft/lbs, and velocity becomes 24.12 fps. We're talking hand-numbing recoil.

Now, I'm pretty recoil-resistant. I've shot a lot of ammo over a lot of years, and a bunch of it has been of reasonably high energy. Shooting a .454 is still work for me. Gloves help. Soft replacement grips help. But nothing can prepare you for the kind of recoil the .454 Casull can generate, nothing except the .454 itself. It isn't something "you get used to." You can buildup to it, but it will take its toll regardless of how you prepare. All you can do is shoot some in each practice session, but not enough to hurt yourself or build a flinch. Then rest, shoot something else and try the .454 again on the next range session. If you shoot too much in one session, all your practice is wiped out by the last few shots.

As if that wasn't enough, there's an even bigger brother, the .480 Ruger. The idea was to build a cartridge that delivered a bigger bullet without the onerous increase of recoil that more velocity generates. Mass is bad on your hands, but recoil velocity is the real pain-maker. In the Super Blackhawk, the factory load is tolerable. Here we're talking about a 325-grain bullet at 1,350 fps, or a

You can have a Super Redhawk in .44 or in .45 Colt/.454 Casull. The Colt is a great big-bore plinker. The Casull is for poking holes through big game.

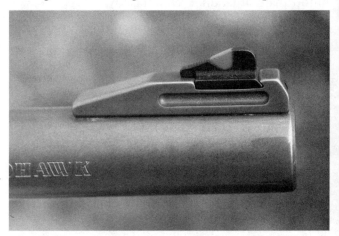

The front sight base is induction-brazed on. The front sight blade is held in by a spring-loaded plunger, so you can change it whenever you want to.

The scope rings of the Super Redhawk both attach to the frame, not to the barrel.

400-grain bullet at 1,100 fps. (If by "tolerable" you mean you'd prefer shooting the gun than letting Mr. Bear chomp on you.) That's still a 438 Power Factor, and 21.97 ft/lbs or 19.93 fps (the 325 load) or a 440 Power Factor and 20.51 ft/lbs and 19.26 fps (400-grain load) in recoil.

However, there is another entire world of abuse waiting for you. If you reload, you can find truly heavy bullets, weighing 420 grains, and loading data to jolt them out the muzzle of your Super Redhawk at 1,250 fps. The numbers? You had to ask, didn't you? The Power Factor of that load is 525. You might recall that a stout load for shooting bowling pins is 195 to 215. A factory .44 Magnum posts a 300 at the upper end. Recoil energy and velocity of the .480/420-grain load are 32.58 ft/lbs and 24.28 fps. You might look at those and remark "they don't seem

The cylinder is clearly marked with the caliber (or in this case calibers) it will accept. Note that this will also accept the .45 Schofield, which is getting pretty low on the energy scale for such a big gun.

that much more." After all, the factory loads are only a few ft/lbs or fps behind that. A few? If you took a .44 Magnum and a .45 ACP, you'd be up to the low end of where we're talking. Add in a .38 special and you might reach the total here. This is really stout stuff, and you have to ask yourself a question: "Is there something out there I really desire shooting enough, that I'll learn to hit with this load?"

You see, you can't simply buy the gun, a few boxes of ammo, and after checking the sights go off hunting. Well, you can, but the guide will know it right away. If you've ever read any hunting stories you'll know the ritual "checking of the sights" after a long trip. Yes, sights do come loose when in the care of airline baggage handlers. But it is also a chance for the guide to size you up. If it is clear to him that you're afraid of your handgun, and can't manage the recoil, he's going to have to lead you to just out of arm's reach of whatever you're hunting. In some cases he may not even take you out. If you're unskilled with your handgun, and unprepared for the shooting, no sane guide is going to lead you to within handgun distance of a big grizzly. Or a small one, either.

Hunting with the biggest loads requires a lot of work, planning and effort. You'll have to become conversant with reloading your own ammo, as commercial loaders don't do much of it. You'll have to practice a lot and get used to the recoil. And you'll have to exercise to get into the kind of shape you'll need to hike after critters big enough to require such loads.

Don't just sit there, go for it!

The Super Redhawk lying on my desk is the 9-1/2" barrel in .45 Colt/.454 Casull, in the Low Glare Stainless, or what's known as the "titanium" finish. The barrel and cylinder are both marked with both calibers, just so no one misses the point:

Loading and unloading is easy and safe and you can quickly tell if you've gotten them all.

The Low Glare stainless finish doesn't look stainless, it looks titanium. Cool.

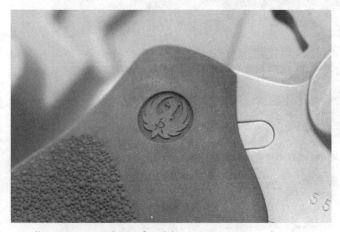

You'll appreciate the soft rubber Hogue grips that Ruger puts on the Super Redhawk.

you can practice with mild ammo. Indeed, with .45 Colt ammo the Super Redhawk is a pussycat. A big, heavy pussycat, but a purring one indeed. Even with the stout stuff, Corbon 200-grain JHPs, and factory hunting ammo, the recoil is not much more than mild. Going up to the .454 Casull, however, is like

stepping into another dimension. The only thing I can compare it to is the martial arts: The .45 Colt is like sparring with someone a grade or two lower in rank than yourself. The hits are relatively soft and easy to avoid or roll with. The .454 Casull is like taking on someone several ranks higher in sparring: the hits come fast, you can't avoid them, and rolling with them doesn't work much. All you can do is add padding. At least in the martial arts you can get stronger, faster, better-timed. With the .454 Casull all you can do is take it. Ouch.

One aspect of the Super Redhawk that Ruger changed for the better was the scope mounting system. The Redhawk and Super Blackhawk Hunter have their barrels machined to take the Ruger scope rings. But the result is a muzzle-heavy gun, and one that is not as pleasing to the eye. (You think looks

Accurate enough for you? Fifty yards, iron sights, .45 Colt ammunition. I can't shoot a six-shot Casull group this tight; the recoil is just too much for sustained precise work.

I shoot for a living (pretty much) and I do not find the .454 Casull at all fun. And no, my left thumb does not get scorched by the gases coming from the cylinder gap.

aren't important? Boy, you haven't spent much time around shooters. They'll swoon over a matted rib on a barrel the way fashion mavens might swoon over a Gucci bag or Manolo shoes.) The frame is extended forward from the front to give both the scope ring some place to be, but to give the barrel more support. The longer frame supports the barrel shank and allows Ruger to make the threaded portion of the barrel just over an inch in length. Unlike other revolvers, the threaded portion of the Super Redhawk barrel is longer than the barrels' diameter. That makes it very securely attached. The barrel is also a simple cylinder with a front sight base induction brazed on it, so fabricating barrels is simplicity itself. It could only be simpler if you got rid of the front sight, but more on that in a bit.

The Super Redhawk sent me was the Low Glare stainless model, and it looks very gray, very titanium, very chic.

Accuracy was pretty good. With the .45 Colt ammo it was like plinking with big bullets. The 100-yard gong found no rest, the targets got perforated right where I wanted them to be perforated. When shooting the Casull, it was like I actually had to work for a living. I had to focus on the trigger and sights, and make sure my grip was consistent from shot to shot. Otherwise the quick and heavy recoil would spoil an otherwise good group.

The serial number prefix of the Super Redhawk began with the "550" series. The model has sold well enough that in the twenty years it has been available Ruger has gone to the middle of the "552" series, and has begun the 530 series for the Alaskan.

Alaskan

There has always been a desire for a short-barreled big-bore handgun with a lot of horsepower. Notice I did not say "need" but desire. The idea is to have a handgun while out hunting that is relatively compact (at least, "compact" in the realm of .44 Magnum handguns) and unobtrusive while you're doing some other outdoors activity. Like hunting with a rifle, fly fishing or just ambling around, say, Alaska.

The "typical" gun has been a 4" S&W M-29, or to send a Blackhawk or Super Blackhawk off to a gunsmith and have him or her shorten the barrel. There was a time when the firearms manufacturers didn't make many short-barreled handguns. At least not those in the big bores. (I shudder to think of a 2" .38 Special as a "bear gun" while hiking.) In fact, until the CNC machine revolution, handguns typically came in two or three variations, and maybe your choice of blued or nickel finish. However, with the use of computers to control inventory and computers to manufacture, it is possible (although not always practical) for manufacturers make many different variants.

At 41 ounces no one is going to mistake the Alaskan for a pocket gun. Not unless your idea of a pocket is the exterior layer, the pocket of a heavy coat meant to keep you warm in sub-zero temperatures. With a 2-1/2" barrel you aren't

The Super Redhawk was built with recoil in mind. You, on the other hand, might not have been. Start with light loads and work your way up as you get used to the recoil.

Practice, practice, practice. It isn't just the way to Carnegie Hall.

going to get the full velocity of your cartridge. But then the hunting loadings of the cartridges in question do not do their magic through velocity alone. Let's say you were in the habit of loading the ammo for your Super Redhawk in .44 Magnum with 180 grain bullets for whitetail deer, and were getting almost 1,900 fps out of a 9-1/2" barrel. Out of the 2-1/2" barrel of the Alaskan you would not be getting nearly 1,900 fps. You'd be getting quite impressive fireballs (as in, avoid dry grass) and probably not much more than 1,400 fps. However, if you were using a penetrating load, say a 305-grain hard-cast lead bullet trundling along at 1,200 out of the long barrel, you'd be better off. Out of the short barrel you could still count on almost 1,000 fps and

quite impressive penetration. Oh, the recoil would be beyond impressive (the load that delivered 1,200 in a 9-1/2" barrel would be stout) because in shortening the barrel from 9-1/2" to 2-1/2" you'd be dropping the revolvers' weight from 58 to 41 ounces. That's (for the math-challenged among you) a new weight that is only 70 percent of the big guns. Lop 30 percent of the mass off of any gun and the new recoil levels will be impressive compared to the old. Do it on a heavy-recoiling gun and you can bring things to a whole new level of abuse.

The Alaskan is currently offered in .44 Magnum and .45 Colt/.454 Casull. I imagine in the fullness of time (and the urgent requests of some shooters) Ruger will offer it in .480 Ruger. If they don't, it would be an easy enough conversion for Hamilton Bowen to perform, as the barrel is an easy enough swap and he already knows how to make new cylinders.

When I visited the plant they were in the midst of making a batch of Alaskans. For the most part it is simply a matter of making Super Redhawks with a different barrel. The roll marks are different, so part of the set-up and planning is to make sure you have the right rollstamps and such. (To mess it up would be to make a short run of instant collectors' handguns, if they even left the factory.)

The Alaskan assembly process is the same as that of Super Redhawks: the frames get trigger guards and cranes fitted, then they get their finish applied. A cylinder gets fitted, and the lockwork then goes in. The barrel? That's where it gets tricky. In case you haven't noticed, the barrel of the Alaskan is flush with the frame, and recessed to protect the crown. From the moment I saw one I was curious as to how they got the barrel screwed in and tightened. Was it a mandrel that fit the rifling? Did they have a fore-and-aft hydraulic fixture that clamped the barrel at forcing cone and crown? No, much simpler. When they make the barrels, the lathe profiles the blank and cuts the threads for the shank – a long shank, as that was one of the design goals of the Super Redhawk. The threaded portion of the barrel is just over an inch

Oh, to be able to get frames ready to go, for experimental gunsmithing projects.

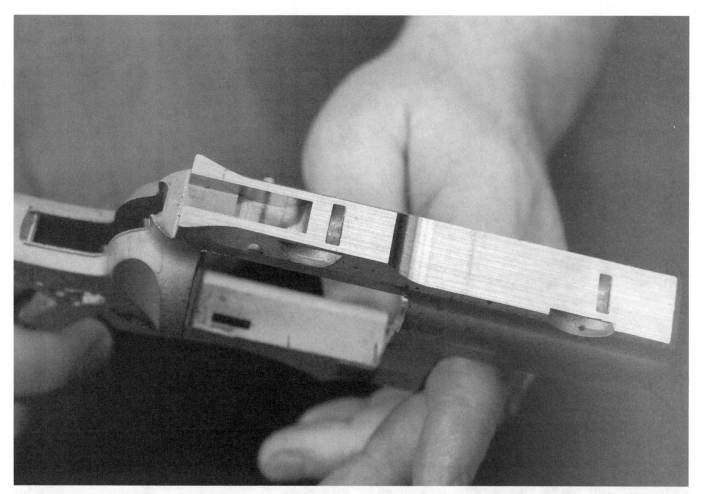

The flats cut, and the slots, let us know this is a Super Redhawk of the normal kind, and not an Alaskan.

in length. The last step of the CNC lathe work on the blank is to mill two flats on the muzzle end. You see, they cut the blanks over-long. There's an angled step as the torque shoulder, and then the slab-sided wrench flats. Yes, wrench flats.

The barrel installer of the Alaskans has the easiest barrel fit of them all. You see, the barrels are simply wrenched in to a standard torque value, and then the rear of the barrel is cut to adjust cylinder gap. Then all the Alaskans take a very short trip back into a special CNC machine that lops off the wrench-flat extension of the barrel and crowns the muzzle. I'm sure the custom gunsmiths who work on Super Redhawk Alaskans (or who had made some before Ruger had made any) had that figured out. But I hadn't, and I think it's pretty trick.

Oh, there is one extra step to making Alaskans that Ruger has to deal with: the front sight. They have to mill a slot for it and drill the hole for its retaining pin. In the world of CNC manufacturing that is stupid-simple. And as a bonus they get to leave out the scope mount machining steps, so the tradeoff is actually to the production lines benefit.

How is the Alaskan? Simply put: a handful. At 41 ounces it isn't that much heavier than an S&W Mountain gun M-29, and is actually lighter than a 6" standard M-29. The Alaskan at 41 ounces has a bit more weight on a Mountain Gun at 38.5, and is lighter than the 6" M-29 at 48 ounces. So with anything over factory-level loads, you're going to pay for your fun and protection. With factory loads in .44 it is a fun handful. With .45 Colt loads in the .45 version it is a big-bore plinker.

Here an assembler is putting the lockwork together. Once done, the DA trigger pull will be useful in an emergency, and the single clean enough to hunt with.

The assemblers know what fate awaits each Super Redhawk: recoil, and lots of it. They build them tough.

With .454 Casull loads it is a beast.

While I'm looking at the Alaskan, I wondered why the 2-1/2" barrel? Yes, I know it makes the barrel flush with the frame, but so what? Except for the looks (which are notable) the barrel length doesn't help all that much. Were I designing my own Alaskan model, I think I'd be happier with a 3-1/2" to 4" barrel, partly to add maybe 50-75 fps to muzzle velocity, but also to add weight and make the package easier to keep in a holster.

As short as it is, you have to have some sort of retaining strap or retention system on your Alaskan. Otherwise it will likely fall out when you move. A 3-1/2" to 4" barrel would be a lot easier to keep holstered.

But Ruger doesn't ask me about such things. I guess if I really want a 4" Alaskan, I'll have to get in line with all the others ordering high-grade custom guns from Hamilton Bowen.

REVOLVERS

— PART EIGHT —
The Old Army

The Old Army was introduced when I was heavily into black powder shooting. We went on the two-week family vacation in 1973 with an impressive load of rifles, handguns, shot, powder and caps, planning to spend the two weeks doing nothing but shooting. Just before we left I picked up a copy of *Guns & Ammo*, with the cover article the brand-new Ruger Old Army revolver. I failed to pick up much else to read. As we were in a cabin in the woods, in the days before cable, satellite TV, cell phones and pretty much any other modern electronic gear, that magazine was all I had to read.

By the end of the two-week vacation I could just about quote the articles at length. For a long time afterwards I could tell you who had what advertisement, on which page. And I had a burning desire for a Ruger Old Army. The only problem was, they were hard to find. As a college student there wasn't much in the way of discretionary income for new guns. So I read, and bided my time. I

As with all other Ruger handguns, you get your Old Army in a 21st century plastic box. Hmmm, a 21st century box, holding a 20th century-alloy of a 19th century-style handgun.

The hammer is flat, but there is no transfer bar. The hammer impacts the percussion caps directly.

was able some time later to get my hands on an Old Army. I was working as a gunsmith, and the poor thing had been brought in for repair. How someone could break an Old Army was beyond me. Well, they hadn't broken it, exactly. What they had done was turned it into a "paper bag" gun. The owner had taken it apart and couldn't get it back together again.

Putting it back together again wasn't a big deal, as the old Army was obviously a Blackhawk modified to work as a cap-and-ball revolver. And by "modified" I mean redesigned so it works that way, not re-built at the factory from Blackhawks that failed QC inspection. Honest, I once had a guy at a gun show (I used to go to them, not so much any more) explain to anyone who would

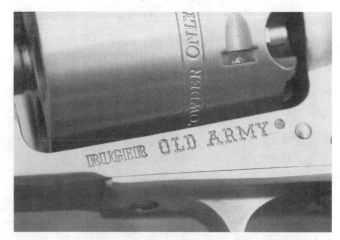

The Old Army is clearly marked, even if the ramrod weren't a big clue.

listen that Bill Ruger was so cheap, and such an un-friend to gun owners, that he made the plants take rejected Blackhawks and turn them into Old Army revolvers.

Not true. Anyone who took more than a few seconds to look at an Old Army would see that the frame is longer in front that that of a Blackhawk. It has to be, to give the loading lever a place for the pivot pin. And that isn't the only difference. But there was no dissuading this guy, so I left. A lesson learned that I have often returned to: "Arguing with a fool makes it difficult for bystanders to see the difference."

The original Old Army was in blue steel with adjustable sights, just like the Blackhawk. As it came out after 1968, all Old Army revolvers have serial number prefixes. They started with Blued guns in the "140" series in 1973, and in 1983 switched to "145." The stainless Old Army started production in 1976 with the "145" series and in 1983 the blued guns were simply folded into the 145 series. In 1994 the "148" series were added. Ruger first offered (and still does) the Old Army in stainless in 1976, a prudent choice for black powder shooters. It isn't that black powder residue in and of itself is corrosive. It simply is hygroscopic. That is, it attracts moisture. In a dry environment black powder residue won't rust, any more than corrosive primers in cartridge firearms

will. But let the humidity rise above a certain level and all bets are off. That said, the stainless steel Ruger uses isn't any more resistant to corrosion than other stainless steels used in the firearms industry. Nor any less. It simply is a lot more resistant, but not rust-proof. As I've mentioned many times before, if the metallurgists added enough chromium and nickel to the iron to make the resulting steel truly rust-proof, it wouldn't be hard enough for use in firearms.

If you don't clean your Ruger Old Army after shooting even the stainless ones will rust. You'll have no one to blame but yourself, because the rest of us have either been there, or warned you. A brief aside: back in the 1970s, when the first of the stainless guns were appearing, a friend of a friend brought his new S&W stainless revolver to me for repair. This was before I was a full-time gunsmith, but everyone knew I loved to work on guns, and his was locked shut. After a bit of struggling I managed to get it open, to find it rusted. Solid. He had shot some blanks through it for the 4th of July. Cheap blanks, made of molded plastic and using black powder. His "cleaning" had been to wipe it off and put it away. July being the

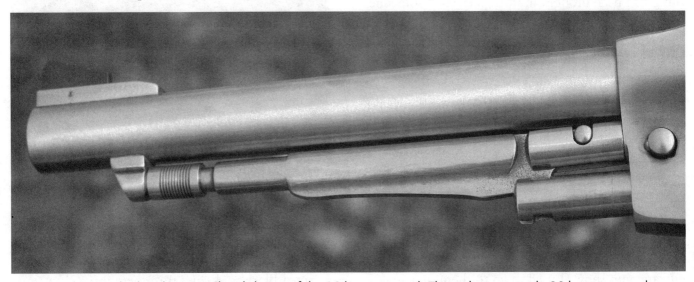

The ramrod is attached and is an updated design of the 19th century tool. The sights are purely 20th century on the adjustable-sight version. (As is the alloy.)

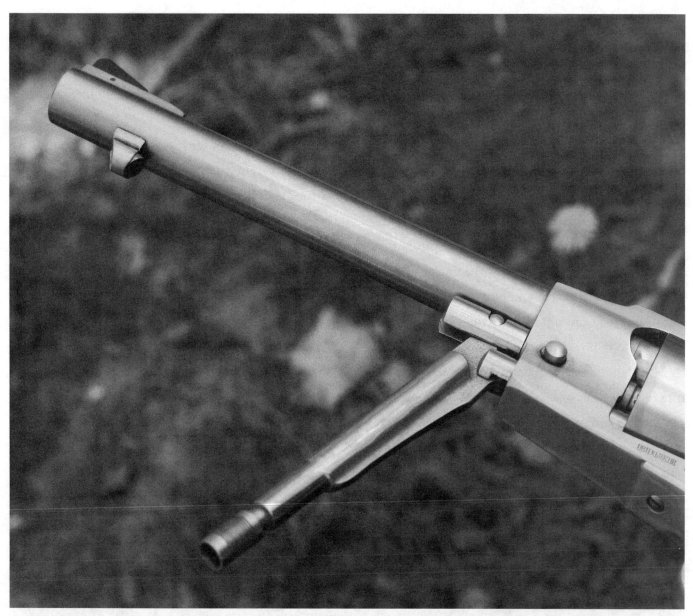

To ram the balls each home over their powder charge (loading each chamber in turn, not all six at once) you unlatch the ramrod and lever the bullet into place.

"desert" part of the weather here, it hadn't rusted right away. But by September the humidity had risen, and the interior was locked shut with rust. The empties had to be pounded out. The chambers and the bore each had a strong resemblance to so much sewer pipe. No rifling, no visible front step on the chambers where the case ended. Just rust. Why hadn't he cleaned it? "Stainless doesn't rust." Was his reply. Well. Maybe the soft 18/8 alloy in silverware doesn't, but firearms steel is harder, and it will rust. End of lecture.

Note the clearance cut in the frame for access to the chamber for the ball and how the ramrod tip is coming down towards the cylinder as the lever moves.

The Old Army is available in blued and stainless, and with adjustable sights and fixed sights.

The one Ruger sent me was an adjustable sight model, stainless, and it looked like an odd Blackhawk. The hammer actually has a nose on it, albeit a flat one. Underneath the barrel is the ramrod. The button in front of the cylinder, that usually holds the center pin in on a Blackhawk or Super Blackawk, holds the whole center pin/ramrod assembly of the Old Army. Press the button in, hinge the ramrod down, and pull the whole thing out. Once the center pin is out, you can work the hammer to remove the cylinder.

The cylinder has six charge holes, each with a nipple screwed in on the rear of it. When you clean, use a slotted wrench to unscrew the nipple and clean them. Cock the hammer, capture the strut, and remove it. Use a screwdriver to remove the action screws, grip frame and anything else you can

remove. Unlike other Rugers, where cleaning after a day's shooting is to remove the cylinder and wash things, with the Old Army you have to be diligent. You'll have to know how to take it all down, scrub it, oil it and reassemble it.

Loading is another interesting difference. With rimfires or centerfire handguns, you simply load the correct cartridge into the firearm. The ammunition manufacturer has done all the hard work for you. Cap and ball revolvers require that you do all the work each time. So, you have to know the drill. First, you'll need lead balls, black powder and the correct-size percussion cap, a #10 or #11. Why the "correct" and two sizes? Not because Ruger can't get the nipple size right, but because the cap makers are not as concerned with precise sizes. The lead balls will have to be pure lead sized .457" and the black powder will have to be black powder granule size "Pistol" or FFFg. (Known at "Three-F" powder.) Some people like to use a loading stand. A loading

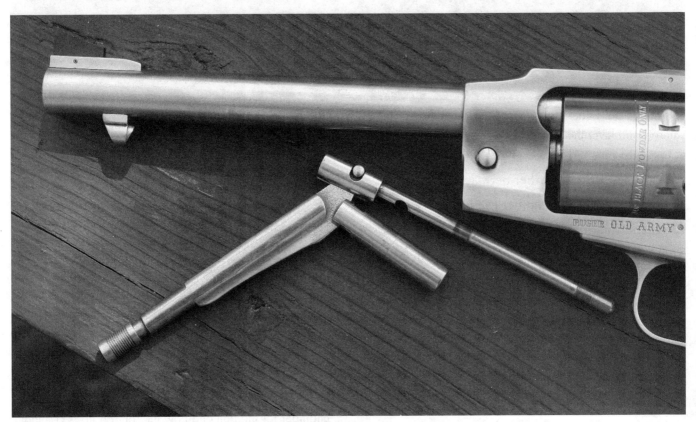

The ramrod assembly comes out for cleaning. Everything comes out for cleaning.

The nipples (which you'll have to remove to clean) are where you place the percussion caps. Note the safety slots between the nipples. That's there you rest the hammer once it is loaded.

stand holds the Old Army (or other black powder revolver) muzzle-up.

Back in the old days we would take a powder flask and use the lever to deliver a charge into the tube (holding the flask upside down with thumb blocking the tube) and then close the lever and pour the powder directly into the chamber. Looking back, I can see where that might get people in trouble. So, the new method is to use the flask the same way: Thumb over the tube. Turn it upside down. Press the spring-loaded charge lever and let the tube fill. Let go of the lever. Turn the flask right-side-up. The tube now has a charge of black powder in it.

Decant the powder into another dish, and then pour from the dish to the chamber. Why do all this? If you're pouring directly into the chamber, and a spark or hot powder granule left over from shooting comes in contact with the powder, the powder will ignite. If that happens while you're holding the flask against the gun, the whole flask might go up.

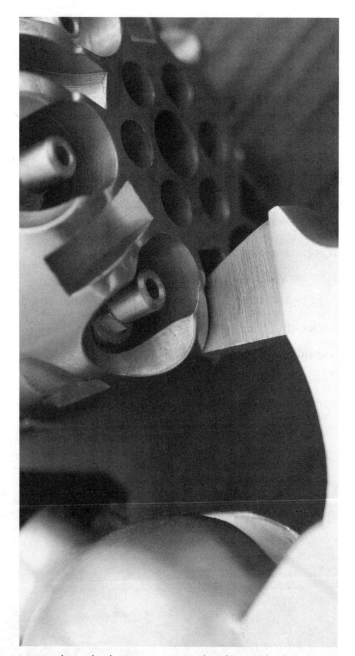

Notice how the hammer rests in the slot. (Cylinder removed from the frame to show the orientation clearly.)

If you're pouring from a dish of 20-30 grains of powder, only the powder in the dish will go up.

Having carefully decanted the powder into the chamber, you place a lead ball on that chamber, rotate it to line it up with the ramrod, and with the rod press the ball home. You can place a wad of grease-impregnated felt under the ball first, or smear lubricant over the ball after it is in place. If you use the correct-size lead balls you'll have a tiny ring of lead shaven off from the ball's circumference. That indicates not only that you have a good seal in the chamber, but you'll give the rifling a good bite on the ball when you fire it. Repeat that, one at a time, until you have all six chambers charged. Now pull the Old Army from the loading stand. Point it downrange (it is loaded, after all) and push a cap onto each nipple, one by one. Once they are all in place you are ready to go.

The Old Army is unique in New Model revolvers in that it does not have a transfer bar. It is, however, safe to carry with all six chambers loaded. If you look at the back if the cylinder you'll notice that the nipple recesses have substantial shoulders on them. Between those shoulders are slots. Each slot is just the right size to accept the hammer nose of the Old Army. Once you've loaded it, you carefully align one of the between slots

under the hammer, and release the hammer to rest inside that slot. Once in place it isn't going to come out of alignment, nor can the hammer nose come in contact with the caps on the nipple on either side.

The same process, in the centerfire guns, is what got a lot of shooters in trouble in the past. If it wasn't OK for them, why is it OK now? The short answer is simple: "A lot of steel vs. a little bit of brass." The shoulders keeping the hammer nose in place are substantial. Those shooters depending on resting the hammer between chambers were counting on the tip of the firing pin, resting between the case rims, to keep the cylinder from turning. It doesn't take much to rotate the cylinder with just the firing pin tip and case rims blocking it. I'm not sure, with the hammer nose in the slot

The cylinder pin is also the ramrod assembly, all held in by the front lateral plunger.

Accurate? You bet. There's a reason the casualty lists were so long after Civil War battles: black powder firearms can be very accurate.

Even after a few shots the Old Army gets lots of fouling. Shoot all day and you'll have to clean it a couple of times even before you go home.

of the Old Army, that you could turn the cylinder with a pipe wrench. (And attempting it would make it an ugly firearm, so please don't try.)

With the Old Army loaded up, and the hammer resting between nipples, you can holster and go about your business. What business would that be, exactly? For the adjustable sight version, plinking hunting and just having a heck of a time. The fixed-sight version was made for the Cowboy Action Shooters. There, they have to have five shots and the six chambers of the Old Army work just fine. CAS competitions have a plethora of divisions or categories. You can shoot one handed or with two, you can shoot one-handed with a gun in each hand, you can use black powder or smokeless.

And you can shoot black powder, cap and ball. That's where the Old Army shines. It is a lot tougher than the open-topped Colt clones. The lockwork of the Old Army is tougher even than that of the Remington cap and ball revolvers, the 1858. I liked those a lot better than the Colts when I was shooting black powder, as they were more resistant to fouling, and less likely to break. The Old Army is a lot tougher, but even it will quit if you don't clean the fouling off now and then during your shooting session. As for it breaking, get real. Rugers don't break. At CAS competitions, you don't have to ask who shoots black powder and who shoots smokeless. If the powder residue and the buckets of scrub water don't give it away, the odor of black powder and its bullet lubes will. Not

Yes, I lusted after an Old Army when they came out. I'll probably have to own one eventually, but the cleaning requirements of black powder always drive me away.

that it's anything bad (they don't refine skunk fat or anything like that to create black powder lubes) but it is noticeable.

Stainless? It makes cleaning easier, but it doesn't eliminate the need. Once you're done shooting, start scrubbing. You will be appalled at the amount of powder residue left behind. If the modern firearm is the equivalent of a gas-burning furnace, your black powder firearm is a charcoal grill. So little of the black powder is actually consumed, and so much is turned into smoke and ash, that it is no wonder smokeless swept the world when it was invented. But sometimes you've just got to step back in time and give the old ways a spin.

— PART EIGHT —
The Vaquero

Cowboy action shooting (CAS) went big-time in 1982, with the organization of the Single Action Shooting Society – basically IPSC with cowboy guns. Now, IPSC in 1982 was still in its infancy. The first .38 Super guns were yet to appear, and compensated guns were still brand-new. We were all shooting single-stack 1911s. (At least those of us who weren't marching to a different drummer, with Browning High Powers, MAB-15, DA revolvers and any old gun we had lying around.) Crossdraw holsters were the rage, and you were considered a demi-god if you could shoot a Par El Presidente on demand.

To shoot IPSC with cowboy guns was to be very eccentric indeed.

The CAS guys found out what had been known a generation before by the quick-draw shooters: the Colt SAA was not up to a whole lot of shooting. Since then we've gained a whole new crop of gunsmiths. These new artists can tune a Colt so it is as reliable as it can be, and a lot more durable than the guns were

The CAS guys and gals insisted on a bright-polish stainless finish to match their nickeled guns.

The high-gloss stainless is a good match to nickel, and if you have a fondness for nickel (I own a few nickel guns) then the New Vaquero will be to your liking.

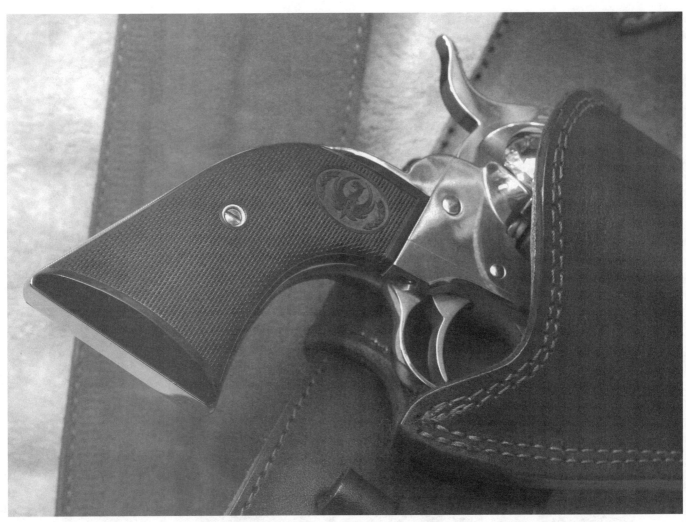

If the original cowboys could have bought a gun like this, they would have. Don't kid yourself, they appreciated progress when it it was something that helped them survive.

before. But even a tuned Colt is not as durable as a standard Ruger. The problem with the Ruger wasn't the advances that made it more durable, it was the advance that made it more modern: the adjustable rear sight.

You need not have been around competitive shooters very long to be unsurprised that some even went so far as to have gunsmiths remove the rear sight. Not just remove the rear sight, but remove any trace of it, and make the Blackhawk look like it had left the factory as a fixed-sight single action, like the SAA. As you can imagine, that takes quite a bit of money. But once it is done, it is done, unlike tuning a Colt and then needing to do it again before the next shooting season.

The Vaquero was a strong seller for a bunch of reasons. One it was as anvil-tough as any other Ruger, and thus even CAS shooters couldn't break it with practice and match shooting. The action was smooth enough, and could be made much smoother via a bit of judicious gunsmithing. The grip frame was steel instead of aluminum as the Old Model Blackhawks had been, always a selling point to the traditionalist. Also, being steel, it was easier to fit new grips to the Vaquero. In fitting grips you might have an occasional "oops" or slip of the file or sanding block. On a steel-frame gun you can take care of those minor "oops" episodes when you refinish the gun after the overhaul. Rugers with aluminum frames needed an anodizing job to refinish them, more expensive and harder to match to the rest of the gun. Steel is also useful in dampening recoil, although the roughly 40-ounce weight of the Vaquero didn't need much help there.

The Vaquero could be had in stainless, which could be buffed up to look like nickel-plating, or you could order it in blued and faux color case-hardened. Topping all that off was the price. In 1993, an Italian clone of the Colt SAA ran you just over $400. The Colt itself was listed at $1,200, but you might wait a long time for yours to appear once you'd special-ordered it. The Vaquero has an MSRP of $30 *less* than that of the Italian clone. You could buy a pair of Vaqueros and with the money saved from not having

bought that one Colt you could buy enough practice ammunition to make you a quite competent CAS competitor.

Introduced in 1993, the Vaquero was an instant hit. Basically it was what the custom gunsmiths had done: a Blackhawk with a fixed rear sight. The frame contours were very much like those of the Colt. However, shooters were not entirely happy. (And if they ever are, you'll recognize it as one of the signs of the coming apocalypse.) The problem, if it was a problem, was the Vaquero's size.

The Vaquero was basically the Blackhawk with fixed sights. But remember back in 1956 when the Blackhawk was chambered in .44 Magnum? Ruger

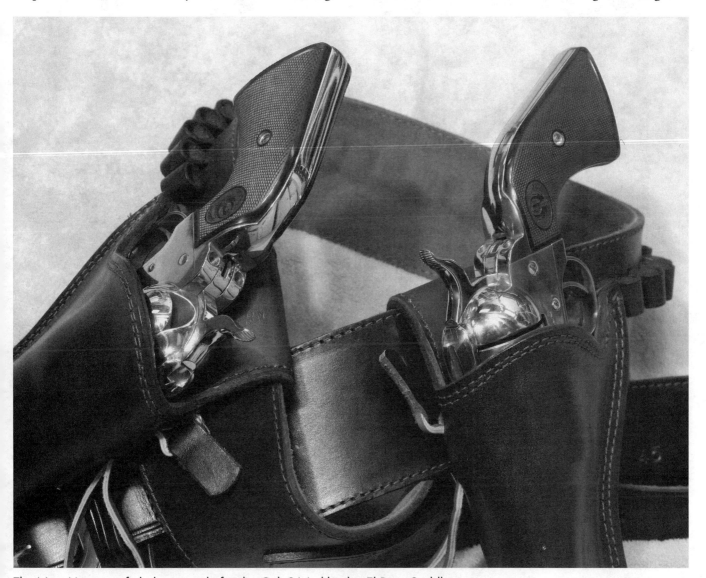

The New Vaqueros fit holsters made for the Colt SAA, like this El Paso Saddlery set.

New Vaquero frames, ready to be transformed into America's favorite new cowboy gun.

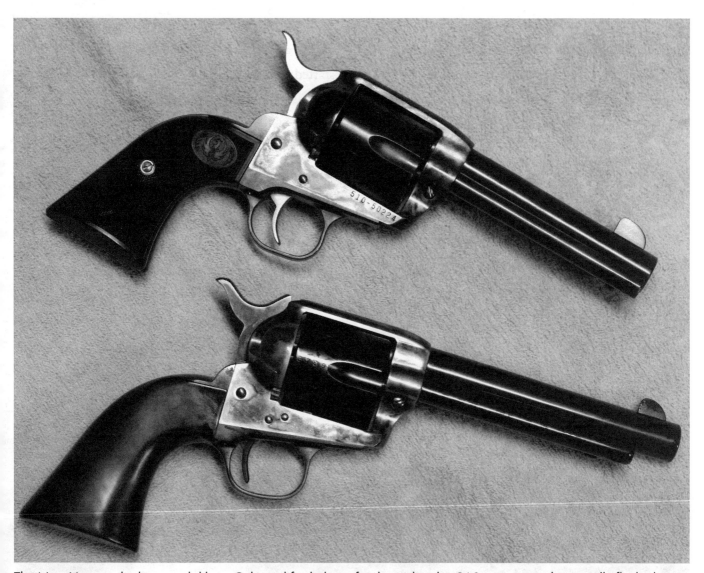

The New Vaquero looks enough like a Colt, and fits holsters for them, that the CAS competitors have really flocked to them.

slightly increased the size of the Blackhawk to fit the .44 Magnum cartridge into what had previously been a .357 Magnum revolver. And then went larger-still with the Super Blackhawk. The Vaquero, since it could be had in .44 Magnum, was made on the Blackhawk .44 Magnum frame pattern. Since most of those buying it were shooting mild .44 Special level reloads, or even lighter loads in the .357 Magnum version of the Vaquero, the gun was too big. And, it didn't fit the holsters the cowboy action shooters had for their Colt SAA revolvers.

Still, Ruger tried to keep CAS shooters happy. In 2000 they changed the Vaquero's ejector rod housing from aluminum to steel, making the CAS shooters happier by adding a fraction of an ounce to the weight. The calibers offered were .357 Magnum, .38-40, .40 S&W, .44-40, .44 Magnum and .45 Colt. The traditional cowboy cartridge left out in the cold was the .32-20, and no one seriously expected those to ever appear. The Vaquero was a large revolver, and making it in .357 Magnum produced a heavy revolver that had inconsequential recoil with the soft loads CAS competitors loved. Despite their grumblings about it being just a tad too big for what they wanted, the cowboy shooters bought them by the truckloads, while complaining that what they really wanted was something smaller. The original Vaquero arrived with a "55" serial number prefix, and in the twelve years it was available Ruger progressed through the "58" prefix block almost in its entirety. As I said, they made a lot of guns.

The New Vaquero has a crescent ejector rod head, like the Colt and clones do. The sight is correct, and the warning markings are on the bottom of the barrel.

In 2005, Ruger came out with the New Vaquero. The New Vaquero received a new prefix, "510," and started over with serial number one. The frame and cylinder were made smaller, the same size as the Colt SAA. In fact, the New Vaquero will fit into holsters designed for the Colt. The frame size is also the same (although not so the sights) size as the 50th Anniversary Blackhawk .44 Magnum that I've also covered in this book. With minor differences in some of the parts – such as the hammer, ejector rod head and the grips being made of checkered black plastic – the New Vaquero looks a lot like a Colt SAA in size and shape.

One change was made specifically for the Cowboy Action Shooters. In some stages (although not many) you have to reload the gun you're shooting with. Usually in Cowboy Action Shooting,

Instead of the two-line patent dates of the Colt, the Ruger has its model name on it: New Vaquero.

The New Vaquero hammer is a close copy of the Colt in shape and length of spur.

especially in SASS matches, you shoot five shots from each of two guns you are wearing, which is why every CAS competitor you've ever seen is a two-gun cowpoke. But occasionally the stage designer will require a reload against the clock. One big strike against the original Vaquero (and the New Model Blackhawk and Super Blackhawk) is the ratchet. As you rotate the cylinder to show each chamber for loading, you'll hear a "click." On a Colt SAA or its clone, the click means you are at the point where the chamber is lined up with the loading gate, and you can load the round.

On the New Model Ruger single actions, however, the click means you *just missed* the point where you could load the chamber, and you can't rotate it back. At that point you can't insert a fresh cartridge if you are loading, and you can't kick the

The cylinder is beveled. Not as much as some SAA revolvers have been, but enough to make re-holstering easy.

empty out if you are unloading. If you try loading anyway, the round will bind and jam in place in the gate. If you try to eject an empty, the rim of it will strike the edge of the loading gate and not leave the cylinder. Cowboy-action gunsmiths made a bunch of money installing "free-spinning" pawls that allowed shooters to rotate the cylinder slightly back and still insert the cartridge.

Now a lot of shooters didn't notice, or care, that the Vaquero had this little problem. Most aren't or weren't CAS competitors. But a bunch were, and they complained. (And also kept gunsmiths busy modifying or installing the pawl that would allow "proper" loading and unloading.)

For the New Vaquero (Does this mean we can call it the "New Model New Vaquero?") the pawl was modified so the click now means you're on-center and can load the cartridge.

Barrel lengths were as before: 4-1/2, 5-1/2 and 7-1/2 inches. Also, the finishes available are as before: bright stainless (which can be buffed up like nickel) and blued/color case-hardened like the original Colts. Calibers so far are fewer; you can have a .357 Magnum or a .45 Colt. But you can't have a .357 Magnum with a 7-1/2 inch barrel. Hey, there are only so many variations they can make at one time. Be patient. If enough shooters ask there will be more.

You can always buy a .357 Magnum and have Hamilton Bowen re-chamber and re-bore it to the bigger caliber of your desire. I would not be the

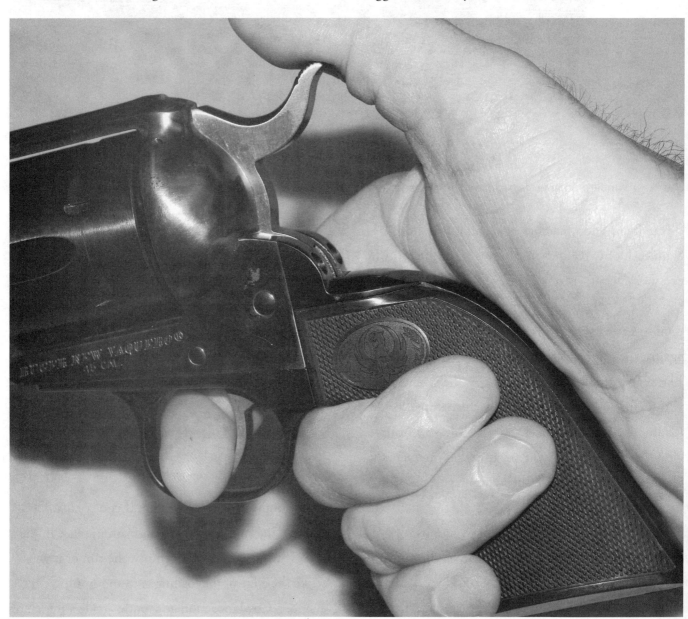

You can see, the hammer spur is easy to reach and gives you lots of leverage in cocking the action.

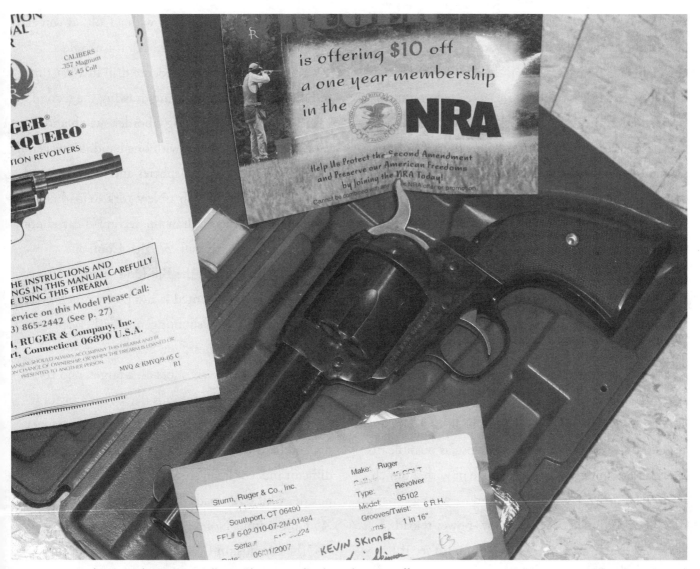

Yes, it was such a good gun I actually made out a check and sent it off to Ruger.

least bit surprised to know that Hamilton has on his workbench a New Vaquero in .357 Magnum with instructions from a customer to re-bore the cylinder and barrel to .44 Special. Those .44 Special guys are just a bit touched in the head and will spend a lot of money to get a gun just the way they want it in .44 Special.

The color case-hardened finish on the Vaquero, New and Old, is an interesting bit of work. The original Colts were made that way as a means of both hardening them and providing a more-durable surface for the frames. The Vaquero and New Vaquero, being made of modern alloys, had no such need, either for hardness or for durability.

But shooters wanted the old finish. You cannot case-harden alloy steel. The alloy is already hard, and the process simply doesn't induce the alloy to absorb any more carbon. So Ruger found a chemical process that produces the wavy colors of color case-hardening. The prototype stainless guns had the customary brushed Ruger stainless finish on them. I can well imagine the looks the cowboy shooters gave those when they saw it at the first trade show. For the first time, the production people had to figure out how to get a bright finish on stainless guns so the cowboy shooters could have a Ruger that looked like it was nickel-plated.

The New Vaqueros are marked with the name

on the left side and the serial number on the right side of the frame. The original Vaquero had "55" through "58" prefixes, while the New Vaquero has a "510" prefix. Best of all for those really hung up on aesthetics, the warning label rollmarked onto every Ruger firearm, is done on the underside of the Vaquero barrel. You don't have to look at it, or as some have had done in the past, get it polished out.

I test-fired the pair of New Vaqueros in the usual manner, and then in an unusual manner. First I shot them to see how they felt (like Colt SAA revolvers, by the way) and for accuracy. The handling, feel, recoil and accuracy were what you'd expect: they felt like a Colt SAA, and they shot as well or better than Colts do. I then tested them for use as home-defense guns. People might look at cowboy action shooters and conclude that the funny getups (you have to dress period-correct, or as close as possible, to shoot in a SASS match) mean you're in with a bunch guys and gals who can't shoot. You'd be wrong. They can shoot. But they usually use low-power reloads. I wanted to test using full-power ammo to see if I could successfully shoot some practical shooting drills using the New Vaqueros.

I started with the classic El Presidente drill. There, you start with your back to the three targets at ten yards. Hands up. On the signal you turn, draw and fire two shots at each of them. Then reload and fire two shots again. In the early days of IPSC, if you could get all "A" zone hits and do the drill in the "par" time of ten seconds or less, you were a really good shooter. If you could do it on demand, you were a demi-god. Now, top shooters with Open guns (optics and compensators) can do it regularly under five seconds. Your average club shooter with a USPSA "B" card, working on moving up into "A," can do it. I did not reload; instead I used the second

gun. You cannot do this drill with a Colt, as you can't have it loaded in all six chambers. It isn't safe.

I cannot do the El Presidente drill in a Par time re-holstering the first gun and drawing the second. I can't get all "A" hits doing a border switch and shooting the second gun with one hand. However, if I mix my centuries, hemispheres and locations, and do the El Presidente with a New York Reload (simply drop the first gun and draw the second) I can shoot a Par El Presidente with all "A" hits. Cool.

The second drill is the Bill Drill. Named after Bill Wilson, who invented it and pretty much began the modern practical shooting gunsmithery/parts manufacturing business, you draw on a target at seven yards. You fire six shots on a target, and try to get all "A" hits in two seconds flat. With a pistol it is a pretty easy thing; with a double-action revolver, not too hard. With a single action revolver it is very difficult indeed. I can sometimes manage it with powder-puff CAS loads. But a Vaquero using factory .45 Colt ammo? No.

The conclusion I came to is that a single action revolver in general, and the Vaquero in particular, is an entirely suitable defensive gun if you have practiced with it. It or they also have the advantage of being innocuous, almost quaint, when it comes time for the inevitable legal proceedings. Where the local DA might look more closely into your shooting incident were you to use a "practical" pistol with a hi-cap magazine, or surely would do so if you had used an AR-15 or AK, using cowboy guns he's much less likely to. If the report he gets indicates, and the briefing from the investigating detectives tells him, that you used a pair of single action revolvers and (maybe) a lever-action rifle, he's likely to conclude there's no political or PR traction there for him and move on to the next case.

No, a digital watch isn't exactly "cowboy" but then I don't worry about that. I worry about shooting fast and hitting well. With a pair of Ruger New Vaqueros, both are easy.

The new Ruger Vaquero.

I was so impressed by the New Vaquero that I broke the cardinal rule of gun writers: I bought one. Where the ones Ruger had sent for testing were a pair of stainless guns, I bought a blued and case-colored one. The grips are plastic but look like the hard rubber of a Colt. The grip is so similar to that of a Colt that you'd be hard-pressed to tell them apart with your eyes closed. The ejector rod head is a crescent shape, and I'm sure some CAS shooters will replace that with a button-head rod, "just because." The pawl allows for loading and unloading when you've reached the click. The hammer spur on the New Vaquero is a bit longer than that of the Vaquero, for easier reach and cocking. And, the front edge of the cylinder is beveled, like many of the Colt models were. Beveling is not just a cosmetic issue,

but it also makes the cowboy action shooters work easier. Unlike my El Presidente, a CAS competitor is not allowed to drop his first gun when he goes for his second gun. (Don't worry about me, I used a cardboard box with an old blanket in it.) He (or she) must re-holster. The beveled edge of the cylinder makes re-holstering much faster and certain.

The transfer bar of the New Model action means it is safe to carry with all six chambers loaded. And I got mine in the only correct barrel length, as far as I'm concerned: 4-5/8". Yes, Colts were made in a bunch of lengths, and those cowboys dressing as period-correct ex-cavalry troopers would pack a 7-1/2" barreled gun. But to my taste and preference in balance, the 4-5/8" barrel length is the only one.

RUGER

— PART TEN —
The Convertibles

The idea is as old as cartridge firearms: if you have a firearm with a common bore size, you find a way to have it fire more than one particular cartridge. In most firearms, the idea comes up short, as the cost of converting from one to another is too great. One example might be trying to take a .45 ACP pistol and converting it to 9mm, to take advantage of cheap surplus ammo. The problem becomes much too expensive, and pretty quickly.

Why? The 9mm and .45 ACP are too much different in their case diameters. The .45 ACP rim is nominally .480" in diameter, and the 9mm Parabellum is .394". Asking an extractor to reach in the .040" difference and reliably extract empty cases is just asking too for much. Not to mention that the slide and recoil spring are probably proportioned for the .45 and thus too heavy and too strong. Another approach would be to convert a 9mm Parabellum to accept 9mm Largo, having found a stockpile of that surplus and cheap. However, while that appears

The convertible case comes with all the usual stuff, plus an extra cylinder.

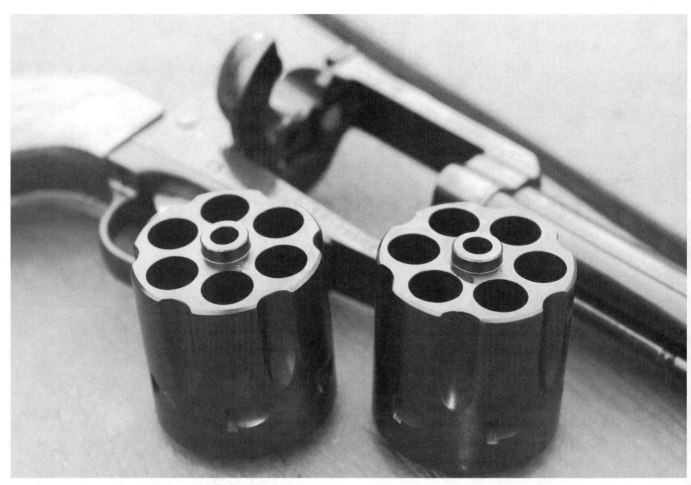

You can swap calibers by changing cylinders, but you must do it only with the cylinders unloaded.

easier, it might not be. The 9mm Parabellum's rim is .394" and the Largo's is .392". Hey, things are looking up. However, the 9X19 case (another name for the 9mm Parabellum/Luger) is .754" long, while the Largo is .910" long, the overall loaded length that each is allowed to be are 1.169" for the 9X19 and 1.320" for the Largo.

The Largo is too long to fit into magazines designed for the 9X19 cartridge. You could convert something in .38 Super to accept the Largo, as the Super has an OAL of 1.280" and you might find the Largo ammo has enough leeway to fit. However, as there are no Ruger pistols chambered in .38 Super, that doesn't give us much joy.

In fact, about all you can do with Ruger pistols is fit a new barrel (if you can find one) in a

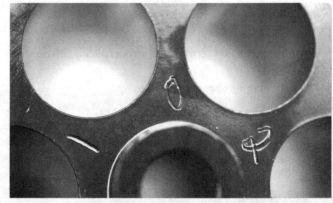

The two cylinders are marked with the last three digits of the serial number, so you won't mix them up with other Rugers you might own. (It also helps Ruger's assemblers.)

necked-down version of an existing caliber. That would mean a 9mm with an extra barrel in .30 Luger, which Ruger did. The KP89X, a stainless P89, could be had with an extra, .30 Luger barrel. The .40 S&W case has the .357 SIG's head dimension, but there have been no Ruger barrels in that caliber. You'd have to find a custom barrel maker and convince him to make you a .357 SIG barrel for your Ruger – which would likely cost you more than the Ruger did. In .45 ACP we have the .400 Corbon and the .40 Super. Not only would they probably cost you as much as a new Ruger, like the .357 SIG barrel, the .40 Super is an orphan with no makers offering loaded ammo. You can, however, get brass from Starline. But the .40 Super is such a hot cartridge that even the tough Ruger pistols would be hammered by it. No, pistols aren't convertible-friendly.

Which leaves revolvers. Convertible double action revolvers are not in the cards. The fabrication of a new cylinder isn't too bad, but making a new crane is a real bit of work. It would be a gunsmith's ordeal to make one, and he'd be showing off if he did.

So we are left with single action revolvers, the natural home of convertible handguns. All we really need are two cartridges with identical or close-enough bore dimensions. As long as the cases are both short enough to fit in the cylinder, and the rims of the cases aren't so large they'd overlap on the back end when loaded, you can do it. And Ruger has done it on their Blackhawk frames. As the first didn't arrive until after the New Model action, all convertibles are New Model Blackhawks, and are safe to carry with all six chambers loaded. There were some Old Model Blackhawks made in .45 Colt, (not convertibles) and if someone has fitted a spare .45 ACP cylinder to it they could

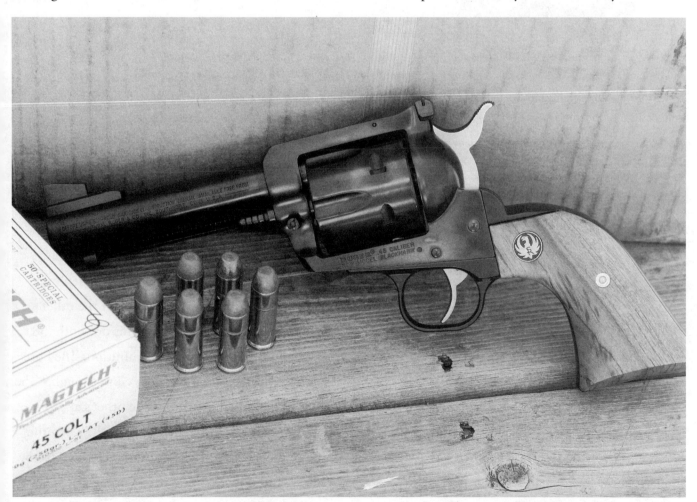

The Ruger Blackhawk in .45 Colt has always been a very nice, handy and powerful handgun. Now you can have it in the ubiquitous .45 ACP, too.

They do differ in length, and the cylinders for each are machined accordingly. If you plan to go to the range, take both ammos and both cylinders.

With the two cylinders side-by-side you can see how closely the two .45s match.

have a faux "Old Model" Blackhawk convertible. Always look for the transfer bar when handling any single action Ruger, regardless of caliber.

The first of the convertibles was the .45. The .45 Colt and the .45 ACP have bore diameters close enough to work. The old dimensions of the .45 Colt called for a .454" groove diameter, but modern-production .45 Colt revolvers (the Ruger being one of those, naturally) now use .451" bore diameter grooves. The .45 was followed by the 9mm/.38 /.357 Magnum conversion. The 9mm cylinder only takes 9mm rounds, but the other cylinder uses (as all .357 Magnums do) both .38 Special and .357 Magnum ammunition. The bore diameters of those two are also "close enough." The 9mm is a nominal .355" and the other's a .357". Two thousandths difference isn't much, when the lands (the part that sticks up in the bore, grabs the bullets, and imparts the spin) are a total of at least ten thousandths high. Sometimes more. The other two convertibles are not so common, and they offer entirely different uses, but the option is the same in both: use the older cartridge for nostalgia, and the newer one for power. Those combinations are .32-20/.32 Magnum and .38-40/10mm.

The .32s are close enough in that the dimensions of the older cartridge, the .32-20, have varied over a large enough set of numbers in the near century and a half since its inception that the new cartridge fell right into the "acceptable" spread of .32-20 specs. The .32-20 is a persnikity cartridge to reload and can have the sloppy reloader tearing his (or her) hair out in short order. It is best reserved for nostalgia shooting and use in cowboy action matches. The .32 H&R Magnum is thoroughly modern, easy to reload, and can be pumped up to brisk pressures and velocities. If you need small-game or light-recoil defensive loads, the .32 Magnum is your choice, not the .32-20.

The .38-40 and the 10mm use the same diameter bullets for a simple reason: the developers of the original .40 pistol cartridge; the .40 G&A, used .38-40 bullets in their R&D. As they and everyone else who followed needed bullets with which to load and experiment, they all stuck with a .400" diameter bullet. So those two cartridges are a perfect fit in the bore. However, the .38-40 makes the .32-20 look easy to reload, and the 10mm makes the .32 look puny in power. If you want power, but not .44 Magnum recoil, the 10mm is yours. If you want big-bore nostalgia with light recoil, the .38-40 can be your option.

Which brings us back to the two .45s, the gun Ruger sent me.

The choices are not many. You can have your convertible right now blued or blued. You can have the 9mm/.38/.357 in a 4-5/8" or a 6-1/2" barrel. You can have the .45/.45 in a 4-5/8" or 5-1/2"

barrel. And you can have adjustable sights. I chose the .45/.45 with 4-5/8" barrel. What can I say, I'm a sucker for the barrel length. It comes with two cylinders, one in .45 ACP and one in .45 Colt. Ruger did miss one trick and that is on the .45 ACP cylinder. It is not reamed to accept the rims of .45 Auto Rim cases. As I have a good supply of it on hand and Black Hills loads it, I think I'd want that option. Luckily it is an easy enough task. Someone like Hamilton Bowen could probably do it in his sleep, but any competent gunsmith with a lathe and the knowledge of how to use a four-jaw chuck can do it.

The two cylinders have the last three digits of the serial number marked on their fronts. That way if they are separated during assembly or bluing, they can be matched back up. To swap them you simply press the center pin latch, pull the center pin out, open the loading gate, lift out the old cylinder, install the new one and re-install the center pin. Until recently I would have assumed that "Unload it before you swap cylinders" part was not necessary to explain. However, I found a guy at the local range doing just that a while back. He looked at it as a "combat reload" of his convertible. Needless to say I was surprised, almost even struck speechless. So, I'll put it here for you, the editors, and anyone who cares to research this book if they ever think to drag Ruger into court: DO NOT SWAP LOADED CYLINDERS IN YOUR CONVERTIBLE REVOLVER. Unload it first.

One complaint some have is that the differing weight bullets will strike to different points on the target. Maybe with the 9mm/.357 combo that could be a problem. A high-velocity 9mm 115-grain bullet and a 158-grain .357 Magnum load just might do that. However, the .45 ACP bullet

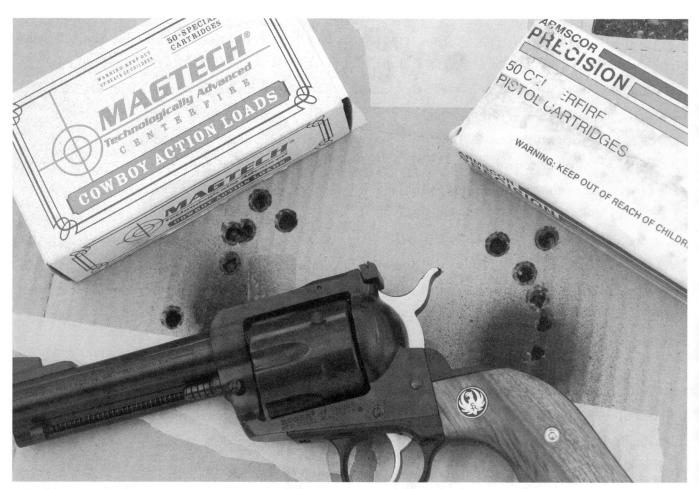

I did not have a problem with point-of-impact differences between the two calibers.

weight range (185 to 230 grains) and the .45 Colt range (225 to 255 grains) overlap so much that it isn't much of a problem. Indeed, I didn't have a problem when I was testing. I used Magtech 255-grain lead bullets in the .45 Colt, and Armscor 230-grain FMJ in the .45 ACP. The group centers were close enough to call them the same.

They ejected easily, the Blackhawk handled nicely, and the concept was once again proven to be useful. Blackhawks have not been the only convertible Rugers made. There have been Bearcats in .22LR/.22 Magnum, Single Sixes in the same combo, and Single Sixes made in the .17 HMR/.17 Mach II. The

convertibles are listed only in the 9mm/.357 and the .45/.45 right now, but given enough demand Ruger will no doubt make the others again. If you can't wait, then get out and get the one you want now, before the collectors bid the prices up. One thing to note: if you have a convertible, and you plan on going to the range, be sure and pack both ammos and both cylinders. Otherwise, Murphy's Law ("Anything that can go wrong, will") will have you at the range with the ammo for one and the cylinder for the other. (Ask me how I know this.) The best thing to do is keep the conversion cylinder with the parent revolver at all times.

Chapter 5

Reloading for Rugers

Y ou might ask "why?" Why would you want to reload for your Ruger handgun? For some, reloading isn't possible. Even if it were technically possible to reload a .22LR cartridge, there wouldn't be any cost savings. But cost isn't the only reason to reload. The best way to answer the question is to pose two questions in return: Have you priced ammo lately? Or have you found a situation where the ammo you could buy wasn't what you needed?

Price first. The quick and easy place to put the blame on spiraling ammo prices is on those "gouging ammo companies, looking to make a quick buck." Someone will do the calculation of just how much copper goes into a bullet (or loaded cartridge,) calculate the current market price for copper, and immediately start blaming the companies. Or just blame them, calculations be damned. There is more than just the cost of copper that goes into ammo. There is also the cost

Some have had good luck with .38/.357 belling stems as large at .355" I prefer smaller, and even use a .348" for lead 9mm bullets in the .38/.357.

.38 Specials that get old and tired usually crack at the case mouth.

of transporting the copper, the lead, the powder, the cost to fabricate all those into a form that can be loaded as cartridges, and then the shipping to get it to your door or store.

As if the simple cost of gasoline going up wasn't enough, there's a war on. The US government went from buying roughly half a billion .223 cartridges to one and a half billion .223 cartridges a year. And they still don't have enough. Quick soapbox time: if you think you're going to need a lot more of something, wouldn't you line up suppliers for it? Or say, build more ammo plants? We're in the same fix in ammo that we are in gasoline: we have no new plants to make any. We haven't built any new oil refineries for over thirty years. We also haven't built any new ammo plants, at least not those capable of producing the kind of ammo, in the volumes needed, for the military. Anyone who can make ammo finds it sucked away by big buyers. All excess capacity goes to training ammo, while the lone US military ammo plant, Lake City, produces combat-needed ammo. We should have built a new plant or three as soon as we decided we had to start shooting people.

Law enforcement is in the same boat. Due to the war, agencies are shooting more. They either have to, to deal with more agents or more requirements, or they feel the need to because they have to be ready. It is an iron law of economics that when the demand for something exceeds its supply, price skyrockets. You can call it gouging, black market profiteering, or any other name, but it is an immutable law. It is the same as if you fall off a cliff: Gravity works.

Now, as if all this wasn't enough, throw China into the mix. The Three Gorges Dam project is requiring a noticeable percentage of the world's production of steel rebar and concrete. That's just one project. China is building the equivalent of a new million-person city at a brisk clip. I've seen estimates of their building as anywhere from a million-person city equivalent every two weeks to one a day. Now, they aren't building them for new people, as the population is relatively static. But all those Chinese want to be in the 21st century with the rest of us. That means buildings for people and powerplants to supply electricity to the buildings. Oh, and all that electricity has to go through copper wires. Every skyscraper you see on the Shanghai or other major Chinese city consumes more copper than is found in all the ammo you and your buddies at the gun club (heck, the whole gun club) shoot in a years' time.

Where did you think copper prices were going to go?

Now that I've scared you, how about this: have you gone to the range, or shot in a match, and wanted a particular kind of load, but no one made it? Then make it yourself. If you want to teach a new shooter how to shoot, but all you have is a .357 Magnum Blackhawk, buying a new gun is fun

The police are shooting more and more these days, and that puts a lot of stress on ammo deliveries.

but kinda throws the budget out of kilter. If you reloaded, you could make the ammo you needed: ammo that was soft in recoil for your new shooter, and easy on the wallet too.

One of the biggest lures of reloaded ammo, and the cost to do so, is that "It costs less to shoot." Which is true, but not what happens in the end. What really happens is that you end up shooting more for the amount of money you would have spent anyway, and probably end up going to the range a bit more often because "reloaded ammo is so cheap to shoot." The end result is that for the most part, those who reload end up as better shots than those who don't reload. Reloaders shoot more often, and shoot more volume. With ammo

on hand, reloaders are more likely to give in to the temptation to shoot a match at the gun club, and thus learn even more than the guys who don't reload. Become a better shot; reload.

"But reloading is arcane, dangerous and there are laws against it." Not so. First, the arcane part. Back in the old days it may have been less than transparent. There weren't many reloading manuals and there weren't many good tools to use. In a lot of cases you had to make your own stuff. When I started reloading it was still possible to buy crappy dies, presses and components. A lot of people either just didn't know or didn't care. And they were the ones making the stuff. Now the situation is a lot easier. First, there are a lot

The 9mm Parabellum comes from the German Army adoption of the Luger. They weren't happy with the .30 Luger, and wanted something bigger.

Progressive presses often use die plates. Once the dies have been adjusted and locked into the plate, the whole assembly can be removed and re-installed without needing to do any more adjustments.

of reloading manuals, some might even say there are too many. You can buy manuals from people who make bullets, from people who make powder, from people who make ammo, and from people who don't do anything but make manuals. The reloading components field is an embarrassment of riches. You can buy your bullets, powder, primers and cases based on economy, performance, brand name or any combination of those variables. You can be the scrounger at your gun club, the one who never lets an empty hit the ground unless someone has already claimed it.

At my gun club you're required to at least pick up your empties and throw them in a recovery bin if you don't want them. Most of the time it works. Occasionally it doesn't. More than once I've gone out to practice or test guns, found one or more of

the ranges with brass on them, and started my day by recovering a gallon of empties. Once I picked up a gallon each of 9mm, .40 and .45 ACP brass. Here's what the police call a "clue:" the empties are the expensive part. Obviously, someone who did not reload went out and shot a thousand rounds or so and left the empties. Works for me; I got them.

Free brass makes your reloads that much less expensive. Question: how long does brass last? As with so many things in life, the answer is not always a satisfactory one: "It depends." If you shoot a low-pressure round at low pressures and your chamber is tight and your sizing die (this will all be explained in a bit) is not too tight, they will last a long time. I have .45 ACP empties that have been reloaded so many times you can't read the headstamps on the case any more. They work fine. At the other extreme, if you run your reloads right to the maximum pressure, and your brass expands a lot due to a large chamber, it won't last so long. A couple of dozen cycles, maybe less. An example of that would be the popular hunting loads in .44 Magnum, with a heavy hardcast bullet at high velocity. If your brass cost you $20 (a decent price, at the 500-piece rate for the bigger calibers) and they only lasted you a dozen loadings, you would have spent a grand total of less than a tenth of a cent on each empty, for each shot fired. That's $20 for the brass to shoot 1,200 rounds. The powder alone will cost you more than $20. No, the cost of brass, if your treat it well, is inconsequential to your shooting.

Dangerous? The question is not is it dangerous, but how dangerous is it compared to other things?

People think of a pound of gunpowder and go "Ohmygod, a stick of dynamite!" No. In fact, the burning energy of that pound of powder is a lot less than the gallon can of gasoline you have in the garage for your lawn mower. The powder will burn, yes. If it didn't it wouldn't be of much use to us. But what it won't do is turn into vapors and explode when the garage burns. It won't leak out and start fires in other locations. What gun powder won't do is explode. (Black powder will. Be very, very careful with it, and don't let your guard down.) Gun powder burns merrily, but that's it.

Primers can detonate, which is why you leave them in their little sleeves until you go to load them. Bullets? Bullets are just heavy. The lead in them is not a problem unless you suck on them

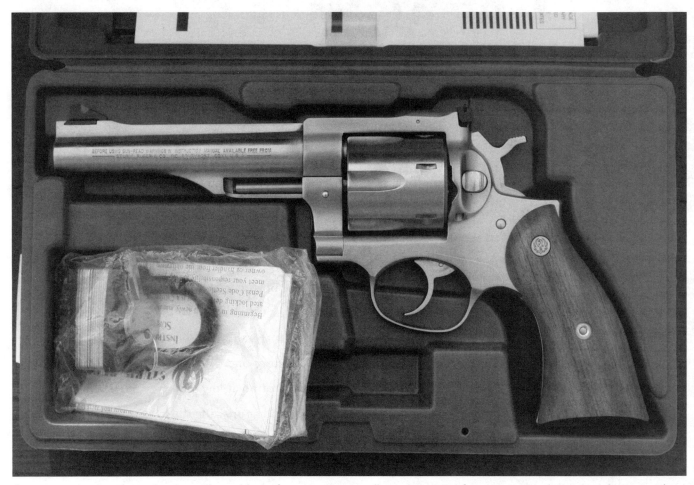

If you go to a shooting school you'll need lots of ammo. Some will insist you use factory ammo, but many don't. Just be sure your ammo is reliable, or you'll be the butt of many jokes.

The .41 Magnum does not share a bullet diameter nor case with any other handgun cartridge. It is a great cartridge with a limited future.

like breath mints, or you fail to wash your hands after loading but before eating.

Laws? Against reloading? I suppose there are, in such places as New York City, but who wants to live there and own guns? There are National Fire Code recommendations for how to store powder, but those are pretty commonsense things: Don't store it near heat, sparks or open flames, don't stockpile a thousand pounds, keep your brother-in-law away from the powder at all times. (OK, I made that one up, but a lot of you were nodding your heads, weren't you?)

Tools

To reload, you need tools. The basics of the reloading process are as follows: Sort, clean, size,

deprime, reprime, neck size/bell, powder charge, bullet seat, crimp, gauge, and label. You do these things with specialized tools.

To save money and time, you should think of reloading as a volume operation. Yes, you can load on a single-stage press (one that holds a single die at a time) but you won't be making a lot of ammo that way. Also, to save money you should buy in volume. As an example (the actual prices will vary depending on your location and the state of the metals market) a box of primers (100 of the little initiators) could cost you $2.99 at the local gun shop. A carton of primers (1,000) of them will cost $21.99. A sleeve (5,000) will cost you $89.95. The peR-00100 primer prices of those units are as follows: $2.99, $2.19 and $1.79. That is why some reloaders get together and buy ten sleeves at once. They get them for $1.59/100 (as of the Spring of 2007). Ditto powder, bullets, and in the rare times they have to buy them, empty brass.

Brass starts the process. With the components on hand, you sort your brass that you picked up at the range. You sort because even if you only wanted your own brass, and the range is relatively clean, you'll still have one or two (or more) "other brass" on our collection. That other brass may simply be a lone .357 Magnum empty in your pile of .38 Specials. Or, you arrived, found the place knee-deep in brass, and scoured it all up before shooting. You want to sort in order to make sure you only process the caliber you want in your loading stream. Having a .357 Magnum empty hit your sizer, bell and bullet seat dies will put the brakes in your loading. Getting a .40 mixed in with the 9mms will bring things to an immediate halt, as it won't fit the sizer.

You can sort and remove all the brass that isn't yours: the exact brand, type and load you fired in your session. Or, you can accept all the brass of the correct headstamp. For our example, that would be all brass with ".38 special" on the case head, and not worry about Federal/Winchester/CCI, etc. There are times to fuss over exact details, and times to not bother. The time to fuss is if you are loading "to the max." An example would be the .44 Magnum, loaded with 300+-grain grain bullets, to maximum hunting velocities. There, a few percentage points difference in case capacity or neck tension could make a difference. When not to? When loading .38 Special plinking ammo. You'll be loading that at not much more than half the maximum pressure, and there minute differences in

case capacity, neck tension and the like won't matter at all.

With your brass sorted, you must clean it. If you don't, the dirty brass will scratch your dies. Scratched dies then scratch brass, which then only last a few loadings before they split along the scratches. You can chemically clean, you can tumble/vibrate, or you can do both. The chemical cleaners are the Birchwood Casey brass cleaners. Mix the concentrate, and pour it into a container. Dump your brass into the mixture. Leave for five minutes or so. Decant the liquid into a storage container (a properly re-marked one gallon milk jug works fine here) and then rinse your brass in

Reloading can save you money, or get you more shooting for the money you spend. But to get the best of reloading, you need to buy in volume. Don't buy primers or bullets in less than a 1,000 and powder in less then 8-pound jugs.

hot water from the tap. As hot as it comes. Pour the water out and spread your brass on an old towel in the sun. On a hot, dry summer day the brass will be dry in a few minutes.

To tumble/vibrate clean, you partially fill a tumbler or vibrator with ground corn cobs, ground walnut hulls or rice. Then dump in your brass. (Each model and size will have different requirements for how much "full" full is.) You can add some brass polisher, too, if you'd like. Avoid the aggressive brass cleaners like Brasso. They contain ammonia, which can chemically work-harden the brass. Run the machine for at least a couple of hours. The grubbier the cleaning media, the longer you'll need to run the machine. Even when the corn cob/walnut/rice is so grubby you don't want to touch it, it will still be cleaning your brass. It will just take longer.

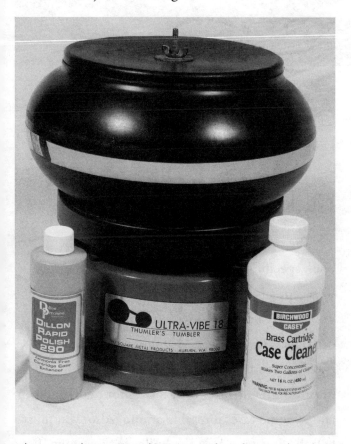

Clean your brass. Dirty brass scratches dies, and it also makes for low-quality ammo.

You can chemically clean and then tumble/vibrate your brass for that "like new" shine. That's what I do. I do not do it because I'm eager to have the shiniest brass, but because I'll typically run the vibrator day and night to clean piles and piles of brass, and then dump the clean brass into clean plastic storage bins with lids. There it can wait as long as needed before being loaded, clean and dust-free.

Sizing

Sizing (reforming the fired brass to proper dimensions) and decapping, in almost every reloading die set or press, are done in a single operation. When you fire the round, a powder burns, pressurizes the case, and expels the bullet. The brass expands to the limits of the chamber and, being springy, relaxes to a slightly smaller size. But that relaxed, post-firing size is larger than the pre-firing size. So you have to squeeze the empty back down to the original size. That is re-sizing. While you're at it, you might as well punch out the fired primer. The die does that for you. You should resist the temptation to save a few bucks by buying the less expensive steel-only sizing dies. Buy a tungsten carbide (T-C), plated steel or other heavy-duty dies. Their sizing rings are much harder than steel and will last longer. it also won't need sizing lube. Sizing lube definitely speeds things up in a T-C die, but isn't needed except for the extremes. Again, if you're loading super-heavy bullets in .44 Magnum (or .45 Colt) cases to the max pressure, you might want to use both a T-C or plated die and lube, or you'll find yourself having to stand on the press handle to resize those cases.

Reloading can be relaxing, enjoyable, and turn out lots and lots of ammo for your practice and competition needs.

Reloaders who load for Rugers are in particular need of T-C dies and lube, for exactly that.

regularly, and make sure grit or powder doesn't build up in the feed system.

Re-priming

Having punched out the old primer, you need to put a fresh one it its place. You can do this with a hand primer or the priming arm on the press. Progressive presses, which either require hand-advancement or auto-advance the rounds, will have a priming system built-in. Hand-seating is the precise method, but it is used only by those crafting the top-end loads, who want everything absolutely exact. If you use a progressive press, keep your priming system clean. Strip and wipe it down

Neck Sizing/Belling

The case has now been sized down to the book specification minimum. It may be too small to accept a bullet, the right size or too large. Too small can be lived with for most, but not all cartridges, just right is what you want, but "just right" depends on the caliber and use. Too big must be attended to, for it makes for poor ammo, and in some cases unusable ammo. Also, you must bell the case mouth so the bullet seats cleanly. If you don't, you can (and will) shave bullet lube or bits of bullet off, which will wedge in place in the round or the die. After enough of that, the die gets gunked up, or you start having bullets/rounds that won't chamber. Or the base of the bullet catches on the mouth of the brass, and when you go to seat the bullet you crumple the case. Bell enough to cleanly seat all bullets and no more. You'll have to take the bell out when you crimp, and doing too much belling simply means more work for you and the brass.

Bullets are kept in the case by neck tension, the "just right" diameter of the belling stem. Not crimp. In the extreme cases you need both, but you can't keep a heavy bullet in the case with crimp alone.

If your belling stem leaves the inside of the case too large, the bullet won't be held properly; it will either set back in pistols when feeding or jump forward on recoil when firing. A bullet set back in the case increases pressure. In some cases it has been known to increase pressure enough to blow a hole in the case. Yes, that is just as messy and exciting as it sounds. Bullets that "jump" the neck, pull forward on recoil, can become long enough to stick out of the front of the cylinder and keep it from rotating. Remember, the sixth round in your

If you make good ammo, it will work reliably for you even under bad conditions. Many shooting schools follow the training schedule, rain or shine. (Later on it got really muddy on us. Or should I say, under us.)

You can get this kind of performance if you want. But most shooters don't need that much ammo like this, and just buy it.

revolver has had five jolts from recoil before it has its turn at the barrel.

Powder Charging

You need powder to burn and to launch the bullet. You need the right amount of the right powder for the cartridge and bullet you're firing. Too much of a fast powder increases pressure past a safe level. Too little of a slow powder means inefficient combustion, and lots of ash and unburnt powder flakes. The various reloading manuals will list combinations of bullets, powders and primers for each caliber. One thing to keep in mind when selecting a loading manual: you should have several. Use them as a guide, and work your load up from a safe low level. Also, if you want to load up full-power heavy bullets for hunting, you really should have a chronograph. It measures bullet velocity, and tells you what you're getting.

If the readings are anomalous for the load you are shooting, then something is wrong. Don't just shrug it off. Find out why.

Don't have more than one type of powder on your loading bench at once. If you are loading the classic .44 Magnum load of a 240-grain Keith bullet over 16-17 grains of 2400, you DO NOT want to risk inadvertently loading 16-17 grains of Bullseye. Store your powder across the room, and only bring over the one powder you want for that particular loading session. Or have only one brand and type of powder at all.

Progressive presses such as the Dillon and Hornady bell and inside-size the cases as they drop the powder charge. The belling stem is what activates the powder dispenser. So this stage actually does the two (or three, depending on how you look at it) steps at this one location. This is a good combination of steps.

Bullet Seating

You must insert a new bullet into the primed, powder-charged case. As the case neck is smaller than the bullet diameter, you can't just thumb the bullet in. The press must seat the bullet. The straighter you set the bullet on the case (and the less the seating die has to correct) the more accurate your loaded ammunition can potentially be. Seat to the crimp groove, or to the correct overall length if the bullet does not have one.

Crimping

Crimping is removing the bell and adding bullet retention to the assembled cartridge. You can crimp too little, just right, or too much. For most loads

Progressive presses can't load accurate ammo? Don't tell this handgun, which just fired the group you see from a Ransom rest at 25 yards.

you can crimp as little as possible. That way your brass lasts longer. Some combinations of bullet and cartridge are more sensitive to crimp than others. The 9mm in particular can be very touchy about crimp. Crimp too much, on plated bullets, and accuracy goes all to heck. Crimp too little and you will have failures to feed.

Crimping too much overworks the brass, which leads to early cracking. But on the extreme heavyweights, you must crimp aggressively. Shorter brass life is just part of the cost of running 300+-grain bullets out of a handgun at 1,200+ fps.

Gauging

You should have a loaded-round gauge to check all your ammo. Measure the first few rounds to come off the press, to make sure nothing has changed since the last loading session. Drop the rounds in one at a time. See that they fall in all the way. Turn the gauge over and let them fall free onto a padded surface. If they do not drop in, or drop free, clean the inside of the gauge and try again. If they still don't, find out why. You may have crimped too much (expanding the case under the crimp) or not enough. The bullet may be the wrong one. The brass might just be an overworked one you should have already retired. Find out and fix it. With "just plinking" ammo you can gauge now and then. I like to gauge the first and last few of each box of primers. (Progressives need the primer feed tubes re-filled every 100 primers) For ammo meant for use in matches, or hunting/extreme performance ammo, I gauge each and every one of them.

Labeling

What _is_ this box of ammo? Yes, the headstamp says ".44 Magnum" but is it full power? Plinking? How old is the brass? Whose bullets did I load it with? When did I load this stuff, anyway? Unless you have a single load for your only gun, you have to label stuff. Labeling depends on just how many loads you have, and how detailed you feel compelled to be. If you simply load the same load all the time, and stuff the ammo back into the little 50-round boxes they came in, don't bother. But add another load, and you need labels.

Me, I load in volume (some say extreme volume) and use shoebox-sized plastic containers. Each gets a masking tape base and then load info on the end. I'll have the caliber, bullets, powder type and charge, powder level and any restrictions on what firearms it can and cannot be used in. That way I'll be highly unlikely to grab the .357 Magnum 180-grain bowling pin load, loaded up to a 215 Power Factor, for a plinking session. And since the bullets look similar, I won't find myself

on the firing line with wimpy 158-grain bullets, loaded to a 145 Power Factor, when I need to be whacking pins.

Ruger loaders may not have as much need for firearms restrictions, but you need to remind yourself of some things if you have other firearms. For instance, pistols that have polygonal rifling are not at all happy with lead bullets. If you own one of those as well as your Rugers, you should mark your ammo so you don't have a mix-up. That way, your brother-in-law doesn't dip into the wrong ammo bin at the range and run a bunch of lead-bullet reloads down the barrel of your XYZ pistol.

Trimming

Someone is bound to point out that there is something missing: the trim stage. Rifle-caliber reloaders measure and trim on a regular basis. Not so handgun reloaders. For almost all applications, measuring and trimming is an utter waste of time. All handgun brass will be under-max length. It

.38 and .357 rounds use bullets from 125 to 158 grains in weight.

.357 Magnum cases that expire crack in the sidewall, sometimes like this.

doesn't stretch when you shoot it. And all chambers will be over-long and there is no chance of a case mouth being out in the chamber neck area. How extreme is it the handgun situation? I measured a bunch of .45 ACP cases once, and a bunch of .45 ACP chamber. The max case/minimum chamber dimension is .898" the longest case I measured was .891" long, and the shortest chamber I measured was .905" Those two would still leave a gap of .014" between them.

No, there is only one instance where you will have to worry about case length, and perhaps trim. That is the extreme-heavy hunting loads. Launching a 320-grain bullet at 1250 fps, you want lots of crimp. For that you need consistent case lengths. However, anything within a few thousandths of the same length is good enough. You could literally sit down with a notepad, digital-readout dial calipers, and a bag of new brass, and sort out the ones you needed in an evening. With a bag of 500 empties, you could easily find 100 that were close enough. Do you really think you're going to need more than 100 of those in the next year or two?

Presses

There are single-stage and progressives. The single-stage are the traditional ones: the press holds a single die at a time. You insert your sizing die and re-size all the brass in a batch. (You also re-prime at this point.) Remove the die (they screw into place) and install the belling die. Bell all the brass. Then use a separate powder charge tool to drop a measured powder charge into each case. Remove the belling die and install a seating die. Seat a bullet on each case. Some die sets have the seating die as the crimp die, too. However, it often works out that seating and crimping in one step produces ammunition that is not as accurate as doing them as separate steps.

In a single-stage press, every 100 rounds you load require 400-500 press actuations, plus 100 steps at the powder-drop tool. And lots of time. When I was loading on a single stage press I spent several nights each week in the basement pulling the handle of a press. For that, I'd have 200 rounds to shoot in the weekend. When I got a progressive, I didn't look back.

A progressive press has locations for four, five or more dies in the press. Each pull of the handle processes a case at each of those stations. So one

9MM MIXED MULTIPLE USES
CLEAN SORTED
NO MILITART CRIMP

Cleaned brass can be stored in sealed containers for a long time and still be ready to load.

pull sizes and deprimes (you re-prime on the downstroke). It also does the other operations at the other stations. So starting from empty press to last finished round, 100 loaded rounds requires abut 110 handle pulls. If you load 500 rounds in one session (easy enough to do) you only pull the handle 510 times or so. You also only have to install the dies once each. So you save all the time spent removing and installing each die. They automatically drop powder, saving that time also. The slowest progressive will run at 200 rounds an hour, and the fester ones can top out (with an experienced operator) at over 1,000 rounds an hour. With a progressive setup, you can literally amble down into the basement when your wife's

Label your ammo bins with all the info you think you'll need.

The 40 and 10mm can use the same bullets. Just don't load the .40 with heavy bullets and fast powders.

favorite sitcom comes on, and when the show is done have your 200 rounds loaded for the weekend practice session.

Some say progressive presses are more prone to mistakes. Mistakes happen when operators are tired, bored, distracted or lazy. Which is going to tire and bore you more, a press that makes the 200 rounds you need in half an hour or one that takes four separate one-hour sessions? Some also say progressives don't make accurate ammo. Don't tell that to the guys who win the big matches: Bianchi Cup, Steel Challenge, USPSA Nationals or Camp Perry. They almost to a man (and woman) load their ammo on progressives. How else do you think they got good enough to win?

I have had good luck with Dillon and Hornady progressives. Which particular model and with what features you select will depend on your budget and needs.

Payback

The biggest drawback to reloading is the cost of the tools. You can easily drop $1,500 on a reloading setup. You can also do it for $500 or so. If we use the example cited earlier of using a .22LR handgun as a training gun, and saving $10 per box of ammo compared to the cost of .38 Special, we figure 5,300 rounds to pay off the .22LR. After that it is money in your pocket. If we take the .38 Special at $12 per box ($240 per thousand rounds) and we reload, what do we get? If you buy in volume, and you pay $1.79 per box of primers, $42 per 500 bullets, and powder at $18 a pound, we come up with a plinking load that costs us $117 per thousand rounds. That's a savings of $123 per thousand rounds. The brass? .38 Special lasts so

The cracked 9mm (on the left) would not work well, were you to load it. Inspect your brass as you use it.

long, through so many loadings, that the cost is next to nothing. Even bought new, and long using it for ten loadings, the cost per thousand rounds loaded is about $10.

We'd pay off the inexpensive reloading setup in 4,065 rounds loaded. We'd pay off the expensive one in 12,195 rounds. I know what some of you are thinking: "Holy cow, that's a lot of ammo." Perhaps. Let's say you want to get better at shooting. You determine that you should practice once a month, and shoot at the gun club once a month. Your practice sessions, at 200 rounds per, use up 1,200 rounds in a year's time. If the club's matches are only 50 rounds, you'll shoot another 600 rounds. That's 1,800 rounds, almost half way to paying off the press and tools. But remember

what I said about shooting more? When I went from a single stage press and shooting about 5,000 rounds a year, to a progressive, I found myself in a few years shooting over 35,000 rounds a year. And the loading of all that ammo still took less time than the 5K I had shot before.

Reload, and you'll shoot more. It's almost a guarantee.

Caliber Specifics

Some calibers are easy. .45 ACP, for instance. It is a very forgiving round, and there is some much loading data available, that you could load it blindfolded and come up with useable ammo. Some calibers don't play well. The .38-40, for instance is a loading hassle if you're new to the game, and a picky round to load if you're experienced.

.32

The .32 H&R Magnum is a pretty straightforward little round. As it is a straight-wall design (no bottleneck) you use T-C sizing dies, and you simply make sure your expander stem and bell-crimp operations are in order. The standard bullet diameter is .312" for jacketed and .313" for lead, so a belling stem diameter of .308" should do just fine. If you plan to use rifle-diameter bullets (I can't imagine why, unless you lucked into a lifetime supply of free .308" diameter bullets) you'd want to use a .304-.305" diameter belling stem.

Bell just enough to cleanly seat all your bullets. Some lead bullets may require a slightly larger diameter of bell than jacketed ones, so you'll have to spend a little time experimenting. The basic clue is; if your seating die gets packed with bullet lube and lead shavings you aren't belling enough. Crimp diameter on the .32 Magnum (and the .32 Long, if you use it) is .329".

The .32-20 is a different beast altogether. First, it is a bottlenecked case. The case tapers down from the base diameter to the bullet diameter. The shoulder of the case will require a great deal of attention. First, because of its shape you won't be able to use a T-C sizing die. You'll have to use a steel die and case lube. The usual process is to clean, lube, size and ten clean the lube off.

Then feed the prepped cases into your progressive loading machine, where you deprime, etc.

.32-20 case shoulders "blow forward" on firing. The manufacturers of the rifles and handguns have traditionally made the shoulder longer, to accept any and all cases. The ammunition manufacturers have traditionally made the shoulder shorter, so they'd fit in any and all chambers. The result is a short shoulder that gets blown forward by the chamber pressure of firing. When you re-size the case, size the shoulder back just far enough to chamber in your Ruger. That way you aren't

A good round, in the gauge. It drops in flush, and drops out (when turned upright) of its own weight.

A bad round in the gauge. It won't drop flush. If you see this, find out why it happens.

Once the old primer has been removed, (right) you need to install a new one (left).

excessively working our brass. If you have more than one, (and they have different chamber shoulder dimensions) either segregate your brass for those two, or size your brass for the shorter chamber of the two.

Case necks are thin. If you get to fast in working the press handle, the normal rocking motion of the brass on the shell plate will throw one occasionally out of line enough to cause the case mouth to catch the belling stem and crush it. Also, if you aren't careful in setting a bullet on the case, you'll catch the case mouth and crush it as you seat the bullet. You can only bell so much, due to the thin brass wall, and if you bell too much you'll quickly crack case mouths.

Loading the .32 H&R Magnum is like loading little .38 Specials: easy as pie. Loading the .32-20 is for the advanced reloader who really likes a challenge.

9mm

For a long time, no one bothered to reload 9mm Parabellum. It wasn't very powerful, it wasn't very accurate, it was cheap and common, and there weren't any competitions that really required it, so why bother? My first attempts at reloading the 9mm were not fun. First, the case is tapered. Think of a cylindrical wedge. Sizing dies in the 1970s were not really designed for that, and the resulting cases looked odd. They fed badly, and accuracy?

Too big a belling stem and you have no neck tension. You can't keep the bullets in place with crimp alone.

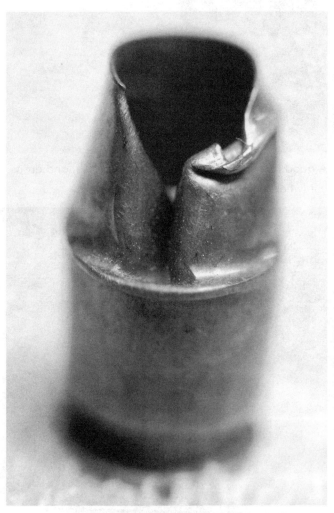

Another example of too-little belling. Here the bullet crushed the case when it was seated.

Here is an example of trying to get too much crimp. The case buckled at the cannelure (the impressed ring at the mid-point) and became useless except as an example.

It sucked. I dropped it and didn't pick it up for fifteen years. By then, IPSC and Steel Challenge shooting had moved onto the scene. Then IDPA came along. Many, many police departments switched to the 9mm. They all wanted accuracy, and by then the guns could deliver. I tried it and adopted it for some uses. By then the reloading die manufacturers had solved the problems, and loading was relatively easy. Not as easy as .45 ACP, but easier than my hair-tearing episodes.

9mm bullets are .355" for jacketed and .356" for lead.

The 9mm is particularly critical of a few things: each pistol likes a particular neck belling stem, although many are very forgiving. Some will be

Here is what can happen if you don't bell enough. The case caught the base of the bullet and sheared off a bit of the jacket.

fussy over crimp: crimp too much and accuracy goes away. Crimp too little and they feed badly. One aspect of the 9mm that I have not seen in any other caliber is a particular combination: fast-burning powders and lead bullets. In some pistols, if you load a lead bullet and (just to pick one) Bullseye powder, you won't get groups. You'll have bullets going sideways through the target. They tumble, and they tumble right away once they leave the muzzle.

None of the Ruger 9mm pistols I tried did this. However, it is an individual pistol thing, not a brand or barrel length thing. If yours does it, consult the powder burning rate chart in your loading manual. Select any powder that is slower-burning than Winchester 231 on the chart, and start loading. The problem will go away.

For belling stem, the diameter I have had great luck with is .350" For crimp diameter, anything between .372" and .377" works in my guns. However, some guns (again, it is a particular gun thing), will not tolerate too tight a crimp with ammo loaded with plated bullets. If your otherwise accurate 9mm Ruger starts throwing shotgun-like patterns when you load plated bullets, look to your crimp.

.38 Special & .357 Magnum

The .38 Special cartridge is so easy to load you could work up a load using a dartboard and a loading manual. It is incredibly forgiving, and your brass will last a long time. Resist the temptation to load it to near-Magnum power levels, even if you are loading for a .357 Magnum. Your ammo might find its way into a .38 some day, and you wouldn't want someone touching off a 30,000 psi load in a gun meant for a steady diet of sub-17,000 psi ammo.

The .38 and .357 are also very fond of lead bullets, which are usually a lot less expensive than jacketed ones. (At least as long as OSHA and the EPA leave us alone.) The jacketed bullets are .357" and the lead .358". Your belling stem should be (mine is) .352". Crimp diameter is 373". Long ago I acquired a huge supply of 9mm lead bullets. What I found was that most .38/.357 revolver were decently accurate using those bullets. But to get them to load right and work I had to use a sub-9mm belling stem (.348" and shorter than the .38/.357 one) with the same crimp I used with .358" lead bulelts. With that setup I was able to load and shoot the 50,000 lead 9mm bullets I had.

Here is what happens if you use dirty brass, and scratch your dies. This round has been crimped with a scratched taper-crimp die, and it shows.

The .38 cases tend to break by cracking at the case mouth. They last a very long time, and the less belling you can get away with the better. The .357 cases either crack at the case mouth like the .38s with brass cases, and they crack in the sides with nickeled cases. I have been told that the cracking is due to the acid bath the brass cases get just before they are nickel-plated, but haven't been able to verify that with the ammo companies. (They are quite close-mouthed about some things. Imagine that.)

Inspect your cases when you handle them after cleaning. If you shake each handful, those that

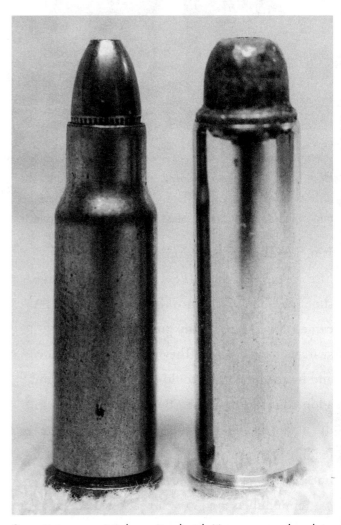

Sometimes you simply must reload. Yes, you can buy lots and lots of .357 Magnum for your GP100. But when was the last time you found ammo on the store shelf for your Hawkeye? And do the collectors know you're shooting it?

You must buy a good measuring caliper, either digital (very, very handy) or dial. Otherwise you wouldn't know this 9mm round was over the max length until you tried to get it to feed. Not a problem if it is the first one off the press. Big problem if you've loaded 1,000 of them before measuring.

contain a cracked case will clink at a different pitch than those where all the cases are unbroken.

.38-40

The .38-40 is like the .32-20 only more so. The brass and chamber dimensions wander more than with the .32-20, and the necks are thin, but with bigger bullets. You have to have a careful hand in loading the .38-40 or you'll be scrapping cases with merry abandon. It should be run at moderate pressure only, as a cowboy action shooting load. There are those who like to "pump it up" but I see that as a waste of time and loading. If you want that kind of power, your Blackhawk convertible (the only place you'll be shooting a .38-40 in a

Ruger) has a cylinder for 10mm. Load *that* to the max and have fun.

.38-40 bullets are .401" in diameter and lead. You'll have a whopping big choice between a 180-grain and a 200-grain flat-tipped round nose bullet. The bullets will have a crimp groove. Use a belling stem of .396" diameter at the smallest, and crimp as little as you can and keep the bullet sin place. Any more crimp than .409" is probably too much.

.40 & 10mm

The other .400" bullet launching calibers, the .40 is the new little brother of the 10mm. They use the same sizing dies, and can often use the

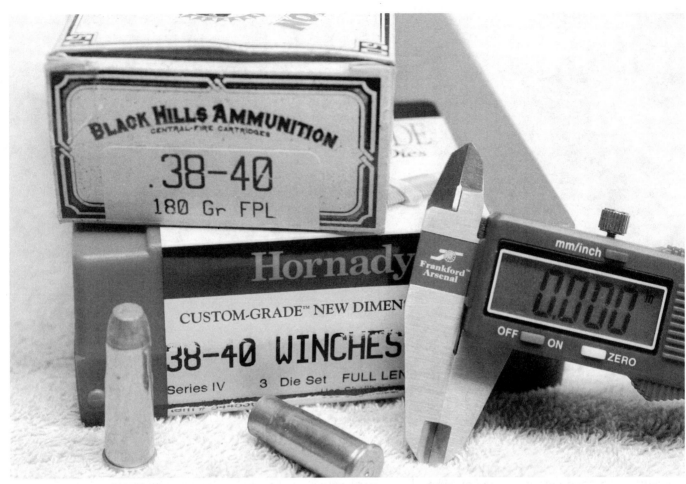

The .38-40 requires that you pay attention, measure everything, and not get too enthusiastic.

same seating and crimping dies, but not at the same time. If you plan to load both, get two sets of dies and adjust them: one for the .40 and one for the 10mm. You use jacketed bullets of .400" and lead of .401" (the same diameter as the .38-40 but different bullet designs). Bullet weights can range from 135 grains to 220. However, the heaviest are 10mm-only bullets.

When the .40 was introduced, IPSC shooters immediately jumped on it. Loaded in 1911-platform pistols, it gave shooters more shots for any given magazine size. When faced with a field course, more ammo meant less reloads, which meant less time. Less time was better. In an attempt to make the felt recoil as soft as possible, they loaded heavy (200-grain) bullets with fast-burning powders. The combination is not forgiving

of mistakes. The pressure was at the maximum, and fast-burning powders are known in some cases to be "spiky" as far as pressure is concerned. When things went awry, cases blew out. A blown case at the least means a trashed magazine. The case blows on the bottom, and the gases are directed into the magazine, usually blowing out the baseplate. Worse incidents resulted in bulged frames, slides, and cracked barrels.

I repeat: DO NOT LOAD HEAVY BULLETS AND FAST POWDERS IN THE .40 S&W.

The 10mm is much more forgiving of that kind of load, but you won't need it. Use slower powder in the 10mm to get the kind of performance for which you bought a 10mm handgun.

Belling stems on the .40 and the 10mm should be .395" and the crimp should be in the .410" region. Again, go with what your pistol tells you it likes.

.41 Magnum

A pretty simple one to load for. Bullets: jacketed .410", lead .411". Belling stem of .405", crimp of .420" or so. That is, unless you're loading the heavy bullets at max pressures and velocities for hunting loads. Then you'll need to sort or trim cases, use a belling stem of .404" or .403" and crimp as hard as you need to, to keep the bullets in the cases under recoil. And not lose accuracy when you do so. Buy lots of aspirin.

.44-40

The biggest of the triumvirate of bottlenecked cases (the .38-40 and .32-20 are the others) the .44-40 suffers all their faults and one more besides: an odd bullet diameter. The accepted bullet diameter of the .44-40 is .427" jacketed and .428" for lead, although older (that is, non-Ruger) guns are bored for even smaller bullets, down to .425". .44 Special and .44 Magnum lead bullets are .431". Can you load the larger bullets in .44-40 cases? Sometimes. If you get away with it, great. But expect split case necks (the .44-40's case is thin, also) and perhaps on our revolver they won't seat in the chambers. Beg or buy a single .431" lead bullet, load it as a dummy, and see if it will fit your chambers. If it does, you can keep one size on hand. If not, you'll have to buy two different diameter bullets for your .44-40/.44 convertible.

Belling stem diameters will be .422" for .427" bullets and .425" for .431" bullets. Crimp diameter will be .436" for all of them.

.44, Non-hunting

The .44 Russian, Special and Magnum use the same bullets, diameters, crimp and belling. The bullets are .430" jacketed and .431" lead. Belling stem diameter is .425" to .427". (Use the tighter figure if you load to higher velocities.) Crimp to .441".

.44 Hunting Loads

With the heavyweights at high velocities, you need to control bullet jump. That means a tight neck diameter, heavy crimp, and consistent case lengths. Polish your belling stem down to .424" or buy one that small. Crimp as hard as you can without harming accuracy. A too-heavy crimp can distort the bullet and harm accuracy. For accuracy

.38-40 case necks measure .007" to .008". Standard modern cases run .010" to .011".

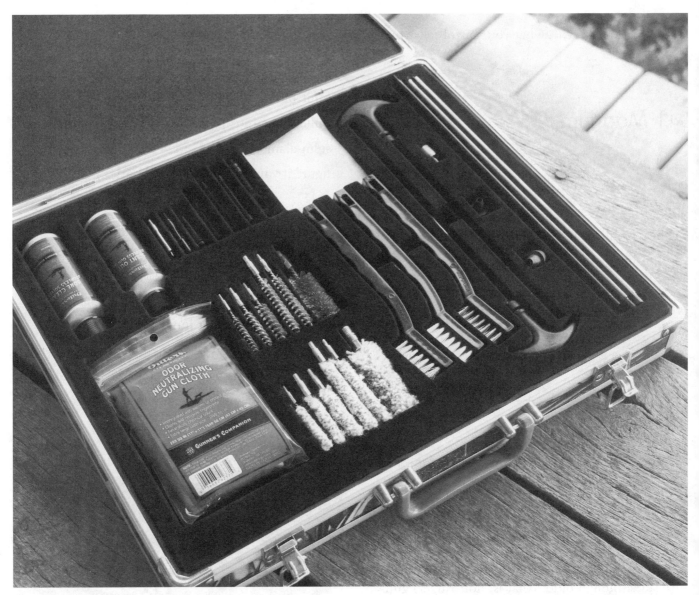

You should clean your reloading dies and press, just as you clean your guns. You do clean your guns, don't you?

testing you should consider a Ransom rest or Caldwell hammer. You can check accuracy without subjecting yourself to the recoil of the heavy loads.

Inspect your brass after every firing, and look for looser primer pockets and cracked case mouths.

.45 ACP

Easy as falling off a log. The .45 is even more forgiving than the .38 Special. Your bullets will be .451" jacketed and .452" lead. A belling stem diameter of .446" is perfect, and crimp to .472" Load buckets of ammo, and practice all day long.

.45 Colt

A little less easy, but more so now than in times past. In the old days the .45 Colt was allowed to wander. That is, bores (and thus the bullets for them) were allowed to be as big as .454. "The ammo of today is closer to, or is, .451" jacketed and .452" lead. As with the .44-40, you can load the .454" if you want, if they'll fit. But as Ruger revolvers have always been made to the newer dimensions you'll find things a lot happier with bullets, belling stems and crimps the same size as the .45 ACP. At least I do.

A good press, a clean bench, and lots of components. The evening's reloading will be fruitful.

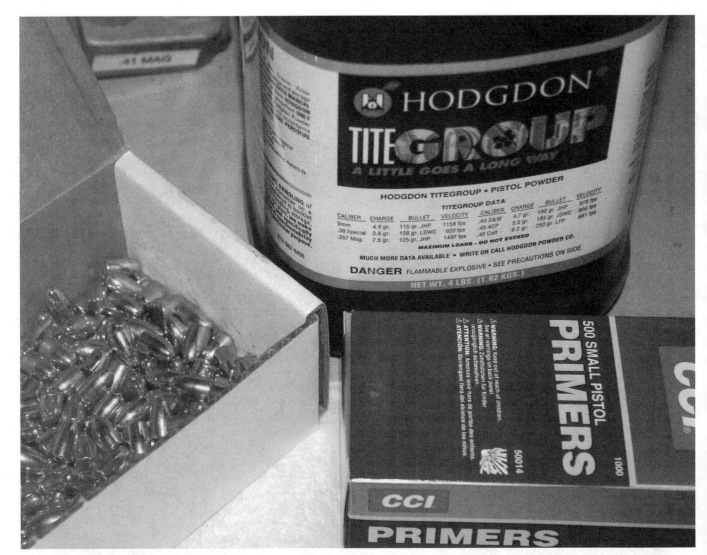

TITEGROUP DATA							
CALIBER	CHARGE	BULLET	VELOCITY	CALIBER	CHARGE	BULLET	VELOCITY
9mm	4.8 gr.	115 gr. JHP	1158 fps	.40 S&W	4.7 gr.	180 gr. JHP	978 fps
.38 Special	3.8 gr.	158 gr. LSWC	920 fps	.45 ACP	5.5 gr.	185 gr. JSWC	956 fps
.357 Mag.	7.5 gr.	125 gr. JHP	1497 fps	.45 Colt	6.2 gr.	250 gr. LFP	881 fps

Pick a powder. Use it. Pick another and use it too. Just keep them apart and have only one of them on the loading bench at a time.

.480 Ruger

As a heavyweight, there are no "light" loads for the .480. The lightest loads you'll load will be at full-power .44 Magnum performance. So you want tight dimensions all around. Bullets will be .475" jacketed and .476" lead. Belling stems should be tight; do not accept anything larger than .470" and if you find any creep at all with one that size, get it polished down or replaced. Crimp diameter should be tight, tight, tight. You need as much as you can get without distorting the bullet or case, to keep the bullet from jumping forward during recoil.

RUGER

Chapter 6

Ruger Safeties

When it comes to self-loading pistols, everyone wants a safety. Some people point out that a revolver usually doesn't have a safety (outside of bad mystery novels) but that isn't true. A single action revolver does have a safety. In the case of the New Model Rugers, the transfer bar acts to keep the firing pin isolated from the firing system. Unless you cock the action and pull the trigger, the revolver won't fire. Load the gun and leave the hammer down, then bash the hammer with a ball-peen hammer. It won't fire. With the older designs you simply leave the hammer down

The Mark I's safety is like a 1911's safety: it blocks the firing mechanism but does not return it to rest.

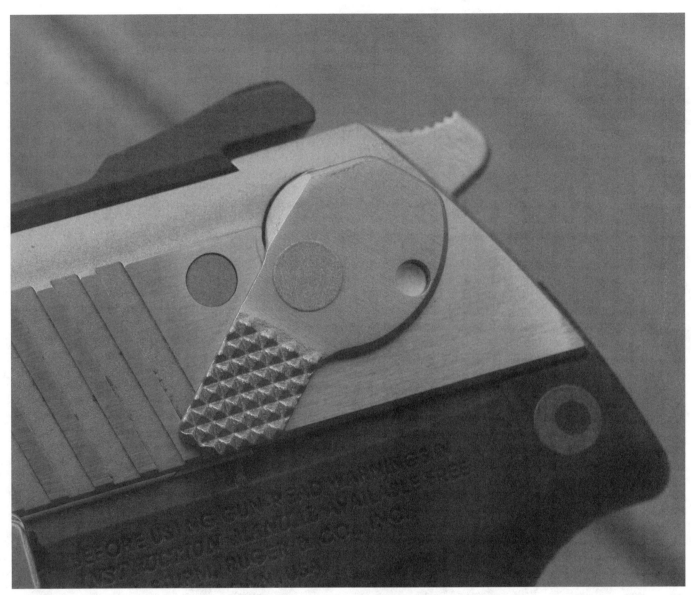

The traditional double action's safety stays down when you lever it down, and the pistol will not fire with the safety down.

on an empty chamber. The same result, except with a five-shot revolver instead of a six-shot.

Double-action revolvers are much the same way. While the Colt remained unchanged, double-action revolvers had some sort of internal block or rebounding hammer, since before the dawn of the 20th century. For them, you needed to pull the trigger, either by pulling the trigger itself or cocking the hammer and pulling the trigger. Simply dropping the gun would not make it discharge.

Pistols have the same sorts of safeties built in; they are simply more obvious.

The customary safety system of pistols was for a long time the Colt 1911. The safety blocked movement of the sear, which kept the pistol from firing. The grip safety blocks movement of the trigger. But to fire a 1911 (or similar -design pistol) the hammer must be drawn back. Either initially when loaded (and the safety applied) or later, in a manner we now know to be less safe than originally thought. There, the hammer is lowered after the pistol is loaded, and then the shooter must cock the hammer before firing the first shot. The problem is, anything that causes your hand to slip (should you be doing this, which I advise against in strong language) will drop the hammer, firing the pistol. Ouch.

The desire for a pistol that worked like a double-action revolver was quite strong. Designers started in the 1930s, with Walther and the PPK. By the time Bill Ruger got around to designing and manufacturing pistols, there were three main types of safeties, which he adopted.

DA/SA

Also known as the Traditional Double Action safety, it works like this: with the chamber loaded and the safety on, you have to push the safety off, and then use the trigger to cock the hammer and release, firing the pistol. Once fired, the hammer stays cocked and subsequent trigger pulls are much easier and lighter. Once you are done firing, you push the safety back to Safe, which mechanically drops the hammer and brings it to rest but does not fire the chambered round. The safety stays down until you push it back to Fire. You can do that right away, and carry it with the safety off but the hammer down. Or you can leave the safety on, and push it to Fire only as you draw. When the safety lever is in the Safe position, pulling the trigger will not fire the pistol.

Decocking safeties are spring-loaded and will not stay in the Safe or non-firing position.

The pros and cons of this system have been debated for half a century, and will likely continue to be so debated.

Decock

Here the safety is spring-loaded, and does not remain on Safe. It can be mounted on the frame (some other brands use that method) or on the slide, which is what Ruger does. Other than the safety lever being spring-loaded, the system works like the traditional double action safety. You must press the trigger through a long heavy first pull to fire it. Then it cocks itself on each shot, and subsequent shots require a much lighter trigger pull.

DAO

Double-Action Only. No external safety lever. Here, each shot is fired is as if it were the first shot on a traditional double action or a decock. The hammer does not stay cocked but follows the slide down to rest and is re-set only when you release the trigger. No safety means much less training to use. Basically, the DAO pistol is a magazine-fed revolver, in that you must pull the trigger a long distance each time to cock the hammer, drop it, fire and then release and repeat.

Which is best? Whichever one fits your expectations, skills, and safety habits. None is bad, some have shortcomings that others don't, but none of them is perfect. They are designed and made by human beings, so of course they aren't perfect.

Serial Numbers

"**O**nce upon a time, in a land far away, there was a reasonable attitude towards firearms...." Then things changed. Ever wonder why firearms have serial numbers? They weren't required for the longest time. Yes, we all know that collectors obsess over serial numbers of Colt SAA revolvers: "Was this made in 1889 or 1898, or when?" Springfield rifles were numbered right from the beginning, in 1903. Why? Because of the military obsession with inventory, accountability and maintenance. Hey, we're talking about taxpayer's money, after all. (Wags will point out that while the Springfields had serial numbers from 1903 onwards, the federal income tax wasn't voted into effect until 1913. Still, the money came from citizens, and had to be accounted for.) You can't keep track of rifles for issue, use, repair and replacement unless each has a unique identifier. So the military was first.

The Mark I, II and III have all had the same serial number locations: on the receiver tube, right side, in front of the ejection port.

The original location of the serial number was forward on the right side and it lacked a prefix. Collectors lust after early-production guns, like this four-digit Blackhawk.

However, there was no law requiring serial numbers on civilian firearms. Many manufacturers didn't bother to serial number their firearms. Lots and lots of shotguns, .22LR rifles, and even scads of handguns, were made without serial numbers. I started working in gun shops in 1977, and almost right away I began running into guns without numbers. Nowadays, a lot of people would jump to the conclusion that they were somehow illegal guns, made without numbers to avoid tracing. Those really in the tinfoil hat ranks would think they were special CIA-made guns for use where they can be dropped and left without tracing,

"sterile" guns.

Oh, get over it. For many manufacturers, it was simply a cost item. It takes equipment, time and labor to stamp a serial number on firearms. It also takes more labor in shipping and inventory to keep track of numbered items than simply numbers of items. Say you have 50 .22LR rifles on the shelves. Great, count 'em up. Fifty? Fifty. Done. If they are all serial-numbered, however, you not only have to count them, but match the numbers (at least on the boxes) to the numbers on your inventory. Who needs that hassle, when you're selling them at wholesale for $34 each? (Just to pick a number, but one that would be about right in the mid-1960s.)

Some guns made without serial numbers *were* "bad guns" but collectors also want them even more for it. During WWII, "lunchpail specials" trickled out of the arms manufacturers. The workers could easily divert a slide here, a frame there, a barrel next week, and at home put it all together. Two or three workers who worked in different parts of the plant could trade parts to match them up. The slide guy could "appropriate" a slide or three, and trade them to the frame guy. The two of them would trade to the guy on the barrel aisle, and they'd all offer cigarettes to the guy with hammer, triggers, etc. Considering the torrent of arms coming out of the manufacturers during WWII, it isn't like they were actually harming the war effort. And some of those parts may have even been snatched out of the reject bin, tossed there by the Army Inspector who rejected it as "not good enough" for the war effort. When those guns come

The Bearcat has such a small frame there's room for the serial number only. The model designation has to go on the cylinder.

Metal-frame pistols get their serial number underneath the ejection port.

up at auction, collectors really jump all over each other. But I digress.

The casual attitude towards serial number (or the lack therof) all changed with the Gun Control Act of 1968. A lot of things changed with that act, but the one we're concerned with is serial numbers. The Act required that all newly-manufactured firearms, and all firearms imported to the United States, have a serial number. Those made before the act's passage, lacking a serial number, were not required to have one affixed. I can only imagine that such a requirement was dropped when the high-class skeet and trap shooters realized they'd

have to have someone stamp some icky numbers on their expensive, engraved shotguns. But then, on some subjects all of us risk veering into tinfoil hat territory.

No problem, right? Ruger firearms had had serial numbers on them since Day One, right? Well, almost. What Ruger had done was give each production item a model name, and then start the serial numbers at 1 for each. In fact, there are collectors who collect (and are listed with Ruger to receive) firearms of each model when they come out with their serial number. You could be the collector of Rugers #119. Or #2701, or whatever. For us gun guys (or gals) it isn't any big deal to keep them straight. We have Mk I #119, and Blackhawk #119, and Super Blackhawk #119, etc.

The bureaucratic mind is not so flexible. Anything that increases the potential for confusion is bad. Anything that decreases the potential for confusion is good. Ruger was told to make serial numbers unique. Rather than assign production blocks of serial numbers Ruger went another way. Serial number blocks are a traditional military approach: "Remington, make weapons numbered from one million to two. Colt, make weapons from two million to three. Winchester, make weapons from three million to four. Let us know when you are getting short and we'll set aside more for you." But in a single company, trying to assign blocks, keep them straight, and not get in trouble, isn't easy. (One can't help but note the immutable nature of confusion. It is sort of like energy in that regard, neither created nor destroyed, simply moved from one location to another.) Making firearms with non-unique serial numbers is not just "a mistake" in the eyes of bureaucrats, it is a crime. If Ruger screwed up (which is a near-certainty for any company) then someone might

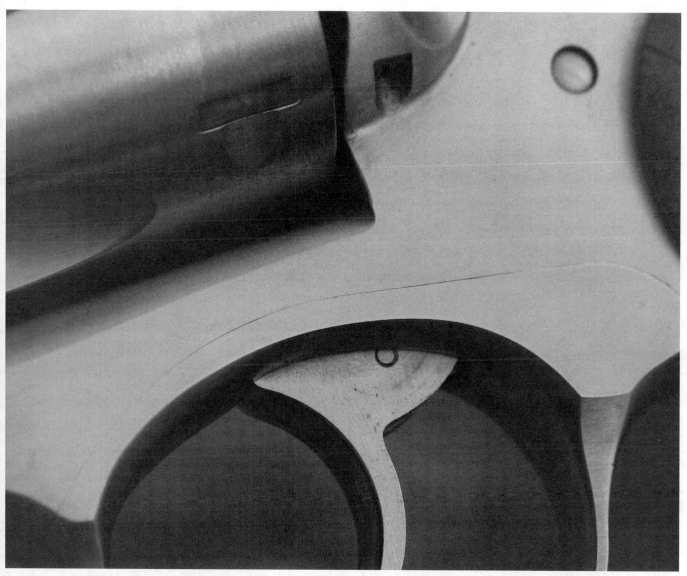

Nothing appears on the left side of the frame on Ruger revolvers. This Redhawk has the serial number down on the bottom of the butt.

go to prison. If Ruger tried to simply assign serial number blocks, and keep production lots within blocks, they would sooner or later overlap blocks. Not funny, to the government.

Hence the model prefix. By assigning each model a unique prefix, Ruger could still sequentially number production (important for QC, recalls and tracking production changes) but satisfy the small-minded who need a simple method of keeping things sorted.

It also has the benefit for Ruger of quickly identifying modified guns. If a model comes in for warranty repair, and the prefix says it is this model and caliber, but the cylinder and barrel (to pick a revolver) are of a different caliber, someone did some changing.

Which means, for you aspiring Ruger collectors, that you need to be aware of the serial number process. First, there are the bare-number models. These will be models and individual Ruger handguns (and rifles and shotguns, too) that were made before 1969. Up through 1968, they all got a sequential number, starting with one, for each model. As before, the Blackhawk was viewed as a separate model in each caliber, so you could have a (just to continue the use, not because I know the guy with this particular number) Blackhawk made in 1955 in .357 Magnum with #119. You could have a Blackhawk made in 1956 in .44 Magnum #119, and a Blackhawk made in 1965 in .41 Magnum #119. However, a New Model Blackhawk made in 1983, in .357 Magnum, would be numbered starting with a "32" prefix, and the first one recorded is #32-33639. The Blackhawks in .41 Magnum got the prefix "40" in 1969, and a re-start in sequence, so you could have a pair of Old Model Blackhawks in .41 Magnum, #119 and #40-00119.

To add to the apparent confusion, the serial number blocks of five digits only allow for one less than a hundred thousand firearms in each block. (00001 to 99,999) So the Blackhawk in .357 Magnum, being a solid and volume seller, has evolved from the "32" prefix through the "37" prefix in 2006. Since the "40" prefix is already taken by the .41 Magnum Blackhawks, what Ruger will do when the digits of the "39" prefix Blackhawks are used up is anyone's guess. I'd bet they'll go with some variant of the "32" in a three-digit number. At the present estimated production/sales rate, it won't be a problem for a few years yet.

The three-digit prefixes came in use in the early 1970s, about the time of the new Model Blackhawks were introduced. Older models kept their two-digit prefixes, but the newer ones received the three-digit ones. With three digits in prefixes, and a five-digit sequential numbers, Ruger has a potential of a hundred million serial numbers at their disposal. I think they're set for a while in that regard. However, it isn't just the total number of prefixes and serial number that provoked the change. As I just pointed out, Blackhawks will run through the "30s" some day and need another prefix. With the three-digit prefix, Ruger doesn't have that problem. Also, the proliferation of models and calibers put a real strain on keeping two-digit prefixes logically and cleanly assigned.

Occasionally you'll come across a Ruger with a "D" prefix or suffix. Buy that gun. No, let me re-phrase it: BUY THAT GUN. Unless the owner knows what it is, and has it priced accordingly, you want to buy it. It is one of the rarest of the rare. The serial number rollmarking machine is an auto-indexing one. (Actually there are many, but we're talking about a machine here.) Each time it stamps a number, it then clicks to the next in sequence. Rarely, very rarely, the machine gets stuck. It stamps the same number. The operator usually picks up on it right away. I have heard rumors from collectors that now and then the operator doesn't pick up on it right away, and as many as a dozen have rolled out with the same number. Or, the starting point or end points are mis-communicated from one day or one shift to the next. You might have a hundred or more with rolling duplicate numbers. Again, the second batch will get a "D" prefix or suffix.

When that happens, and they are caught, the staff stamps the "D" prefix: Duplicate.

The P95, with its serial number plate on the low left, is the odd man out. Why? No one is saying. Perhaps some new machinery required that location. Maybe the first big P-95 contract was for a department or agency that required it. (Stranger things have happened.)

Collectors have been known to lose all grips on sanity when given the chance to buy one. Especially if it is matched with the one without the "D" prefix/suffix. Rarer still are the ones with duplicates lacking the D. A collector with a pair of matching-number model Rugers is a happy one indeed. However, you've got to be careful. I'm not a lawyer, nor do I play one on TV. I've got to figure that the ATFE, lacking a sense of humor, would view such a situation with near-horror. You may find yourself, if you're too public about it, receiving a visit. The ATFE agents will probably be polite, and they may even bring a "D" stamp with them. So do be careful, unless I'm just being a bit over-caffeinated and conspiratorial this particular morning.

Some manufacturers will allow you to special-order custom serial numbers. Ruger isn't one of them. You get whatever the machine stamped out that day. Still, for the solid, near-indestructible machine you're getting for a fair price, not getting a custom serial number is not a big deal.

Serial number locations are pretty consistent through the Ruger production timeline. Single Sixes got them on the bottom of the frame butt. As did Redhawks. Early guns, like the Blackhawks and Super Blackhawks, got the serial number on the lower right side of the frame. Later guns got them on the rear right side.

`Pistols have them in a few locations. The metal-frame guns have the serial number on the right side, under the ejection port. The P345 has the serial number plate (a steel plate inset and molded in with the polymer frame) on the right side above where the grips would be if there were grips. The P95 has it on the left side, down on the frame, near the magazine well. The Mk I and all its progeny have the serial number on the receiver, not the frame, and forward of the ejection port on the right side.

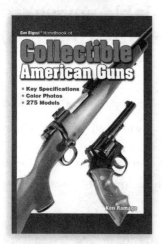

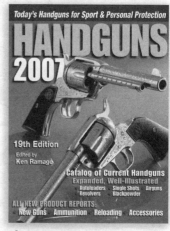